television:

planning, design, and production

by
les satterthwaite

arizona state university
tempe, arizona

with
john maher, jr.

D1308139

KENDALL/HUNT PUBLISHING COMPANY
2460 Kerper Boulevard, Dubuque, Iowa 52001

A special thanks to Frank Conti and Harold Wedell of ITS-Concor who made this book possible.

PN
1992.75
S37
1980

Copyright © 1980 by Kendall/Hunt Publishing Company

ISBN 0–8403–2153–8

All rights reserved. No part of this publication may be
reproduced, stored in a retrieval system, or transmitted,
in any form or by any means, electronic, mechanical,
photocopying, recording, or otherwise, without the prior
written permission of the copyright owner.

31 3 1199 00272 5805

Printed in the United States of America

B 402153 01

CONTENTS:

television:

Chapter III. The Multicamera Television System 89

INTRODUCTION:

television:

In 1975 the TELEMEDIA Project was born. During a lunch with Mr. Frank Conti of ITS-Concor, I made a rash statement that *anyone* could learn to design and produce television programs using a multicamera TV production system. Mr. Conti took me at my word and provided me with a black and white multicamera production unit and a Vega station wagon to carry it around. Contacts with the local high schools soon provided the subjects for the experiment and in just a few short months I had proven my point. The original equipment was redesigned and housed in a special console that would allow it to be easily rolled into the classrooms or left in the van for use as a mobile control room. This original grant evolved into the TELEMEDIA Project in which Mr. Conti provided the equipment and the transportation and Arizona State University provided the insurance and the logistical support. I provided my Fridays and Saturdays.

Our first concern was to find the answer to two simple questions (1) WHO CAN LEARN TO DESIGN AND PRODUCE SIMPLE TELEVISION PROGRAMS? and (2) WHAT IS THE BEST INSTRUCTIONAL STRATEGY TO USE IN THIS TRAINING? The answers became quickly obvious. *Anyone* can learn to design and produce simple television programs in as little time as eight contact hours. This program has been successful with students from the third grade through graduate schools. The only reason we don't include first and second graders is that they keep falling off the chairs that they stand on to operate the equipment. I found that the most appropriate instructional strategy was a full day's experience. Beginning with 24 students at 8:00 in the morning, the class was able to design and produce as many as 15 short programs by 3:30 in the afternoon. We found that the parents were interested in what their children were doing so we initiated a pot-luck dinner at 5:30 after which the student programs were shown. Since 1975 literally thousands of students have gone through the TELEMEDIA Project.

However, as we answered one question another would take its place. Letters from parents, teachers, and even the young people themselves indicated that the participants were learning more than just television production. They were changing from passive viewers of television information to active critics of what they saw. They were learning to be productive members of a group as they interacted in the small society we call a television crew. Positive social skills such as cooperation, responsibility, leadership, and group interaction seemed to be acquired as they went through the process of television production training. We are not sure exactly what happens as the student becomes actively involved in television production but we do know that some very exciting changes appear to be taking place. The TELEMEDIA Project is currently involved in finding ways to measure these changes.

In addition to this continuing exploration of the effects of television production training the TELEMEDIA Project is moving into a new phase. The phase is one of dissemination. This book is the result. It is my hope that through this television production training manual you will be able to establish your own TELEMEDIA Project and to enjoy the excitement that I have found in working with students.

Good Luck,

Les Satterthwaite
ARIZONA STATE UNIVERSITY

CHAPTER I.

PORTAPAK TELEVISION PRODUCTION:

* AN EXAMINATION OF THE EQUIPMENT, PERSONNEL, AND PROCEDURES FOR THE PRODUCTION OF SIMPLE SINGLE CAMERA "PORTABLE" TELEVISION PROGRAMS.

PORTAPAK:
EQUIPMENT, GENERAL

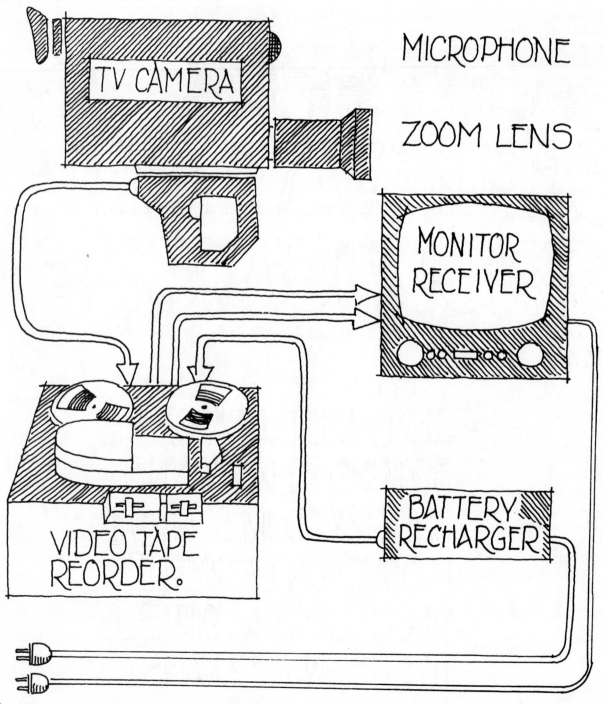

MICROPHONE

ZOOM LENS

TV CAMERA

MONITOR RECEIVER

VIDEO TAPE REORDER.

BATTERY RECHARGER

PORTAPAK EQUIPMENT, A GENERAL INTRODUCTION

The equipment in any television production system must do the following things. First a camera or cameras must translate the images of the real world into video electronic signals. At the same time a mike or microphones must translate the sounds of the real world into audio electronic signals. These audio and video signals must be sent to a console or control center if multiple cameras or multiple mikes are used and then they are sent to a video tape recorder (VTR) where they are recorded on video tape. The video tape recorder then plays back these tapes on a display system called the monitor/receiver where the electronic audio and video signals are translated back into images and sounds that are usable by the viewing audience.

Since the portapak system is designed to operate on battery power and to be used by a single person many of the functions have been modified. For example, when you purchase a standard portapak unit the basic equipment consists of (1) the camera, (2) the video tape recorder, and (3) a battery and battery recharger. Additional elements that you may want to add to the system consist of a monitor/receiver, a sound mixer, and additional microphones. Let's see how these elements are different from the standard pieces of equipment.

The television camera in the portapak actually serves four functions. First, it is a camera that translates the reflected light from the subject into electronic signals. Secondly, it has a built-in microphone that translates the sound waves into electronic signals. Thirdly, it has a viewfinder that also serves as a monitor for viewing your program in the field. Fourth, the television camera has a trigger that lets you control the recording and in-camera editing.

The video tape recorder receives the audio and video electronic signals from the camera and translates these signals to magnetic records on the video tape. Video tape used in portapak systems can range from ¼" to ¾" in size and can be either reel to reel or cassette format. The video tape recorder has a number of functions: (1) passive record (pause mode), (2) active record, (3) rewind, (4) fast forward, and (5) playback. For recording the VTR is placed into passive record and then the camera trigger is used to move from passive to active record and back to passive record. The rewind and fast forward functions are used to cue up the video tape. The playback is used to either send the signal to the viewfinder of the camera or to the larger, separate monitor/receiver. The video tape recorder also contains the battery that powers both the camera and the video tape recorder.

The battery recharger is the third element in the basic portapak system. The battery recharger serves two basic functions. It can be used to recharge the battery overnight to insure that the system is ready for use the next day. It can also provide AC power to the system when it is available in the shooting location.

These three basic elements: the camera, the video tape recorder, and the battery recharger will allow you to produce video tapes. But to improve the productions and to make them more available to an audience there are two additional elements that should be added to the system. To improve the sound and utilize music for the productions a sound mixer, additional mikes, and an audio tape recorder should be added. To allow you to display the programs to a larger audience, a monitor/receiver should also be included. The monitor/receiver should have one diagonal inch for each student it is to serve, i.e., a 19" set will serve 19 students.

PORTAPAK:
THE CREW (GENERAL)

NORMAL CREW

EXPANDED CREW

THE PORTAPAK CREW, A GENERAL INTRODUCTION

A television system is more than just a collection of equipment. The system must also include the personnel that are needed to operate the equipment and to plan, design, produce, and evaluate the proposed production. These people are normally referred to as the production crew. This chapter will be devoted to an examination of these various individuals and their roles and responsibilities in the production of programs utilizing the portapak system. Our examination during this chapter will concentrate on the preproduction, production, and post-production activities for each of these crew roles. The specifics of the planning, design, and production documents will be covered in more depth in the chapter titled THE PRODUCTION PROCESS.

There are two basic types of crews that are used in productions involving the portapak system. The normal crew for portapak production is a single individual. This is what the system was designed for. It was designed to be operated by a single person who would be a combination Producer, Director, Cameraman, Audio Technical Director, Video Technical Director, and Floor Director. The expanded crew is an artificial crew distribution but can involve two, three, or four people directly in the production activity.

The Normal Portapak Production Crew

The portapak system was originally intended for operation by a single individual. The portability of the system, its ability to view productions immediately, and the built-in microphones in the camera all stress this individuality in production. This means that the individual must fill all of the crew roles and responsibilities. He or she must be the Producer, the Director, the Cameraman, the Audio and Video Technical Director, and even the Floor Director. This individual does everything except perform in front of the camera. This application allows that individual to exert a great deal of control over the production but it also is a strictly individual effort that stresses creativity over the group process. This approach seems most appropriate when you are producing inserts for a larger production or when you are doing a program that requires in-camera editing.

The Expanded Portapak Production Crew

In this situation the emphasis is on a group activity rather than on an individual creative effort. The exact number of the crew to be involved is a function of the extra elements in the production equipment. If there is a support system for the camera (tripod or unipod), the roles of Producer/Director and Cameraman may be separated. If the audio system includes a sound mixer with multiple mikes and an auxiliary sound input sources such as a tape recorder, it may be necessary to use separate crew members for the role of Audio Technical Director and Video Technical Director. The roles that have to be filled include the following. The Producer/Director is in charge of the production and the production crew. The Cameraman operates the camera during production. The Audio Technical Director prepares the audio tapes and operates the audio mixer during production. The Video Technical Director checks the equipment and operates the video tape recorder during production. The Floor Director prepares the graphics for the production and assembles the equipment, set elements and props that are needed for the production. This situation allows the crew to be involved in a group creative effort. They will learn the necessity of individual responsibility, cooperation, and leadership as they put their program together.

This is a general look at these various crew positions. Now we will take a specific look at the preproduction, production, and post-production responsibilities of each of these crew positions.

PORTAPAK:

THE CREW, PRODUCER/DIRECTOR

NORMAL CREW ○   EXPANDED CREW ●

PREPRODUCTION

- ○ PLANNING DOCUMENTS   ●
- ○ DESIGN DOCUMENTS   ●
- ○ PRODUCTION DOCUMENTS   ●
- ○ CHECK THE VTR
- ○ CHECK THE CAMERA
- ○ CHECK THE AUDIO
- ○ PREPARE AUDIO TAPES
- ○ PREPARE GRAPHICS
- ○ COLLECT/ARRANGE PROPS
- ○ THE WALK THROUGH   ●
- ○ REHEARSAL   ●

NORMAL CREW o   EXPANDED CREW ●

PRODUCTION

- o OPERATE THE VTR
- o OPERATE THE SOUND SYSTEM
- o MONITOR THE AUDIO
- o CALL THE SHOTS   ●
- o OPERATE THE TV CAMERA   ●

POST PRODUCTION

- o EDITING   ●
- o EVALUATION   ●

THERE WILL BE SOME VARIATION
DEPENDING ON THE NUMBER OF
PEOPLE IN THE EXPANDED CREW.

PORTAPAK:
THE DIRECTOR, PREPRODUCTION

 INITIAL CLIENT CONFERENCE.

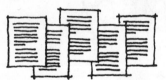 PLANNING AND DESIGN DOCUMENTS.

CLIENT APPROVAL MEETING.

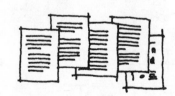 PRODUCTION DOCUMENTS

  WALK THROUGH REHEARSAL

PREPRODUCTION ACTIVITIES OF THE DIRECTOR IN THE PORTAPAK SYSTEM

There are three stages in the production of a television program: the preproduction activities, the production activities, and the post-production activities. To put it another way there are things that need to be done before, during, and after the actual production of the television program. The preproduction activities will differ slightly depending on whether the program originates from an internal need or an external need. For details, see the planning, design, and production section of the chapter titled THE PRODUCTION PROCESS. This will be a very general treatment of these preproduction activities of the Producer/Director.

Initial Client Conference

If the program originates from an external need this means that you are producing the program for someone else, a client. The client has a need to communicate with an audience and you, as Producer/Director, have the communication skills to develop the message for them. In this initial conference with the client you begin the development of the planning documents. These documents are simply answers to the following questions. What do you want to say? To whom? With what effect? Through what channel or medium? The answers to these four questions become (1) the content outline, (2) the audience description, (3) the goals or objectives, and (4) the media selection rationale. During the interchange with the client you need to get the necessary information for a rough set of planning documents. Using additional people, print, and non-print resources these are polished and prepared. Using these as a basis you then prepare the first of the design documents—the treatment. These planning documents and the treatment are then presented to the client in the client approval meeting.

The Client Approval Meeting

During this meeting there are three things that can happen. First, the client can accept your documents and approve them as they stand. Secondly, the client can request some modification in the documents. Thirdly, the client can reject the documents and request that you start all over with the process. Normally, there are few if any changes if you have listened carefully and done a good job of research on the subject of the program. As you become more and more proficient the chance of change grows less and less.

On the basis of the approved planning and design documents you will then prepare the remaining design documents and the production documents. The remaining design documents consist of the storyboard and the script. The production documents consist of the shooting schedule, the prop and equipment list, and the set of studio diagrams. While the client may want to approve the storyboard and the script the production documents are for the production crew.

The Walk-through and the Rehearsal

One of the final stages in the preproduction activities of the Producer/Director is the preparation of the talent and the crew for the production. This preparation takes two forms: (1) the walk-through, and (2) the rehearsal. The walk-through is the Director's opportunity to see the Talent's delivery of the information. This may be based on a storyboard and script or it may be an ad-lib delivery by the Talent. During this time the Director will decide what shots are appropriate and what types of transitions to use between the shots. Any changes that are necessary are shared with both the Talent and the crew. The final rehearsal is video taped and may become the finished production. It is more likely that it will be evaluated and additional changes and/or modifications will be made in preparation for the production.

PORTAPAK:

THE DIRECTOR, PRODUCTION

AND POST PRODUCTION

EDITING

EVALUATION

PRODUCTION ACTIVITIES OF THE DIRECTOR IN A PORTAPAK PRODUCTION

The Director's Role in the Expanded Crew

In both the expanded and normal crews the Producer/Director has a major role in the interaction with the crew and talent. The Producer/Director works closely with the client during the development of the planning and design documents and during the walk-through and rehearsal that immediately precede the actual production. This interactive activity continues during the production activity. A major role that the Producer/Director will play is that of supporting the Talent. In most situations you will be working with untrained Talent who may be appearing on television for the first time. It is the role of the Producer/Director to let the Talent know what they are doing right and what they are doing wrong. However this must be done in a supportive manner to ensure the best possible performance. In the expanded crew situation the Director may serve as the cameraman and call the shots for himself. Or the Producer/Director can look over the Cameraman's shoulder and call the shots for the Cameraman. This latter mode poses some difficulty. First, the viewfinder of the camera is quite small and it will be difficult for both the Cameraman and the Producer/Director to monitor the incoming signal. Also if the Producer/Director calls the shots too loudly they may be picked up by the mike that is built-into the camera. The best approach is to have the Producer/Director also serve as the Cameraman.

The Director's Role in the Normal Crew

The normal crew in a portapak situation is a single individual. This is the way the system was designed. In this application the Producer/Director assumes all of the roles in the production activity. The Producer/Director has prepared the planning and design documents and worked with the Talent during walk-through and rehearsal. In the actual production stage the Director operates the entire production system. This means that the Producer/Director serves as Director and calls the shots, the Producer/Director also operates the camera during production. In addition to operating the camera the Producer/Director also operates the audio system and the video tape recorder.

POST-PRODUCTION ACTIVITIES OF THE PRODUCER/DIRECTOR IN A PORTAPAK PRODUCTION

Even after the production is completed there are things that the Producer/Director must do. First, he or she must edit the production if it is necessary. Secondly, he or she must evaluate the finished production to determine if the technical, artistic, and informational aspects are up to quality.

The post-production editing is only necessary in those situations where the original footage was shot either out of sequence or in a series of interrupted scenes. This post-production editing is not normally available in public schools. If it is available it is usually the less professional assemble editing systems. In these cases the various scenes are rearranged and assembled electronically.

The evaluation of the technical and artistic quality of the production is the responsibility of the Producer/Director. The other members of the production crew may be involved for their input but the final decision is up to the Producer/Director. The evaluation of the instructional, informational, or entertainment quality of the production is up to the client. It may involve the Producer/Director but the client is the one making the final decision.

11

PORTAPAK:
THE CREW, THE CAMERAMAN

○ PREPRODUCTION:
CHECK THE CAMERA
CAMERA ACCESSORIES

○ PRODUCTION:
CAMERA SHOTS (STATIC)
CAMERA SHOTS (TRANSITION)
CAMERA OPERATION

○ POST PRODUCTION:
EVALUATION - ASSIST THE
DIRECTOR

THE ROLE OF THE CAMERAMAN IN THE PORTAPAK SYSTEM

In many situations the role and responsibility of the Cameraman is taken by the Producer/Director in charge of the production. However, there are some types of portapak productions (see page 5) that can make use of both a Producer/Director and a Cameraman. In situations where you are shooting "inserts" for other productions the addition of a separate individual serving as just a Cameraman may have some definite advantages. First, the addition of a separate Cameraman will allow the Producer/Director to spend more time setting up the scenes and working with the Talent. The addition of a Cameraman may also be useful in those situations in which you are shooting footage for post-production editing. Here the Director needs to set up the individual scenes and to keep the shooting schedule operating smoothly. However, in most situations the Producer/Director will also double as the Cameraman. In this section we will look at the preproduction, production, and post-production activities of the Camerman whether he be only a Cameraman or a Producer/Director doubling as a Cameraman.

The Preproduction Activities of the Cameraman

Before the production actually begins the Cameraman should take the time to learn the nomenclature (names) of the various parts of the TV camera and what functions they perform. The actual operation of your particular brand of equipment cannot be covered in detail since there are so many different brands. We will cover the parts of the camera in general and you should refer to the operator's manual for your particular equipment.

In addition to the camera there are also additional pieces of equipment associated with the camera that you should be familiar with. The most common equipment in this category are those that are designed to provide support and mobility to the camera. The support systems include tripods (three legs), unipods (single leg), and the various body harnesses that provide support and mobility for the camera. These are available from most dealers and can improve your portapak programs.

The Production Activities of the Cameraman

Once the Cameraman has become totally familiar with the camera and its operation he or she can then become concerned with the use of the camera during the shooting. In the preparation of the storyboard and during the actual program various camera shots will be referred to. Some of these shots are static shots such as the close-up, the medium shot, and the long shot. There are the other shots that are required to move from one static shot to another. These are referred to as transitional shots and include pans, tilts, zooms, and combinations of these. It is important that the cameraman become familiar with these shots.

In addition to the names and appearance of the various camera shots the Cameraman must also know how to operate the camera to get these shots when the Producer/Director calls for them. Camera operation includes getting steady static shots and smooth transitions. The professional operation of a single camera system is much more difficult than it is in the multicamera systems—and much more important.

PORTAPAK:
THE CAMERA, NOMENCLATURE

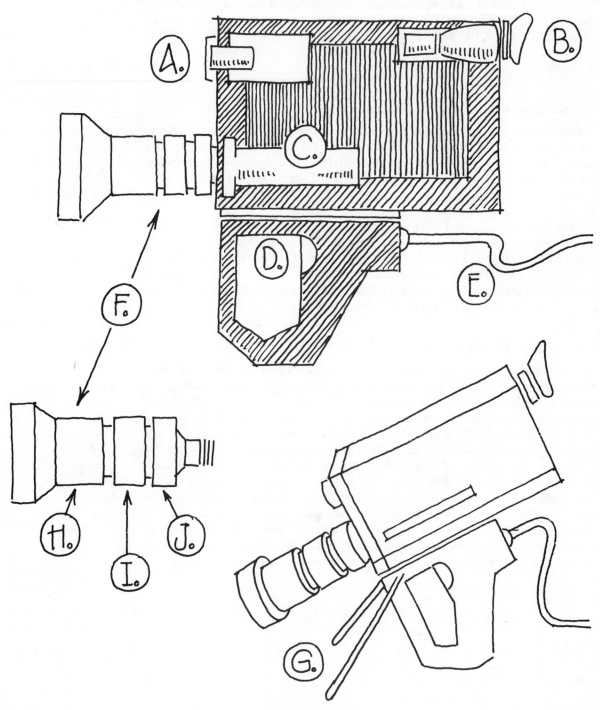

THE PORTAPAK CAMERA, NOMENCLATURE AND FUNCTION

The portapak camera is quite different from most television cameras. In a normal situation the function of the camera is to translate the reflected light from the subject into electronic video signals. In the portapak system this is only one of the camera's functions. To better understand these functions let's first look at the parts of the camera.

The portapak camera contains a built-in microphone (A) which is used to translate the sounds of the talent and environment into audio electronic signals. There is also a monitor (B) in the camera that allows the Cameraman to monitor the program during production and also allows the Cameraman and other members of the crew to view the playback of the tape that was just produced and evaluate the technical and artistic qualities of the production on the spot. The camera also serves the normal function of translating the reflected light from the subject into the electronic video signals that are sent to the video tape recorder. The light passes through the lens of the camera (F) and is focused onto the vidicon or plumbicon tube (C) inside the camera. This tube is the one that actually creates the electronic video signal.

Most portapak cameras use manual zoom lenses. These zoom lenses (F) allow you to zoom into or away from a subject without physically moving the camera. By rotating the zoom control (I) the size of the image can be increased from a close-up to a long shot or decreased from a long shot to a close-up. The zoom lens has two other controls. The one closest to the camera body controls the amount of light entering the camera. This aperture control (J) is changed to adapt to the various light conditions under which you might be shooting. To determine the setting to use just watch the monitor in the camera and adjust the aperture for the best possible picture quality. This can also be used to fade in and out of a scene if this is desirable. The third adjustment that is available on the zoom lens is the focus control (H). This is used to keep the image in sharp focus during the production. Ideally you will zoom in tight on the subject, focus the image, and then you should remain in focus at all zoom settings as long as the subject-to-camera distance remains the same. Obviously one hand is required to operate all of these controls on the zoom lens. The other hand is used to support the camera. The camera handle (D) serves basically three functions. First, it allows the Cameraman to support the camera; secondly, it contains the trigger that operates the video tape recorder; and lastly, it sends the composite audio and video electronic signal to the video tape recorder through the camera cable (E). This cable also supplies power to the camera from either the battery located in the video tape recorder or from the battery recharger that is connected to an AC power source.

Many portapak cameras have built-in tripods to use between shooting rather than during production. These tripods (G) allow you to set the camera down as you are planning the next shot. Often to provide the support for the camera during production, tripods, unipods, and even body harnesses are used to support the weight of the camera and allow the Cameraman to get steady static shots and smooth transitional shots. The tripod is a three legged support system that has a pan tilt head. It attaches to a coupler at the base of the camera handle. The unipod has a single leg that is designed to support the weight of the camera. The body harness comes in many shapes and sizes and provides both support and smoother pans and tilts for the camera.

This portapak camera is intended to be the control center of the portapak production system. Since the system was originally designed to be operated by a single individual both the audio and video operations are controlled from the camera.

PORTAPAK:
CAMERA SHOTS, STATIC

LONG SHOT · MEDIUM SHOT · CLOSE UP

LONG SHOT · MEDIUM SHOT · CLOSE UP

TWO SHOT · EXTREME CLOSE UP · EXTREME LONG SHOT

STATIC CAMERA SHOTS

It is important that anyone involved in television production know both the names and the descriptions of the various television shots. These are the vocabulary of the television program. The Producer/Director needs to know them to prepare the storyboard and to adequately communicate with the other crew members. The television Cameraman needs to know these shots to be able to read the storyboard and to translate the Director's words into acceptable action. Even the Talent must know the names and effects of the shots to be able to anticipate movement patterns and to know when and where to manipulate the props.

These various shots can easily be subdivided into two classes: (1) the static shots, and (2) transitional shots. The static shots are used to feature a person or an object. The transitional shots are used to move the camera from one static shot to another. People who are new to television production seem to think that to maintain visual interest, they must keep the camera in continual motion. It is as if the term "motion picture" refers to the movement of the camera rather than the static camera taking pictures of people in motion. Let's examine some of the basic static camera shots.

First there are basically three static shots: (1) the close-up, (2) the medium shot, and (3) the long shot. The long shot shows the subject and the environment in which it exists. Often it is referred to as the establishing shot—establishing the subject and its environment. The actual size of the shot is a function of the subject. The long shot on the top row on the opposite page shows a Talent in an environment (the corner of a room). It is a wide shot. However, immediately below we see the same shot—a long shot—of a glass of water. In this case it is a much smaller shot but it is still a long shot of the glass of water. The medium shot is treated the same way. It is not the size of the shot that counts but rather what it shows. The medium shot, whether it be of a person or a glass of water, emphasizes the subject and shows only a small portion of the environment. As we move on to the close-up, the emphasis is entirely on the subject and there is little or no environment showing. Generally a program begins with either a long shot or close-up and then moves to the other shots. For example, we might begin with a long shot to establish the subject in the environment and then go to a medium shot and finally to a close-up. Or for quite a different effect we might begin with a close-up and then go to a medium shot and end up with an establishing shot.

There are obviously other shots. Some of the more common static shots include (1) the two shot, (2) the extreme close-up, and (3) the extreme long shot. The two shot is just what the name implies—a shot of two separate elements, in this case two people. The extreme close-up and the extreme long shot are what their names imply. Some other shots that the Producer/Director might call for are waist shots (a shot of the Talent from the waist up), bust shot (a shot of the Talent from the bust up—similar to a medium shot), profile shot (showing only the talent in profile), etc. To ensure that the Cameramen and the other people in the production crew know exactly what shots the Producer/Director wants, they will go through the required shots during the rehearsal. This communication about the various shots is essential and so it is necessary that each person in the crew has a common understanding of what the various shots look like and how to get them effectively and efficiently.

PORTAPAK:
CAMERA SHOTS, TRANSITIONS

THE PAN AS A TRANSITION ▶

OPENING TITLE CARDS

THE TILT AS A TRANSITION

THE ZOOM AS A TRANSITION

TITLE CARD

TRANSITIONAL CAMERA SHOTS FOR THE PORTAPAK SYSTEM

In a multicamera production system the transitions between the various static shots are the switches between cameras. These may be cuts, dissolves, wipes or other special effects. They are the means of getting from one static shot to another. In a program that is designed for post production editing the transitions are provided by the cuts that are inserted in the editing function. In portapak productions that are edited in the camera, the change from passive to active record mode and back to passive record mode provide the same types of cuts between the various static shots. However, in a "live" portapak production where the program is shot from beginning to end without any interruption, these transitions take the form of camera movements such as the pan, the tilt, the zoom, and combinations of these three.

The Pan as a Transitional Shot

On the opposite, you can see one application of the pan as a means of providing a transition between three static shots. The static shots are a close-up of the opening title card, a medium close-up of the Talent and a medium shot of the subject. Beginning with the close-up of the studio card, the camera will then pan right to the Talent. After the Talent has introduced himself and the topic of the program, the Director will again say, "Pan right," and the cameraman will pan to the subject. The reverse of this can be used to close the program. The camera pans from the subject to the Talent who closes the program and then to the studio cards to end the program. In this situation the placement of the studio cards, Talent and subject is important.

The Tilt as a Transitional Shot

While the pan is a horizontal camera movement, the tilt is a vertical camera movement. As shown on the opposite page, the sequence can begin with a static shot of the studio card. Then as the Director says, "Tilt down," the Cameraman will tilt to show the Talent. Again the Talent will introduce the topic and upon the Director's command, the cameraman will tilt down to show the subject. This last static shot will be held steady as the talent manipulates the materials that are the subject of the program. When the manipulation is completed, the Director will again say, "Ready to tilt up; tilt up," the cameraman will tilt up to frame the Talent for his/her closing remarks. Then at the appropriate time the camera will tilt up again to show the closing card for the end of the program. Like the pan shot, this tilt shot must be set up well in advance to ensure that as the Cameraman tilts up or down they are showing the information that the Director wants shown.

The Zoom as a Transitional Shot

Notice that both the pan and the tilt movement keep the same relative camera shot. The zoom, on the other hand, is a change in the relative size of the camera shot. In the example on the opposite page, you might begin with a shot of the studio card, then zoom out to show both the card and the Talent, then zoom out to a long shot of the Talent and finally back into a medium close-up of the Talent. Actually it is almost impossible not to include both pans and tilts when you are making a zoom transiton. Note on the opposite page, that the zoom shown also includes a pan to the left and a slight tilt up. The zoom is the most difficult transitional camera movement to make smoothly. It will require a lot of practice but the results will be well worth it.

These camera shots, both the static shots and the transitional shots, are like the punctuation in a paragraph of good writing. They provide the emphasis that is necessary to make the Talent's performance come alive and communicate the concept that you want communicated.

PORTAPAK:
CAMERA OPERATION

CENTER OF GRAVITY

BODY ACTION

BODY SUPPORT

TRIPOD SUPPORT

OPERATING THE PORTAPAK CAMERA

As we indicated, the camera shots are the grammar of the television program. The static shots are the sentences that are punctuated by the transitions. They can give a meaning or flow to the message that a single static shot would lack. They provide emphasis where emphasis is necessary and they pause for contemplation when contemplation is needed. However, they should never intrude on the program. These camera movements should be executed so smoothly that people are not even aware of them. The point at which the audience becomes aware of the technical side of the program is the point at which they stop watching the content and start reacting to the techniques.

Center of Gravity

The term center of gravity simply means that you should balance the camera so that it forms the center of gravity of the combination of your body and the camera. In the diagram on the opposite page, the Cameraman is balancing the camera over the center of gravity. This will help ensure that the camera can be held steady during the static shot and that the transitional shots will be smooth. The right arm is tight against the body and the hand has a firm grip on the handle. The left hand is either supporting and steadying the camera at the top or it is holding the lens for a possible zoom or focus.

Body Action for Pans and Tilts

One of the common mistakes that a Cameraman makes in portapak shooting is that he or she tries to do pans and tilts with just the hands and arms. These transitional shots will be much smoother if the whole body is used. In the example on the opposite page, you can see how the pan should be done. Notice that the movement is at the waist. The hands and arms are steady and the elbows are, if possible, locked into the upper body. When the Cameraman swings at the waist and shifts the weight of the body to the other foot, the resulting pan should be much smoother. The key to good camera work is simple: practice—practice—and more practice.

Body Support

There are times when a long static shot is required. If you do not have a physical support for the camera, you may need to use your body. Notice in the diagram on the opposite page, the weight of the camera is being supported on the Cameraman's knee. Unfortunately, this may put the camera too low for the type of shot that you want. If this is the case, look for something that you can rest the camera on; a railing, box or even the fork in a tree can give support for the weight of the camera. Note that you do not want to lock the camera in if the static shot is to be followed by a transition.

Tripod Support

Ideally you will purchase a tripod for your portapak system. The tripod attaches to the base of the handle of the camera and has a pan head that will allow smooth pans and tilts. In the diagram on the opposite page, the Cameraman is providing additional support by grasping the top of the camera. While this is a good position for static shots, it is not appropriate for transitional shots. For pans, tilts, and zooms, the hand not holding the camera handle should be holding the lens. It will provide almost as much support for static shots and when holding the lens you are ready for either zooming or focus changes. A good tripod will often make the difference between a good production and a professional production.

PORTAPAK:
THE CREW, TECHNICAL DIRECTOR

- ○ ## PREPRODUCTION

  CHECK VIDEO TAPE RECORDER
  CHECK THE AUDIO SYSTEM
  PREPARE AUDIO TAPES

- ○ ## PRODUCTION

  OPERATE THE VIDEO RECORDER
  OPERATE THE SOUND SYSTEM
  MONITOR THE RECORDING

- ○ ## POST PRODUCTION

  ASSIST IN THE EVALUATION

THE TECHNICAL DIRECTOR IN THE PORTAPAK CREW

The role and responsibilities of the Technical Director in the portapak system are primarily concerned with the equipment, particularly the audio and video systems. The Technical Director has the responsibility for setting up, checking, and operating (1) the video tape recorder, (2) the sound mixer, (3) the microphones, and (4) any auxiliary sound systems such as tape recorders. The interactions with these various systems will vary depending on what's available in your system (the amount of equipment) and the phase in the production process (preproduction, production, post-production).

Preproduction Activities of the Technical Director

The Technical Director's responsibility during the preproduction activity of the production is primarily to get ready. He or she needs to collect all of the necessary equipment (using the prop and equipment list from the Producer/Director). Once the equipment is collected he or she then needs to interconnect the units of the system and check it out. Check the operator's manual that came with your particular brand of portapak equipment for specifics on hooking up the various components of the system. Once the system is interconnected the next responsibility of the technical director is to run a check. Actually make a short tape using all of the audio and video inputs. Then playback the tape and check the technical quality that was recorded. If it is acceptable you can move to the next stage; if it is not acceptable make the adjustments that you can to improve this technical quality.

Once the system has been checked out completely the Technical Director then can attend to the production of the audio tapes that are needed for the actual production. Check the storyboard and script from the Producer/Director and if necessary consult with him or her about the audio needs. Check through the music and/or sound effects that are available and transfer the disc recordings to audio tape or create your own on audio tape (This is only necessary for those systems that include the sound mixer).

Production Activities of the Technical Director

Up to this point the Technical Director has been getting ready for the production. Now the time is here and we put all this preparation into use. You have recharged the battery overnight and assembled the system at the shooting location and checked it out again during the walk-through and rehearsal. The show is ready to go on the air. In this situation the Technical Director moves into the operating mode. He or she will be responsible for the operation of the audio and video components of the system.

The video tape recorder is the easiest piece of equipment to operate since it is normally controlled from the television camera. However, the Technical Director will put it into passive record at the beginning of the production and turn it off at the end. He or she will also rewind it and put it into playback mode so that the Cameraman and/or Producer/Director can view and evaluate the production on the camera viewfinder.

The operation of the audio system will vary depending on what is available. In the normal portapak system all you do is to monitor the sound to make sure that the quality is acceptable. If the system has been expanded to include a sound mixer you will adjust the sound level of the various sound inputs and also operate the auxiliary audio tape recorder with the appropriate sound at the appropriate times. Once the production is completed, there are still two more roles for the Technical Director.

Post-Production Activities of the Technical Director

During the evaluation of the program, the Technical Director will be expected to provide input as to the technical quality of the audio and video recording. Also it is the responsibility of the Technical Director to collect and return all of the equipment.

PORTAPAK:
THE VIDEO TAPE RECORDER

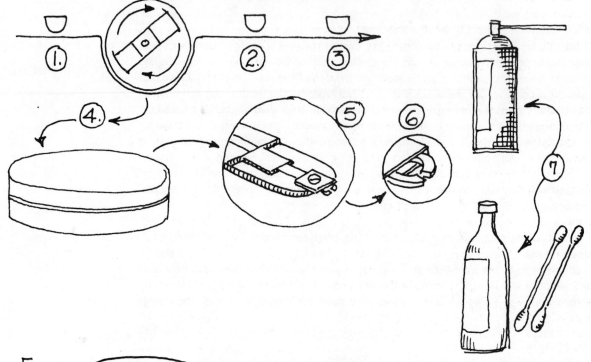

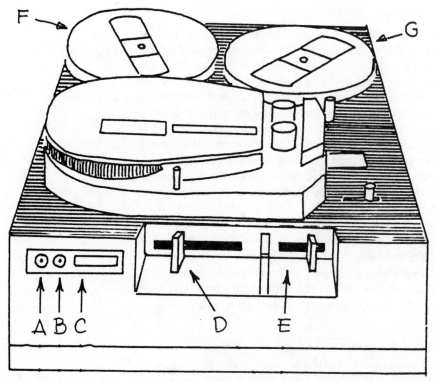

THE VIDEO TAPE RECORDER IN THE PORTAPAK SYSTEM

While you may never look inside the video tape recorder (VTR) in the portapak system you should have some idea of what is happening to the video tape. In the diagram at the top of the opposite page, the tape first passes across the video erase head (1). This is only operative in the record mode and erases any previous information to prepare the tape for recording. Next the tape passes across the video record heads (4) where the video signal is recorded. The next head is the audio erase head (2) which erases previous audio information. This head, like the video erase head, is operative only in record mode. The last head has two functions. First, it is the audio record head (3) and it also lays down the control track for the video tape. During playback both the video record and the audio record heads serve to read the video tape and to translate these magnetic signals into audio and video electronic signals that are sent to the display system. There are actually two recording heads on the video record unit (4). These rotate at either end of an arm (5) in a cylindrical housing. At the ends of the arm is the unit (6) that actually records or plays back the video signal. These elements should be cleaned every time you use the VTR. Either special cleaning solvent in a spray container or alcohol and a soft cue tip (7) should be used to ensure that not only all of the heads are clean, but also that all of the guides and rollers are clean. Check the operator's manual that came with the system to determine the exact cleaning procedure for your particular brand of VTR.

There are two types of portapak VTRs that are currently available. The one shown on the opposite page is an example of the reel to reel format. The video tape is loaded onto the feed reel (F) threaded around the various recording, erase and playback heads of the equipment and onto the take-up reel (G). The other type of VTR is the cassette unit in which the tape is enclosed in a plastic container and simply pushed into the VTR and threaded by the machine when it is turned on.

Normally the controls of the VTR are quite simple. There is a function lever (D) which allows the operator to select between various modes. For example, there will be a setting for forward, another for fast forward, and another for rewind. These control the passage of the tape through the recorder. The record lever is used to change the mode of the VTR from playback to record. Combinations of these two levers operate the VTR. When the recorder is placed in passive record mode—with the record lever in record mode—the tape is not passing through the machine. However, the circuits are open and the Cameraman can see through the camera viewfinder and check his shots. Pressing the trigger on the camera moves the VTR into active record mode in which the tape is actually passing through the machine.

There are other elements in the VTR that you should also be familiar with. The VTR will normally contain a mike jack (A). You can either plug a mike into this jack or you can plug the output of the audio mixer into this unit. The earphone jack (B) is also a normal part of the VTR. This allows someone to monitor the audio portion of the program during production. Usually there is a battery meter (C) which keeps you informed of the charge remaining on the battery that is contained inside of the VTR. Also your VTR should contain some sort of footage counter that will help you locate points on the video tape for cueing the tape for playback or recording. At the rear of the VTR will be the various jacks and plugs to accommodate the inputs and outputs from the camera and the battery recharger.

The form of these items will vary from video tape recorder to video tape recorder so be sure to consult the owner's manual that comes with your particular brand of VTR.

PORTAPAK:
THE MONITOR/RECEIVER, RECHARGER

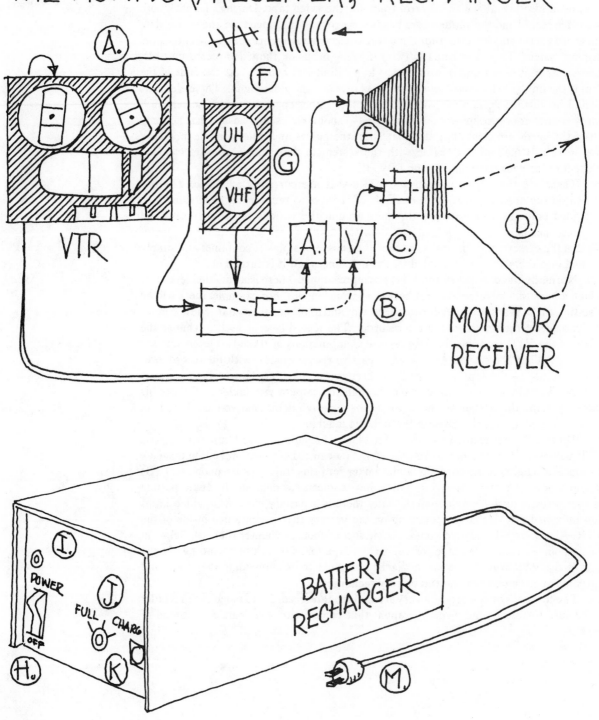

VTR

MONITOR/
RECEIVER

BATTERY
RECHARGER

POWER

FULL   CHARG

OFF

THE MONITOR/RECEIVER AND BATTERY RECHARGER IN THE PORTAPAK SYSTEM

Two other components of the standard portapak system are the display system (the monitor/receiver) and the battery recharger that keeps the battery in the VTR up to charge. While the monitor/receiver is not normally a part of the standard portapak system, it is essential if you want others to be able to see what you produced.

The Monitor/Receiver

The function of the monitor/receiver is to display the audio and video electronic signals from the camera, video tape recorder, or off-the-air broadcast signals. In the diagram on the opposite page we see the output of the VTR (A) being fed into the monitor receiver (B). This electronic signal is a composite of both audio and video signals from the camera and the microphones. These signals are electronically separated inside the monitor/receiver with the audio signal sent to the speaker (E) and the video signal sent to the picture tube (C) where a beam of light displays the image on the phosphorescent screen (D). This is an example of the monitor function of the monitor/receiver. In a similar situation, the camera and mike signals are sent to the VTR. With the VTR in passive record mode the signals simply pass through the VTR without being recorded on video tape and are sent to the monitor/receiver in just the same fashion.

In the receiver mode the broadcast signal is picked up by the antenna of the monitor/receiver (F). These signals travel to the tuner of the television set (G) and the signal from the channel that is selected travels on to the electronics of the receiver where it is again split into both audio and video signals (B). The audio signals are sent to the speaker (E) and the video signals are sent to the picture tube (C). Some television sets are just receivers of broadcast information. Others are just monitors for closed circuit signals. When you are selecting a unit for your portapak system get a monitor receiver that will serve both functions.

The size of the monitor/receiver that you select is a function of the size of the group that you normally serve. A good rule of thumb to use in selecting a monitor/receiver is to pick one that has one diagonal inch for each student. Thus a 19" set should serve a maximum of 19 students while a 24" set would serve a maximum of 24 students.

The Battery Recharger

The battery recharger is a unit that normally comes with the portapak system. It is designed to serve two major functions. First, it is intended to recharge the battery that is carried in the video tape recorder. It is plugged into an AC outlet and then into the video tape recorder. The power switch is turned on and it takes between four and eight hours to bring the battery to a full recharge. When it is in operation the charging light (K) is on and the progress of the charge is shown on the scale (J). You also need to check the scale on the video tape recorder to make sure that the battery is fully recharged.

The life of the battery may range from one-half hour to as long as an hour. This creates a limit on how long you can take to produce the program that you are involved in. But the battery power does allow you to shoot in areas where AC power is not available.

The battery recharger can also be used to supply AC power directly to the video tape recorder and to by-pass the battery in the VTR. In this situation the camera and video tape recorder are not limited in time by the battery life. The limit is rather the length of the extension cord that is available to interconnect the local AC power source and the battery recharger.

PORTAPAK:
THE AUDIO SYSTEM

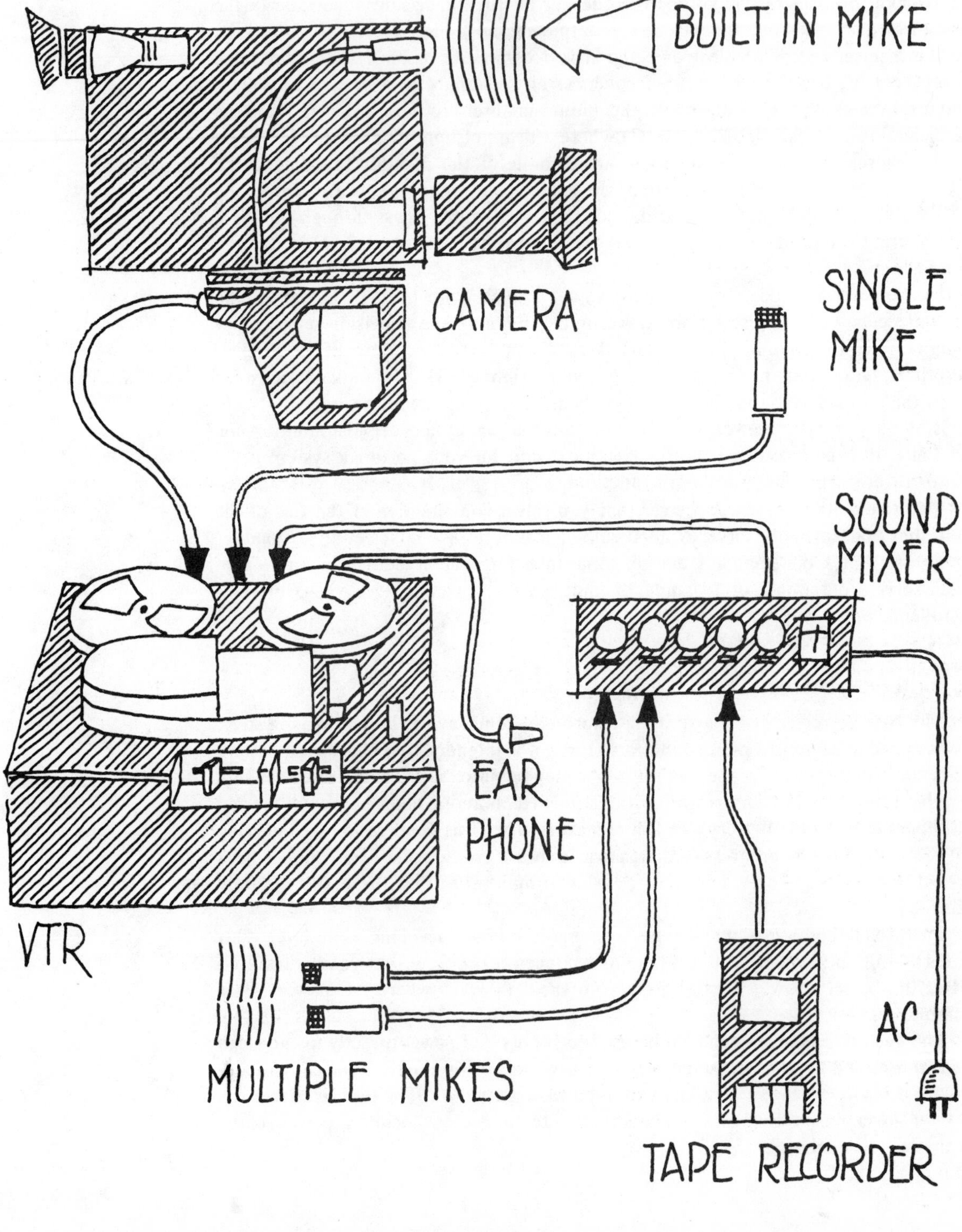

BUILT IN MIKE

CAMERA

SINGLE MIKE

SOUND MIXER

EAR PHONE

VTR

MULTIPLE MIKES

AC

TAPE RECORDER

THE AUDIO SYSTEM FOR USE WITH THE PORTAPAK

There are three types of audio systems that can be used with the portapak system. They are (1) the built-in microphone, (2) the microphone plugged directly into the video tape recorder, and (3) the sound mixer that interfaces between the various sound sources and the video tape recorder. The involvement of the Technical Director ranges from just monitoring the sound signal in the first two types to actually controlling the level of the sound and creating the sound in the third type of system.

Using the Built-in Microphone

When you are involved in a production in which just the built-in microphone is being used the Technical Director has relatively little to do. His or her main role will be to monitor the technical quality of the production and inform the Producer/Director if anything requires that the tape be redone. Occasionally he or she may run a record player or audio tape recorder to provide background music or sound effects that will be picked up by the mike in the camera.

Using the Plugged in Microphone

When a separate microphone is plugged into the video tape recorder this will mute the mike that is built into the camera. The advantage of using this type of mike is that you can get it closer to the talent and thus there is less chance of picking up disturbing background noise. In this situation the Technical Director again simply monitors the sound that is being recorded to keep the director informed of any technical problems.

Using the Sound Mixer

In this system the output of the sound mixer is plugged into the mike input on the video tape recorder. The sound mixer is a unit that is capable of taking the sound from a variety of sources (mikes, record players, tape recorders, etc.) and sending a composite signal to the video tape recorder. The sound mixers will vary in cost from $20 to $100. The more expensive systems will produce a much more professional sound quality. They normally will handle 4–5 input sources ranging from microphones to audio tape recorders. Each input has its own volume control. These signals then go through a master gain control (that controls the output signal) to the video tape recorder. With this system the Technical Director is responsible for placement of the various microphones, the preparation of the music and sound effects tapes, the cueing of the tapes, setting the sound levels for the various sound sources, and then controlling the sound as it is fed into the sound mixer.

It is almost essential that some sort of listening system such as a headset or earphones be connected to the output side of the sound mixer so that the Technical Director can monitor the sound that is being fed into the video tape recorder. Usually the earphone that is plugged into the earphone jack of the video tape recorder is being used by either the Producer/Director of the Cameraman so this makes a separate listening system doubly essential.

The audio playback should be a cassette tape recorder with a digital counter of some sort. This will allow you to have separate music or sound effects on separate tapes and to have them cued up and ready to go. Also it will eliminate threading of the reel to reel type of tape recorder and impossibility of cueing the record players.

As we said the preparation of the audio materials and the operation of the audio system is often the major role that the Technical Director will play in the production of a portapak program.

PORTAPAK:
MICROPHONE PLACEMENT

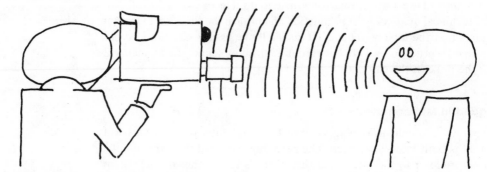

USING THE BUILT IN MICROPHONE.

FIST

USING THE LAVALIER MIKE.

DESK AND FLOOR MICROPHONES

MICROPHONE PLACEMENT IN THE PORTAPAK SYSTEM

The placement of the microphone will have a definite effect on the technical quality of the audio portion of the television program. While the built-in microphone is the easiest to use it does create some very definite audio problems. It is so far away from the Talent that it will pick up a great deal of background noise. The term background noise refers to any sounds in the immediate environment. In some cases this may provide the "atmosphere" you want but in others it may interfere with the ability to hear what the Talent is saying. Actually the audio portion of a television program is least likely to get the attention it deserves. If we want to eliminate the background noise, it is necessary to move the microphone as close to the Talent as possible. In this case we would use the second of our audio systems—the one in which we plug in a mike to the mike input on the video tape recorder.

These microphones usually do not come with the system and will need to be purchased separately. The dynamic microphones seem to be the best choice for television production. They are very dependable and have a smooth frequency response. In addition they are not terribly expensive. Their cost ranges from $40 to $80. You should use a lavalier type of microphone that has a lanyard that goes around the Talent's neck. Your mike should also be a low impedance mike that will allow you to use a long microphone cable.

The microphone is placed around the Talent's neck and then adjusted so that it is approximately one fist's length from the Talent's chin. To improve the mobility of the Talent the microphone cord is usually tucked into the belt so that the cord hangs down the Talent's side (as shown on the opposite page). This helps to ensure that the mike cable will not trip the Talent as he or she moves from place to place in the set. Ideally you will have a microphone for each Talent in the program. In some cases this is not possible and it is necessary to make multiple use of the same mike.

In interview situations the interviewer can often share the mike with the person being interviewed. The movement of the mike should be limited but it should be turned to favor the person who is talking. This will take a little time to do this properly but with practice the interviewer will be able to maintain good audio quality. In situations where there is a panel discussion the microphone may be mounted on a desk stand and placed in the midst of the participants. The exact location is dependent upon the level of the various voices. A similar mike placement can be used with standing groups. In this case a taller microphone stand is used and the people are clustered around the mike. If a sound mixer is available the Audio Technical Director will have to take a sound level of the voice of each participant and raise or lower the volume level of that mike to compensate for the different voice levels of the talent.

The most difficult audio placement occurs when there is music. For example if you place the mike too close to a guitar you will pick up the noise made when the fingers move to a new set of strings at the neck of the guitar. This problem is amplified even further when you try to place the mikes for a musical group. Often the only reasonable solution is to use a single mike and just trust to luck. There are few hard and fast rules for mike placement and that is what makes the job of the Technical Director so difficult. Don't be afraid to try something and check it out on the system.

PORTAPAK:
RECORD TO TAPE TRANSFER

RECORD PLAYER   MIKE

HEAD SET

TAPE RECORDER

THROUGH-THE-AIR DUPLICATION

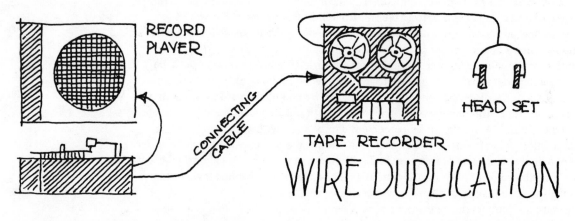

RECORD PLAYER

CONNECTING CABLE

HEAD SET

TAPE RECORDER

WIRE DUPLICATION

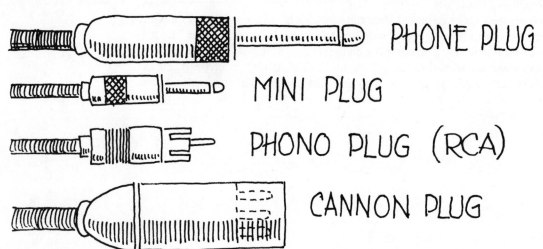

PHONE PLUG

MINI PLUG

PHONO PLUG (RCA)

CANNON PLUG

TRANSFERRING RECORDS TO TAPE FOR A PORTAPAK PRODUCTION

First a word about copyright. Most recorded music is owned by someone else. In some cases there may be a copyright on the words, the music, and even on the arrangement. This copyright is designed to protect the author's property. If you transfer the information on a record to a tape format you are violating the copyright of the people who own the material. If this is the case and you want to use music in your production what are your options? Educational activities tend to fall under what is called fair use. Simplistically this means that if you do not cause the copyright holder to lose money and you do not make money from the process you are not in violation of the copyright. To avoid any problems with copyright you can turn to your own resources. Perhaps there is someone in your school who could create a simple melody and someone else who could play it. All you have to do is record it with a tape recorder and you can stop worrying about copyright. Also there are some records such as SOUNDS FOR A PICTURE EVENING that are available from *Popular Photography* that are designed to be used in local production activities. These can be transferred to tape and used without fear of violating someone's copyright.

But how do you go about making these disc-to-tape transfers? There are two basic systems: (1) through the air duplication, and (2) wire duplication. The first is simpler but will not provide the quality. The second is more difficult but will provide a higher quality. These two systems are diagrammed on the opposite page. In the through the air system the equipment is set up as shown. The record player is set up with its speaker system. The mike from the tape recorder is placed fairly close to the speaker. The tape recorder is turned on and the record player is turned on. The sound comes out of the speaker of the record player and is picked up by the mike and sent to the tape recorder where it is recorded on audio tape. This needs to be done in a quiet environment as the live mike will pick up sounds of traffic, clocks, airplanes or anything else that is part of that environment. The person doing the recording should wear a pair of headsets to monitor the recording and to identify any extraneous sounds that interfere with the music. Even with this monitoring system you should play the tape back to check the recording and to make sure you have what you want.

For a more polished dubbing from disc to tape you should consider the wire duplication system. In this case the output of the record player is connected to the input of the tape recorder by wire. Since there is no microphone the speaker of the record player is used only to monitor the recording. The sound from the record player is sent to two different sources. One set of audio signals drives the speaker of the record player for monitoring and the other is sent, by wire, to the tape recorder where it is recorded. In this case the recording environment may be as noisy as necessary since there is no mike to pick it up. Again a set of headsets should be used to monitor what is being recorded.

Audio equipment may not always have the same input plugs or jacks. This means that you need to know the names of the various audio connectors. On the opposite page we see the four most common audio plugs. The plug is the male connector and the female connector is called a jack. To complete a connection you need to find out what the output jack looks like and what the input jack looks like and then to get a connector that has the right plugs to interconnect the system. These are often available at your local audio store.

PORTAPAK:
THE CREW, FLOOR DIRECTOR

- **PREPRODUCTION**

  PREPARE THE GRAPHICS
  PREPARE SET ELEMENTS
  COLLECT/ARRANGE PROPS

- **PRODUCTION**

  HOLD THE TALENT'S CUE CARDS
  PULL THE STUDIO CARDS

- **POST-PRODUCTION**

  ASSIST THE DIRECTOR
  WITH THE EVALUATION

THE ROLE OF THE FLOOR DIRECTOR IN THE PORTAPAK CREW

In the expanded portapak crew, the Floor Director is an important member. Like all of the crew members, the Floor Director has certain preproduction, production, and post-production responsibilities. These various responsibilities are primarily located in the studio or shooting area. Just as the Technical Director is in charge of the equipment, the Floor Director is in charge of the Talent, props, set elements, and the various graphics that will be used during production.

Preproduction Activities

Before the production begins the Floor Director prepares the various graphics and instructional materials that will be needed. The term graphics refers to the various studio cards that are used at the beginning and end of the program and often in the middle. These graphics may be simple title cards or credits or they may be vocabulary cards that simply name the various elements that the talent will manipulate or demonstrate during the program. The specifics of these studio cards and their production are detailed on the next set of pages but we should point out the relationship between the television image and the subjects that it displays. The aspect ratio of the television image is roughly 3×4. Therefore, anything that is displayed on television must also be a 3×4 ratio. Those things that we can design, such as studio cards, can be designed in a 3×4 ratio but those things that we acquire must still be shown in whole or part in terms of 3×4 ratios.

The Floor Director is also responsible for the collection and arrangement of the set elements. These are those materials that make the environment of the Talent match the environment required by the storyboard and the script. The same consideration is given to the props that the Talent will manipulate as part of the presentation. The Producer/Director will provide the Floor Director with a prop list which can be used as a guide for collecting the appropriate materials and the storyboard is used to assist in the arrangement of the setting. The Producer/Director will also prepare a diagram to show the location of the various set elements and props.

Production Activities of the Floor Director

During the actual production the Floor Director's main role is to be ready to take care of any problems that arise. The Floor Director is the one crew member who has relatively little to do during production. This fact makes the Floor Director extremely valuable. The Floor Director can keep his eyes open to see what may go wrong and correct it before it gets on the tape. The Floor Director has the time to anticipate trouble and by anticipating it prevent it. The Floor Director is available to fill in for all those vital moments in production where an extra hand, or an extra set of ears, or an extra set of eyes are necessary to ensure a polished program.

The Floor Director should always try to make the Talent's job easier. If cue cards are needed the Floor Director will make sure the Talent can see them. If props need to be rearranged off-camera, it is the Floor Director who does it. The Floor Director is an important member of the portapak production crew.

Post-Production Activities

When the production is completed, the Floor Director assists the rest of the crew in the technical and artistic evaluation of the production. While the Producer/Director makes the final decision all of the crew members will have an input. After the evaluation, the Floor Director is responsible for putting all of the props and set elements away.

PORTAPAK :
TELEVISION GRAPHICS

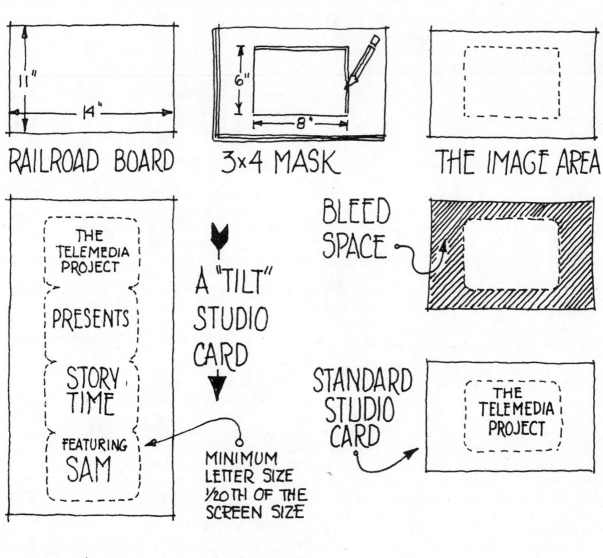

RAILROAD BOARD

11"
14"

3×4 MASK

6"
8"

THE IMAGE AREA

THE TELEMEDIA PROJECT

PRESENTS

STORY TIME

FEATURING SAM

A "TILT" STUDIO CARD

MINIMUM LETTER SIZE ½0TH OF THE SCREEN SIZE

BLEED SPACE

STANDARD STUDIO CARD

THE TELEMEDIA PROJECT

A PAN STUDIO CARD

THE TELEMEDIA PROJECT   PRESENTS   STORY TIME   FEATURING SAM

THE VIDEO TECHNICAL DIRECTOR: PRODUCING STUDIO CARDS

One of the first responsibilities of the Video Technical Director is the production of the studio cards called for in the storyboard and the prop and equipment list. These studio cards are primarily used as opening and closing credits for the proposed production, but occasionally are used for internal information.

There is insufficient space here to go into all of the details on the mounting, lettering and illustration techniques that can be used to produce studio cards. If you feel the need for more information in this area, you might consult GRAPHICS: SKILLS, MEDIA AND MATERIALS by Les Satterthwaite published by Kendall/Hunt. Here we will concentrate on the form and format of these studio cards.

Studio cards should be mounted on railroad board or other medium weight cardboard. Railroad board normally is available in a 22 × 28″ format which cuts into quarters that measure 11 × 14″. This is an excellent size for the standard studio card. The first problem is to locate a 3 × 4 area within the railroad board. This 3 × 4 area corresponds to the 3 × 4 ratio of the television screen. In this case a 6 x 8″ visual area (still a 3 × 4 ratio) should be centered as shown on the opposite page. It might be a good idea to draw diagonal lines, locate the center, then measure up and down 3″ and right and left 4″. The result would be the image area. If this were cutout it could serve as a mask. By simply placing the mask or stencil over other sheets of 11 x 14″ railroad board, you could quickly indicate the desired visual area.

We also need to point out the concern for bleed space. The term bleed space is used to describe the space around the visual area that will allow the Cameraman to quickly get a good shot without showing the edge of the studio card. Without the bleed space the effort to fill the screen with the information in the visual area often results in spending an excessive amount of camera time.

A point should be made about the size of the lettering that can be used within the visual area. To ensure that the audience will be able to read this information it should be a minimum of 1/20th the height of the image area. In the case of the 6 × 8″ image area this means that the smallest letter should be a minimum of 1/20th of 6″ or approximately ¼″.

It should also be pointed out that there are variations on the standard studio card. Sets of standard studio cards can be pulled on the air to reveal successive bits of information. If this is not suitable consider the use of pan and tilt studio cards. The tilt studio card, as the name implies, is designed to be used while the camera is tilting up or down across its surface. Note in the example on the opposite page, the tilt card is designed for a tilt down. The camera begins with a shot of the top title then tilts down to show the intermediate title and then down again to show the last title. This can be done in one continuous smooth tilt or the tilt can pause at each bit of information. In either case it is essential that the information fall into the same 3 × 4 ratio (or image area) that we discussed before.

The pan title is similar except that the camera will pan across its surface either right to left or left to right. In the example on opposite page the pan card is designed to be used with a left to right pan. The camera sets up the shot on the TELEMEDIA PROJECT. Then it pans left to show presents and continues on to show STORY TIME and FEATURING SAM. Like the tilt studio card the pan movement may be smooth and continuous as it moves across the image or it may pause at each bit of information. Notice that the same 3 × 4 image area is still utilized and that there is still bleed space around the information.

CHAPTER II.

SINGLE CAMERA STUDIO TELEVISION PRODUCTION

✳ AN EXAMINATION OF THE EQUIPMENT, PERSONNEL, AND PROCEDURES FOR THE PRODUCTION OF SIMPLE SINGLE CAMERA "STUDIO" TV PROGRAMS.

STUDIO: EQUIPMENT, GENERAL

A. CAMERA
B. PAN HEAD
C. TRIPOD/DOLLY
D. MIKES
E. TAPE RECORDER
F. SOUND MIXER
G. VIDEO TAPE RECORDER
H. TV

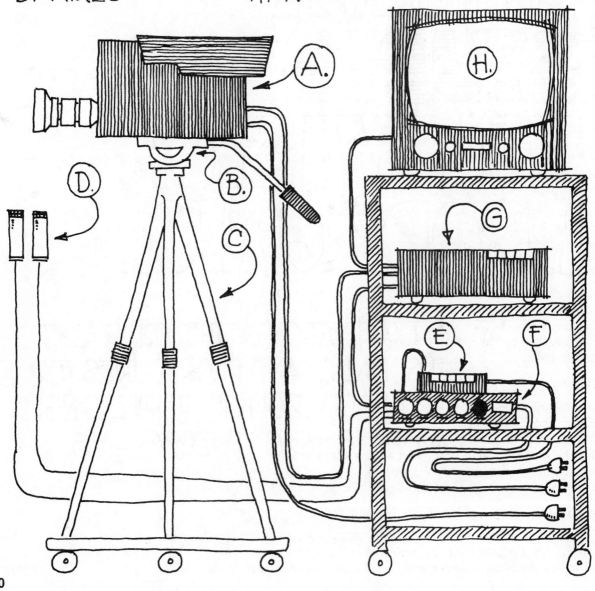

A good deal of care

AN INTRODUCTION TO "STUDIO" EQUIPMENT

The term "studio" is often used to describe a particular type of single camera television production system. This system is the one that is most commonly found in the public schools today. It consists of (a) camera, (b) pan head, (c) tripod and dolly, (d) one or more microphones, (e) audio tape recorder (this is optional), (f) sound mixer (this is also optional), (g) video tape recorder, and (h) monitor/receiver.

The Camera

Like all television cameras this one is designed to translate the reflected light from the subject into electronic signals that may be recorded on the video tape recorder and displayed on the monitor/receiver. For this system you should purchase a viewfinder camera with a zoom lens. In addition you will want to consider the purchase of a camera that can be, at a later time, incorporated into a multicamera system. This will mean a slightly higher initial cost but it will save money as you expand the system.

The Pan Head

The pan head attaches the camera to the tripod or is an integrated part of the tripod. This provides the handle for the camera and allows the Cameraman to pan and tilt the camera as it is being supported by the tripod. While good pan heads are expensive they will increase the smoothness of the Cameraman's actions and thus improve the productions.

The Tripod/Dolly

The tripod provide the support for the camera and should be one that allows you to "boom" the camera by raising or lowering the center post of the tripod. The tripod can be used by itself or a dolly can be attached to the base to provide mobility. The dolly is a three wheeled platform that allows the camera to be easily repositioned between shots or even during a production.

Microphones

Just as the camera translates reflected light into electronic signals, the microphone translates sound waves into the electronic signals. In the standard studio system there will only be one mike. However, in a system which has been expanded to include an audio mixer you may have as many as four microphones.

Sound Mixer

This unit does not normally come with the standard studio system but it can be added at any time. The sound mixer allows the inputs of a variety of microphones and auxiliary audio systems such as the audio tape recorder to be fed into a single source. Here they can be controlled and combined into a single signal that is sent to the video tape recorder.

The Video Tape Recorder

This unit in the system is designed to receive the video electronic signals from the camera and the audio electronic signals from the various sound sources and transfer these signals to a magnetic recording on the video tape. These magnetic records can then be stored, played back, and erased as circumstances require. The video tape recorder may be a cassette system that has the tape encased in a plastic container or it may be a reel to reel system that must be threaded through the video tape recorder.

The Monitor/Receiver

The monitor/receiver is designed to display the electronic signals from the camera and mikes or from the video tape recorder. This unit has two functions: (1) displaying the closed circuit signals mentioned, or (2) displaying broadcast signals.

STUDIO:
THE TV CREW, GENERAL

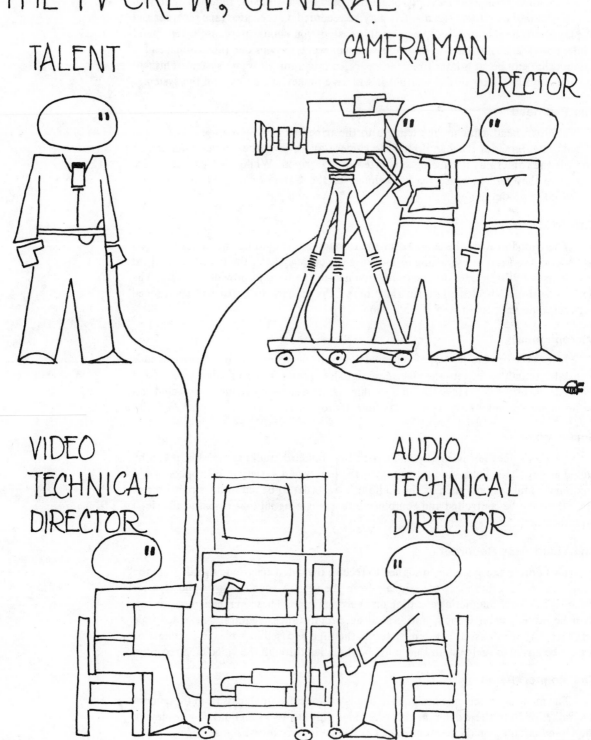

TALENT

CAMERAMAN

DIRECTOR

VIDEO TECHNICAL DIRECTOR

AUDIO TECHNICAL DIRECTOR

THE TELEVISION CREW FOR THE "STUDIO" SYSTEM

While the studio system is a single camera system like the portapak unit, it does have one significant advantage. The portapak system is designed to be operated by single individual but the studio system is intended to be operated by an entire crew. This is an advantage when the goal is to involve a group of students in the production process. The actual number of students in the studio crew may vary depending on the circumstances but a normal crew will consist of (1) a Producer/Director, (2) a Cameraman, (3) a Video Technical Director, (4) an Audio Technical Director, and (5) one or more Talent. Let's look at these roles in a little more detail.

The Producer/Director

The Producer/Director is the person who has the total responsibility and authority for the production—the boss. Because there are so many things to be done, the Producer/Director will often need to relegate some of the various roles but they retain the overall responsibility for the entire production. During the preproduction phase the Producer/Director will deal with the client and/or the Talent and develop the various planning, design, and production documents. During the actual production, the Producer/Director will give commands to the Cameraman concerning the various static and transitional shots that they are expected to get. During the post-production activity, the Producer/Director is responsible for the artistic and technical evaluation of the program and the decision to keep or to reshoot.

The Cameraman

The Cameraman is the assistant to the Producer/Director and is in charge of the rest of the production crew. During the preproduction phase he or she is responsible for making sure that the set, props, and studio cards are on hand and ready for the production. He or she also makes sure the equipment is properly wired and in good working order. During the production phase he or she operates the television camera and gets the various shots that the Producer/Director calls for. During the post-production phase he or she assists in the evaluation of the production and the storage of the production equipment and materials.

The Audio Technical Director

The Audio Technical Director's role will vary depending on the complexity of the audio system used with the production equipment. If a simple audio system (one mike) is used he or she will assist the other crew members. If a sound mixer is part of the system his or her role and responsibility is more complex. During the preproduction phase, he or she will produce any needed audio tapes, check out the audio system, and position and check the mikes and auxiliary audio systems. During the production phase he or she will operate the audio mixer and fade in and out any necessary sound and cue and play any music or sound effects that are needed. During the post-production phase the Audio Technical Director assists in the evaluation of the production and makes sure that the audio equipment is properly stored.

The Video Technical Director

The Video Technical Director is responsible for the preparation of graphic materials, the assembly of the production equipment, and assisting the Cameraman in the assembly and placement of the various props and set elements that are necessary for the production. During the actual production the Video Technical Director will operate the video tape recorder and monitor the production.

Talent

The Talent is responsible for the presentation of the required information in front of the camera.

STUDIO:
THE ROLES OF THE DIRECTOR---

PREPRODUCTION

PRODUCTION

TECHNICAL
ARTISTIC
INFORMATIONAL

POST PRODUCTION

THE PRODUCER/DIRECTOR IN A "STUDIO" SYSTEM

The Producer/Director in a "studio" television production system is the boss of the production. As the boss, the Producer/Director has all of the responsibility for the production. Whatever goes wrong the Producer/Director is the person responsible. When everything goes well who is the person responsible—the Producer/Director. When anyone has this degree of responsibility he or she also needs authority—total authority. If the Producer/Director is expected to be totally responsible for the television production he or she also needs total authority over that production and the crew that is involved. This type of authority is difficult for many people to handle. In some cases they become too authoritarian and make the crew members who work for them angry and uncooperative. In other instances they may fail to take the necessary degree of authority and the jobs just don't get done. The ideal lies somewhere in the middle ground. The Producer/Director must exert his or her authority to the degree that the necessary jobs get done but do it in such a way that the crew is not alienated.

The Producer/Director's involvement with the production begins at the very beginning. If a client comes to the Producer/Director with an idea for a program it is the task of the Producer/Director to assist in the process of putting this idea into a finished television production. The Producer/Director will take the initial client meeting and from this develop the various planning and design documents. Once these are approved by the client, the Producer/Director will then develop the rest of the design documents and production documents and meet with the production crew. During this meeting the Producer/Director will make sure that each crew member knows what is expected and will detail their individual roles in the production. The production documents will be distributed, the equipment and materials collected, and the program rehearsed with the Talent. This walk-through or rehearsal will allow the Producer/Director to make any changes that are necessary and to ensure that all the crew member know what they are doing and what is expected of them.

During the actual production, the Producer/Director will be busy calling the shots for the Cameraman and cueing the Talent. He or she will have to rely on the rest of the crew to do their jobs. This is one of the most difficult tasks of the Producer/Director. Since he or she cannot be directly involved in all of the activities that are necessary to make the proposed television program a reality he must rely on the other members of the crew. He or she must provide the necessary training and guidance to ensure that the program will be a success. In addition to making sure that they are technically ready, the Producer/Director must make sure that the entire crew, including himself are psychologically ready for the production.

When the production has been finally put onto tape the critical part of the job of the Producer/Director begins. At this point the Producer/Director must view the production, evaluate the technical and artistic quality of the program and decide whether to keep the production or to reshoot it. While the Producer/Director may listen to the ideas of the crew and the client it is his or her responsibility to make the final decision.

The Producer/Director works with the client, the Talent, and the crew to make the best possible program. This working relationship requires that the Producer/Director exhibit a degree of leadership that will allow him or her to exert the necessary authority and still maintain the cooperation of the crew, client, and Talent. It is a difficult job but it is a job essential to the production of a successful television program.

STUDIO:
DIRECTOR, PREPRODUCTION ACTIVITIES

THE PRODUCER/DIRECTOR: PREPRODUCTION ACTIVITIES

A television program can be divided into three stages or sets of activities. First there is the preproduction stage that covers all of the activities up to the actual production. Second, there is the production stage in which the program is actually put onto video tape. The last stage involves the evaluation of the production and is the post-production stage. While the Producer/Director is active in all three of these phases the preproduction phase is perhaps the one in which there is the most activity. Let's look at a simple production and see what might happen.

A client approaches you (the Producer/Director) for assistance in the design and production of a television program. During this initial client conference (A) it will be your responsibility to find the answers to some basic questions. You need to determine "What the client wants to say (content), to whom (audience), with what effect (objectives), through what channel or medium (television naturally)." The results of this interaction will be a set of rough planning documents. These are then polished by the Producer/Director (B) and presented to the client during the client approval meeting (C). Specifics on this and other aspects of the preproduction process are covered in detail in chapter IV, THE PRODUCTION PROCESS. The key to these planning and design documents is the simple fact that they are intended to communicate with others—to ensure that the client's ideas and the Producer/Director's perceptions are the same. They form the basis for all future activities and should be dealt with seriously.

Once the client has approved the planning documents, the Producer/Director next prepares a set of design documents including the script and storyboard and a set of production documents including the prop and equipment list, the shooting schedule, and the set or studio diagram (D). These design and production documents are then shared with the production crew and the Talent during the production meeting (E). At this point the Producer/Director make sure that everyone knows what his or her responsibility will be and provides training or explanation that is necessary for each crew member to be able to perform as needed.

Once the crew is trained and informed, they will then do what is required of them. They will assemble and set-up the equipment and check it out to make sure it is operating properly. Other crew members will prepare the graphics and audio tapes necessary for the production. The Talent will work on the script and his/her delivery of the information. Then, when everything is ready, the Producer/Director will call for the walk-through and the rehearsal (F).

There is a major difference between the walk-through and the rehearsal. The walk-through is just the Talent and the Producer/Director. The Talent performs and the Producer/Director checks to make sure that the shots called for in the storyboard are appropriate. Changes may be made in the shots and sequences of shots at this stage. During the rehearsal the entire production crew is involved. Here we have what we might call a dress rehearsal. It is not uncommon to actually roll the video tape during the rehearsal. Each crew member will perform in the same way that he or she is expected to perform during the actual production.

Changes that are identified during the walk-through and the rehearsal are shared with the production crew and the Talent. Once all of these changes are identified and understood the program is ready for the next stage—the production stage. This preproduction stage is vital to the success of the production stage. It is often said that the more time you spend preparing for a production the better the actual production will be.

STUDIO:
DIRECTOR, PRODUCTION AND POST-PRODUCTION

PRODUCTION

POST-PRODUCTION

EVALUATION

THE PRODUCER/DIRECTOR: THE PRODUCTION AND POST-PRODUCTION STAGES

Once the walk-through and the rehearsal are completed and the Talent and production crew have been informed of any necessary changes you are ready for the production stage. The success of this activity will be determined to a large degree by the time and effort that you, the Producer/Director have put into the preproduction stage. However, once the rehearsal is over and everyone is as ready as he/she can be you must then take them through the production itself.

While the main role of the Producer/Director during the production process is to call the shots for the Cameraman, there are many other things that also need to be done. First you need to check out your crew. Even though you have just completed the rehearsal you need to check with each crew member and ensure that he or she is ready and that he or she knows what is expected. Cover the modifications identified during the rehearsal. Then ask if the people are ready:

TALENT READY?	READY! I know what is expected and am ready to deliver the information.
CAMERA READY?	READY! I am set up on my first shot and know the rest of the shots in the program.
VIDEO READY?	READY! The VTR is cued up and in standby mode. I'm ready to monitor the program.
AUDIO READY?	READY! The mikes are checked and the music is cued and ready.
STANDBY!	
ROLL VIDEO!	(Video Technical Director starts VTR)

Now the video tape is rolling and you are ready for the actual production. Probably the first thing you will do as the Producer/Director is to fade in. In this case it simply means that you open the aperture of the camera lens to the point where you get a picture of good quality (preset this before opening the program). Once the aperture is open you then need to cue either the Cameraman or the Talent. Your instructions to the Cameraman can be whispered but you must rely on hand signals to cue the Talent or other crew members.

Let's assume that you have opened on a studio card with music. You would signal to the Audio Technical Director to fade in the music—then to open the Talent's mike. You would whisper in the Cameraman's ear to be ready to zoom out and pick up the Talent and then to zoom out (note the use of both a preparatory and an execution command). As the picture enlarges to include the Talent you will have to cue the Talent to begin his or her delivery. As the Talent begins his/her delivery, you would signal to the Audio Technical Director to fade out the opening music. This process continues until the program is completed.

Once the production is complete you move into the post-production stage—the evaluation of the production. As Producer/Director it is your responsibility to look at the production and to evaluate the artistic and technical quality of the production. While you can and should listen to the comments of the other crew members, it will be your final decision to either accept the program as it is or to reshoot it. The criteria that you use to make this decision are detailed in the evaluation section of chapter IV, THE PRODUCTION PROCESS.

In addition to the technical and artistic evaluation of the complete project there is also the instruction/informational/entertainment quality of the program to consider. However, this evaluation requires an audience. While the client may make a judgement of the *potential* instructional/informational/entertainment value of the production, an accurate determination of the ability of the program to meet the goals or objectives that were established in the planning phase requires that the production be displayed to a sample audience and their reactions be analyzed.

STUDIO:
THE ROLES OF THE CAMERAMAN

PREPRODUCTION ACTIVITIES

PRODUCTION ACTIVITIES

POST-PRODUCTION ACTIVITIES

THE CAMERAMAN IN A STUDIO SYSTEM

The Cameraman in a studio production system is the assistant to the Producer/Director. While the Producer/Director is working with the client and the preparation of the planning, design, and production documents, the Cameraman is working with the production crew to ensure that they are well trained and informed of their various roles and responsibilities. The Cameraman goes through three quite different stages in completing the program. There is the preproduction stage, the production stage, and the post-production stage. While the Cameraman is not involved in the planning and design process, he or she is still very busy during the preproduction stage.

The activities of the Cameraman begin when the Producer/Director distributes the production documents and meets with the production crew. At this point in time the Producer/Director turns the production crew over to the Cameraman. Using the various production documents the Cameraman makes sure that each crew member understands his/her assignment.

The shooting schedule informs the crew when and where the production will take place. The shooting schedule will also include the assignments for each of the crew members. Copies of the storyboard and script are also distributed at this time. The Audio Technical Director will use this to identify the number of mikes that are required and the type of music or other audio tape recordings that are called for. The Video Technical Director will use the storyboard and the script to identify the various studio cards and instructional aids that are required for the program. The remaining production documents (prop and equipment list, set or studio diagram) are used to further identify these items and ensure that they are prepared ahead of time.

As the Cameraman, it is your responsibility to supervise the rest of the production crew. During this preproduction phase you have the responsibility of checking on the activities of the Audio and the Video Technical Directors. You also have your special tasks to perform. While you may use the assistance of both the Audio and the Video Technical Director you hold the prime responsibility for the preparation of the set and the arrangement of the various props and graphics for the production. This brings us to the production stage.

During the production stage you become an extension of the Producer/Director. He will call the shots and you will execute them. But as Cameraman, you must be more than just an unthinking extension. You must know the vocabulary that the Producer/Director will use—the names of the various static and transitional shots. You must know the operation of your particular piece of equipment, the camera. You must know what is going to happen and to anticipate the Director's commands and be ready to execute them when they are given. The Producer/Director will give two types of commands; the preparatory command is your cue to get ready to do something, the execution command is your cue to do it. For example, *ready to zoom out*—a preparatory command; and *zoom out!*—an execution command.

When the production state is over you are ready to move into the next, the post-production stage. As Cameraman, you have two major areas of responsibility. First, you are responsible for assisting the Producer/Director in the evaluation of the completed program. While the Producer/Director will have the final decision you, as Cameraman, may make vital inputs into the decision in the areas of technical and artistic evaluation. In addition to the assistance in this area, you are also responsible for the dismantling and storage of the production equipment and materials. You need to assist and supervise the activities of the crew in putting the production system away.

STUDIO:

CAMERAMAN, PREPRODUCTION

PRODUCTION
DOCUMENTS

MAKE ASSIGNMENTS *

A.

V.

C.

AUDIO.

VIDEO.

CHECK

ASSEMBLE EQUIP.

ASSEMBLE SET/PROPS.

CAMERAMAN: PREPRODUCTION ACTIVITIES

The Cameraman in a single camera studio system has a very busy life but perhaps the busiest time is during what is referred to as the preproduction stage. This stage preceeds the production of the program and usually begins when the Producer/Director distributes the various design and production documents at the production meeting. Since the Cameraman is the assistant to the Producer/Director, it is often this point at which the crew is turned over to the Cameraman.

Making Sure the Crew Knows Their Jobs

This is the first task of the Cameraman and he or she is aided by the design and production documents prepared by the Producer/Director. The shooting schedule will not only describe the time and place of the production, it will also specify the individuals and their general crew responsibilities. One crew member will be assigned as Audio Technical Director and another assigned as Video Technical Director. As needed, additional personnel will be assigned to assist them and the Cameraman. Once the general crew assignments are known, it is then the Cameraman's responsibility to make sure that the individuals know exactly what is expected of them.

Making Sure That Crew Knows How to Do Their Jobs

The Cameraman must check with each crew member to make sure that he or she has the necessary skills to complete, successfully, the tasks to which he/she has been assigned. For example, does the Audio Technical Director know how to make a record-to-tape transfer of the opening and closing music? Does he/she know how to operate the audio mixer and the various audio input systems? If the answer is yes, then he/she can simply go about his/her business. If the answer is no, or even "I think so," it is the responsibility of the Cameraman to provide the training to ensure that he/she not only knows what his/her job is but how to do it. Of course, this means that the Cameraman must be totally familiar with not only his job but also with all of the jobs in the production crew.

Making Sure They Did Their Jobs

The Cameraman is responsible for checking the crew. This involves approving the content and quality of the auxiliary tapes prepared by the Audio Technical Director and the graphics prepared by the Video Technical Director. It also means checking the production system after the Audio and Video Technical Directors have set it up to make sure that it is in proper working order and that it will produce a video tape of acceptable technical quality.

Making Sure You Do Your Own Job

The Cameraman has certain primary responsibilities that must be considered. These evolve around the development of the set called for in the storyboard/script and blueprinted in the set diagram. While the Cameraman may require the assistance of the other crew members to collect and arrange the set elements and the various props necessary for the production, this activity is his primary responsibility. Also the Cameraman must make sure that he is totally familiar with the script and storyboard. He will be the one operating the camera during the actual production and advance knowledge of what to expect is essential. The Cameraman must also know the special language that the director will use to communicate—the names of the various shots and what they should look like.. The Cameraman must also master the operation of the camera so that he or she can get the shots that the Producer/Director calls for. This preproduction period is a busy time but the activities and supervision of the Cameraman will make the program successful.

STUDIO:
THE CAMERAMAN, ARRANGE SET/PROPS.

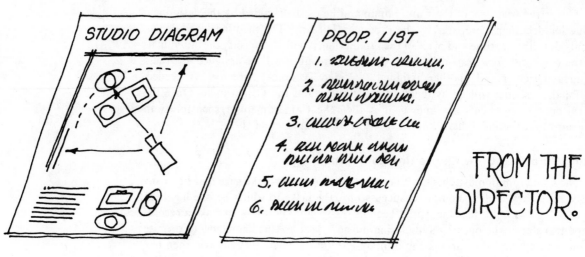

STUDIO DIAGRAM

PROP. LIST

FROM THE DIRECTOR.

THE CAMERAMAN, ARRANGING THE SETS AND PROPS FOR THE PROGRAM

While the Cameraman has the responsibility of supervising the various activities of the production crew, he/she also has the specific responsibility for collecting and arranging the various elements for the set of the proposed production. When the Producer/Director delivers the studio diagram, prop list, and script/storyboard these become the guides that the Cameraman will use to develop the set that is called for in the script/storyboard.

The set for the program may fall into one of three different types. The first is the existing set. In this case you move the production to an area that is just what the script calls for. For a program dealing with a chemical experiment you might logically move into the chemistry lab of the school. If you want an office setting you might ask the principal for permission to use his office. A second type of set might be one in which you can use an existing space but need to modify it to some degree. If your program for the chemical experiment is part of a horror story you might need to add some elements to create the right atmosphere for the school chemistry lab. If the office setting is to be President Lincoln's office then a different group of props might be needed to provide the proper historical setting. The third type of set is that which you have to prepare from scratch. For example it might be difficult to acquire the interior of a submarine or to find a Hobbit's home but these could be constructed by the production crew under your supervision.

A brief word about cost. Obviously the least expensive system is using an existing set and the most expensive is creating the set from scratch. However, the set is essential to the program. It is often the difference between a professional and an amateur production. Often a few extra props such as pictures or drapes will transform an otherwise drab existing set into the proper atmosphere for your production.

This brings us to the production documents that you will use to develop these sets. Basically there are three documents that you need to consult to develop the set: (1) the studio or set diagram is the basic blueprint; (2) the prop and equipment list describes what is necessary for the production; and (3) the script/storyboard may provide an overall idea of the atmosphere that is to be created. While these documents are produced by the Producer/Director, the Cameraman may often be involved in the decision making process in this early stage.

The studio or set diagram is basically a map of where the set and prop elements, the equipment, and the talent will be located. To produce this, the Producer/Director and the Cameraman will often scout the location ahead of time and determine whether the existing location is appropriate or whether it requires some modification. Then their rough sketch is translated into the set diagram which serves as a blueprint for the production. The prop and equipment list is used to identify the special props and set elements that are needed to make the setting exactly right or to provide the talent with items to be manipulated during the production. The script and the storyboard are used in a more general way. A careful reading of these will identify the atmosphere for the entire production.

As we indicated earlier, this preparation of the set is a major responsibility of the Cameraman. While the rest of the production crew may participate in this process it remains the job of the Cameraman in the single camera studio production.

STUDIO:
CAMERAMAN, THE CAMERA

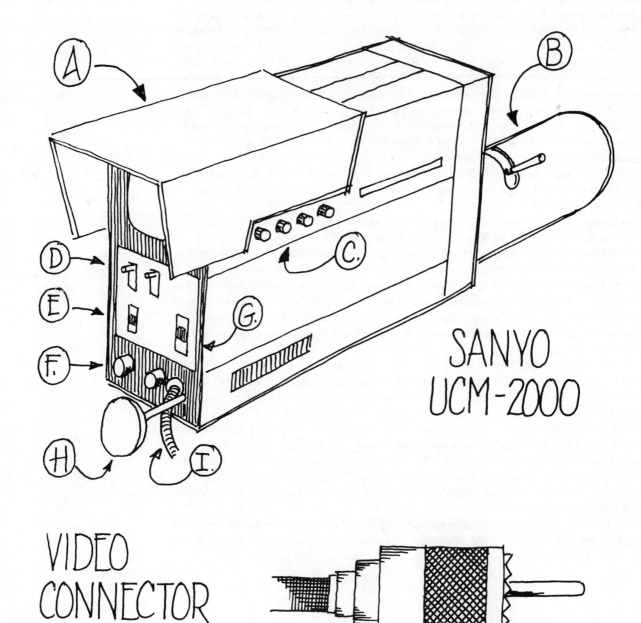

SANYO
UCM-2000

VIDEO
CONNECTOR

THE CAMERAMAN AND THE TELEVISION CAMERA

The Cameraman has a variety of roles and responsibilities in a single camera studio system. He or she supervises the rest of the production crew, is primarily responsible for the preparation of the set in which the production will take place, and is responsible for the operation of the camera during the actual production. This latter role requires that the Cameraman be totally familiar with the camera, its accessories, and the various camera shots.

The television camera for a single camera studio system should have the following characteristics: (1) It should be a viewfinder camera, one with the viewfinder attached to the top; (2) it should have a zoom lens which is remoted so that the operator can zoom and focus from the rear of the camera; (3) it should be capable of operating from both internal and internal sync, for later expansion to a multicamera system; and (4) it should have video outputs suitable for both straight video and multicamera 8 or 10-pin outputs. In addition the camera should be a low light level camera that will allow you to shoot in a wide variety of existing light situations.

I have had a great deal of success with the Sanyo UCM-2000 camera. The diagram on the opposite page shows this particular camera and we can use it to learn the parts of all cameras. The viewfinder (A) is used by both the Cameraman and the Director to monitor the images that the camera sees. The zoom lens (B) allows the Cameraman to enlarge or reduce the image without physically moving the camera. The zoom has a control for the aperture which allows control of the amount of light entering the camera. The zoom and focus controls (H) are mounted on the rear of the camera. In this case you push or pull the rod to zoom in or out and rotate the handle to focus the image. The viewfinder has separate controls (C) that allow you to adjust the image on the viewfinder. These adjustments do *not* control the quality of the outgoing video signal. This particular camera has a camera/monitor switch (D) which allows you to either monitor the camera image on the viewfinder or to monitor the image from the video tape recorder. Just to the right of this switch is the ALC defeat switch. In the on position this switch will allow the camera to compensate for abrupt changes in the lighting situation. The sync selector switch (E) lets the Cameraman select either an internal or external sync source for the camera. In single camera operation this should be on "internal" and in multicamera operation it should be on "external." The video outputs are located just below these switches (F). One is a straight video output that accepts the standard video connector and the other is a multi-pin video connector. The straight video connector is used in a single camera system and the multi-pin connector is used in the multi camera system. The power switch (G) and the AC power cord (I) supply the power that is necessary for the camera to operate.

While any good television camera can be used as the basis for a single camera production system you need to keep in mind the possible expansion of the system to incorporate more than one camera at a later time. Savings on cameras in the original purchase can often result in more expense when you are ready to expand the system. A little extra money spent on the camera for a single camera system will result in the expansion of the system with much less cost. Once you have your camera and know the names and functions of the various parts you are ready to learn more about your role as cameraman in a single camera studio system.

STUDIO:
CAMERAMAN, ACCESSORIES

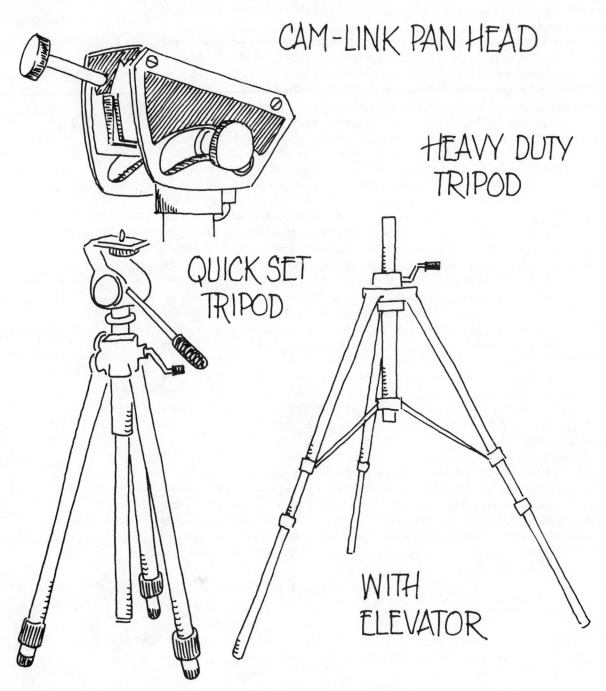

CAM-LINK PAN HEAD

HEAVY DUTY
TRIPOD

QUICK SET
TRIPOD

WITH
ELEVATOR

CAMERA ACCESSORIES

The camera in the single camera studio system, unlike the portapak camera, cannot be hand held. It requires some sort of support system that will provide both stability and mobility to the camera. There are actually three different components in this support system: (1) the pan head, (2) the tripod, and (3) the dolly. Each of these three elements serves a specific function and comes in a wide range of quality. Again we are faced with the situation of cost. You can buy inexpensive support systems, but you have to remember that they are supporting a very expensive piece of equipment. In many instances it is not cost effective to settle for the least expensive item.

The Pan Head

The pan head is designed to be the connection between the camera and the tripod. The camera is bolted to the pan head and the pan head is bolted to the tripod. The function of the pan head is to provide the Cameraman with the ability to smoothly pan and/or tilt the camera as desired. The handle for the camera extends from the pan head and lock nuts are loosened on the sides to allow the desired freedom of movement. Basically there are three types of pan heads available for the support of television cameras. The least expensive is the friction pan head in which the camera is held steady by the friction of the lock nuts on the side of the pan head. There are also gear pan heads in which the tilt mode can be controlled by a gear mechanism. While this will smooth out any tilts that are required for the program they do not aid the pans or combinations of pans and tilts. The cam-link pan head provides smooth pans and tilts and prevents the possibility of the camera nose-diving.

The Tripod

The tripod is the basic support system for the camera. Make sure that you get a tripod that will support the weight of the camera, lens, and pan head. Like the pan heads the tripods come in a wide range of quality and cost. The Quick-Set tripod shown on the opposite page is an example of one of the least expensive tripods. Note that it also has a built-in pan head. Heavy duty tripods like the one shown on the opposite page have lateral supports from the elevator column to the individual legs. The third type of tripod is the pedestal tripod (not shown) which looks like the professional support systems found in broadcast studios. The tripod should have legs that are adjustable in length and it should also have an elevator or pedestal that will allow you to raise or lower the height of the camera. This is generally called "booming"—you boom up or boom down.

The Dolly

The dolly is a three-wheeled support system that provides the entire camera assembly with mobility. It allows you to move the camera from position to position either before the production or during the production. A dolly is essential in a multi-camera system but not in a single camera system. The physical movement of the camera during an actual production is commonly called trucking or dollying. You truck to the right or left and dolly in or out. It is difficult to control these shots and they are not commonly used on the air. However, it is common to reposition the camera that is off the air during a multicamera production. In a single camera system the only real purpose of the dolly is to move the camera to and from the shooting area.

These three elements—the pan head, the tripod, and the dolly—are common accessories that you will find with the television camera. They add to the cost but the smoothness that they provide is well worth it.

STUDIO:
CAMERA SHOTS, STATIC

LONG SHOT   MEDIUM SHOT   CLOSE UP

LONG SHOT   MEDIUM SHOT   CLOSE UP

TWO SHOT   EXTREME CLOSE UP   EXTREME LONG SHOT

STATIC CAMERA SHOTS

It is important that anyone involved in television production know both the names and the descriptions of the various television shots. These are the vocabulary of the television program. The Producer/Director needs to know them to prepare the storyboard and to adequately communicate with the other crew members. The television Cameraman needs to know these shots to be able to read the storyboard and to translate the Director's words into acceptable action. Even the Talent must know the names and effects of the shots to be able to anticipate movement patterns and to know when and where to manipulate the props.

These various shots can easily be subdivided into two classes: (1) static shots, and (2) transitional shots. The static shots are used to feature a person or an object. The transitional shots are used to move the camera from one static shot to another. People who are new to television production seem to think that to maintain visual interest they must keep the camera in continual motion. It is as if the term "motion picture" refers to the movement of the camera rather than the static camera taking pictures of people in motion. Let's examine some of the basic static camera shots.

First there are basically three static shots: (1) the close-up, (2) the medium shot, and (3) the long shot. The long shot shows the subject and the environment in which it exists. Often it is referred to as the establishing shot—establishing the subject and its environment. The actual size of the shot is a function of the subject. The long shot on the top row on the opposite page shows a Talent in an environment (the corner of a room). It is a wide shot. However, immediately below we see the same shot—a long shot—of a glass of water. In this case it is a much smaller shot but it is still a long shot of that glass of water. The medium shot is treated the same way. It is not the size of the shot that counts but rather what it shows. The medium shot, whether it be of a person or a glass of water, emphasizes the subject and shows only a small portion of the environment. As we move on to the close-up, the emphasis is entirely on the subject and there is little or not environment showing. Generally a program begins with either a long shot or close-up and then moves to the other shots. For example, we might begin with a long shot to establish the subject in the environment and then go to a medium shot and finally to a close-up. Or for a quite different effect we might begin with a close-up and then go to a medium shot and end up with an establishing shot.

There are obviously other shots. Some of the more common static shots include (1) the two shot, (2) the extreme close-up, and (3) the extreme long shot. The two shot is just what the name implies—a shot of two separate elements, in this case two people. The extreme close-up and the extreme long shot are just what their names imply. Some other shots that the Producer/Director might call for are waist shots (a shot of the Talent from the waist up), bust shots (a shot of the Talent from the bust up—similar to a medium shot), profile shots (showing only the Talent in profile), etc. To ensure that the Cameramen and the other people in the production crew know exactly what shots the Producer/Director wants, they go through the required shots during the rehearsal. This communication about the various shots is essential and so it is necessary that each person in the crew has a common understanding of what the various shots look like and how to get them effectively and efficiently.

STUDIO:
CAMERA SHOTS, TRANSITIONS

THE PAN AS A TRANSITION ▶

OPENING TITLE CARDS ▶

THE TILT AS A TRANSITION

TITLE CARD

THE ZOOM AS A TRANSITION

TRANSITIONAL CAMERA SHOTS FOR THE STUDIO SYSTEM

In a multicamera production system, the transitions between the various static shots are the switches between cameras. These may be cuts, dissolves, wipes or other special effects. They are the means of getting from one static shot to another. In a program that is designed for post-production editing, the transitions are provided by the cuts that are inserted in the editing function. In a single camera studio production where the program is shot from beginning to end without any interruption these transitions take the form of camera movements such as the pan, the tilt, the zoom, and combinations of these three.

The Pan as a Transitional Shot

On the opposite page, you can see one application of the pan as a means of providing a transition between three static shots. The static shots are a close-up of the opening title card, a medium close-up of the Talent and a medium shot of the subject. Beginning with the close-up of the studio card, the camera will then pan right to the Talent. After the Talent has introduced himself and the topic of the program the Director will again say "Pan right!" and the Cameraman will pan to the subject. The reverse of this can be used to close the program. The camera pans from the subject to the Talent who closes the program and then to the studio cards to end the program. In this situation the placement of the studio cards, Talent and subject is important.

The Tilt as a Transitional Shot

While the pan is a horizontal camera movement, the tilt is a vertical camera movement. As shown on the opposite page, the sequence can begin with a static shot of the studio card then as the Director says, "Tilt down!" the Cameraman will tilt to show the Talent. Again the Talent will introduce the topic and upon the Director's command the Cameraman will tilt down to show the subject. This last static shot will be held steady as the talent manipulates the materials that are the subject of the program. When the manipulation is completed, the Director will again say "Ready to tilt up, tilt up!" And the Cameraman will tilt up to frame the Talent for his/her closing remarks. Then at the appropriate time the camera will tilt up again to show the closing card for the end of the program. Like the pan shot this tilt shot must be set up well in advance to ensure that as the Cameraman tilts up or down he or she is showing the information that the Director wants shown.

The Zoom as a Transitional Shot

Notice that both the pan and the tilt movement keep the same relative camera shot. The zoom, on the other hand, is a change in the relative size of the camera shot. In the example on the opposite page, you might begin with a shot of the studio card, then zoom out to show both the card and the Talent, then zoom out to a long shot of the Talent, and finally back into a medium close-up of the Talent. Actually it is almost impossible not to include both pans and tilts when you are making a zoom transition. Note on the opposite page, that the zoom shown also includes a pan to the left and a slight tilt up. The zoom is the most difficult transitional camera movement to make smoothly. It will require a lot of practice but the results will be well worth it.

These camera shots, both the static shots and the transitional shots, are like the punctuation in a paragraph of good writing. They provide the emphasis that is necessary to make the talent's performance come alive and communicate the concept that you want communicated.

STUDIO:

THE CAMERAMAN, PRODUCTION AND POST-PRODUCTION

PRODUCTION

POST-PRODUCTION, EVALUATION

THE CAMERAMAN: PRODUCTION AND POST-PRODUCTION ACTIVITIES

Once the rehearsal has been completed, the activity moves from the preproduction to the production stage. With this change there also comes a change in the nature of the activities of the Cameraman. During the preproduction activity, the Cameraman has certain individual responsibilities but he/she is also acting in a supervisory capacity. He/she is responsible for the other members of the production crew. This supervisory role changes when the production activity begins.

Production Activities

During the actual production, the Cameraman becomes an extension of the Producer/Director. The Cameraman will operate the camera but will take commands from the Producer/Director. These commands fall into two categories: preparatory commands and execution commands. The preparatory command is designed to allow the Cameraman to get ready for the action that is anticipated. The execution command is the signal for that action. The following is an example of the type of preparatory and execution commands that might occur in a simple single camera production.

READY TO FADE IN.	(Preparatory command)
FADE IN!	(Execution, by Director)
READY TO ZOOM OUT TO THE TALENT.	(Preparatory command)
ZOOM OUT.	(Execution, by Cameraman)
READY TO PAN WITH TALENT.	(Preparatory command)
PAN WITH THE TALENT!	(Execution, by Cameraman)
READY TO ZOOM IN ON THE PROP.	(Preparatory command)
ZOOM IN!	(Execution command)

Even though the Cameraman will respond to the command of the Producer/Director, he/she must be more than just a simple extension. The Cameraman must anticipate the shots that are necessary. To do this the Cameraman needs to be almost as familiar with the production as the Producer/Director. This familiarity is developed by a careful reading of the script and the storyboard and by the careful attention paid during the rehearsal. This preparation will allow the Cameraman to anticipate the shots and even, in certain circumstances, to take over the Producer/Director's role during production.

Obviously the Cameraman must also need to know the techniques for the operation of the camera and the nomenclature of the various shots that are part of the storyboard and script. With this preparation, the Cameraman is ready for the production activities.

Post-Production Activities

Once the production is on video tape, the role of the Cameraman again changes. During the post-production activity, there are two major activities that the Cameraman will be involved with. First, the Cameraman will assist the Producer/Director in the technical and artistic evaluation of the production. Secondly, the Cameraman will supervise the rest of the production crew in the dismantling and storage of the production equipment, props, and set elements. The evaluation role is an advisory role since it is the responsibility of the Producer/Director to make the final decision. However, the Cameraman's input is vital. Can the shots and transitions be improved? Can the moving shots be made smoother? These are questions that only the Cameraman can answer.

STUDIO:
THE ROLE OF THE AUDIO TECH. DIRECTOR

PREPRODUCTION ACTIVITIES

PRODUCTION ACTIVITIES

POST-PRODUCTION ACTIVITIES

THE AUDIO TECHNICAL DIRECTOR: INTRODUCTION

The exact nature of the role that the Audio Technical Director plays in the single camera production system is a function of the type of audio system that is available. Normally a single camera system has a single mike plugged directly into the video tape recorder. In this situation the Audio Technical Director has very few audio responsibilities and can take over the Cameraman's job with the sets and props. In the situation where you have added a sound mixer and an audio tape recorder to the system the Audio Technical Director has many more responsibilities in the area of audio. Let's look at these various roles and responsibilities of the Audio Technical Director with an expanded audio system.

Preproduction

During the preproduction phase of the project the Audio Technical Director is responsible for the following: (1) preparation of auxiliary audio information, (2) the assembly of the audio equipment and interconnecting it to the video system, (3) the wiring of the Talent and the establishment of the various sound levels, and (4) running the audio system during the rehearsal.

It all begins when the Producer/Director has the production meeting and distributes the production documents. With the Cameraman acting as the supervisor, the Audio Technical Director will determine the type of opening and closing music that is required and translate it from disc to tape recordings. The Audio Technical Director will consult the storyboard and script to determine the number of mikes that will be needed and their approximate placement. When the day arrives and the equipment is delivered to the set area, the Audio Technical Director and the Video Technical Director will assemble the system, interconnect the various parts and check it out. Once the system is checked out, the Audio Technical Director will wire up the Talent, check the sound levels and make sure that all audio systems are "go." Then during the rehearsal the Audio Technical Director will make the final adjustments as he/she works with the audio equipment.

Production

Once the problems have been ironed out during the rehearsal, the Audio Technical Director prepares for the actual video taping. During production, the Audio Technical Director will have a good idea of what is going to happen but should rely on the hand signals from the Producer/Director to actually execute the various changes. The Audio Technical Director should also monitor the sound track of the program and keep a record of any problems that might require a reshooting. During this process, the Audio Technical Director will continually refer to the storyboard/script and to the changes and modification identified during the rehearsal.

Post-Production

Once the program has been taped, the Audio Technical Director has two major roles to play. First, he/she assists the Producer/Director and the rest of the crew in the technical and artistic evaluation of the production. Since the Audio Technical Director has the responsibility for the audio portion of the program, his or her input into this aspect of the technical quality of the production is important. However, the Producer/Director will make the final decision to reshoot or to keep the program. Once the program has been accepted, the Audio Technical Director will assist the Video Technical Director in the dismantling of the system and the storage of the various parts so that they will be ready for the next production.

STUDIO:
THE AUDIO TECH. DIR., PREPRODUCTION

SCRIPT

AUDIO

EQUIPMENT SET-UP

WIRE THE TALENT

REHEARSAL

AUDIO TECHNICAL DIRECTOR: PREPRODUCTION ACTIVITIES

The preproduction activities begin at the production meeting. The Producer/ Director normally will turn supervision of the crew over to the Cameraman. At this point, the various design and production documents will be distributed and explained. If you are assigned the role of Audio Technical Director you will be especially interested in: (1) the storyboard/script, (2) the set diagram, and (3) the shooting schedule. The shooting schedule will tell you the where and when of the production. The storyboard/ script will help you determine the number of microphones that will be necessary and the type of opening and closing music that the Producer/Director will require. The set diagram will show where the Producer/Director wants the mikes and the equipment placed.

Probably the first task that the Audio Technical Director should undertake is the transfer of the desired music and/or sound effects from records to tape. This can be done with either a through-the-air transfer or by a wire transfer system. It requires that the sound from a record player be transferred to magnetic recordings on audio tape. Obviously it should be the same format (reel-to-reel or cassette) as the auxiliary tape recorder in the single camera production system. Make sure that either the Cameraman or the Producer/Director approve both the content (the music transferred) and the technical quality of the transfer.

The next task of the Audio Technical Director is to assist the Video Technical Director in the acquisition, delivery, and assembly of the television production system. While the main concern of the Audio Technical Director will be the audio components of the system it will be necessary to be involved with the entire unit since the components must be interconnected. Once the system is ready, a check should be run to determine the quality of the audio and video signal that is being recorded. Nothing is worse than to have to rework the system during the actual production.

Once the system is functioning properly the Audio Technical Director should wire up the various Talent with microphones, play the audio tape, and check the levels and quality of the recordings. In this situation, the Audio Technical Director may have to change the mike placement that is indicated in the set or studio diagram. Changes that are made should be shared with the Cameraman so that he/she can approve of them. This activity is perhaps the most important one that the Audio Technical Director will be involved in. Unfortunately the quality of the audio in a television production is not given the attention that it deserves. Your work with the audio system will contribute markedly to the overall quality of the television production.

The last preproduction activity of the Audio Technical Director is the operation of the audio system and the monitoring of the audio during the rehearsal. This rehearsal will allow the Audio Technical Director to identify any problems in mike placement, music cueing, or sound levels that might affect the actual production. The Audio Technical Director needs to make full use of this opportunity to ensure that all systems are "go" and that the quality of the audio system is acceptable.

While the Audio Technical Director is primarily concerned with the audio component of the production he/she is also a member of the production crew and thus is concerned with the overall technical and artistic quality of the program. The Audio Technical Director works under the supervision of the Cameraman. This means that any questions or concerns that the Audio Technical Director may have should be brought to the Cameraman's attention.

STUDIO:
RECORD TO TAPE TRANSFER

RECORD PLAYER   MIKE

HEAD SET

TAPE RECORDER

THROUGH-THE-AIR DUPLICATION

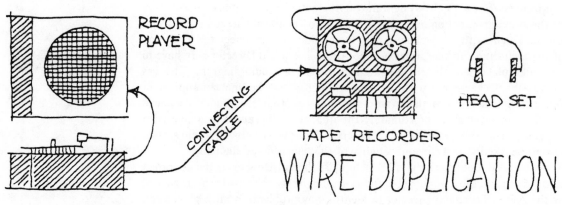

RECORD PLAYER

CONNECTING CABLE

HEAD SET

TAPE RECORDER

WIRE DUPLICATION

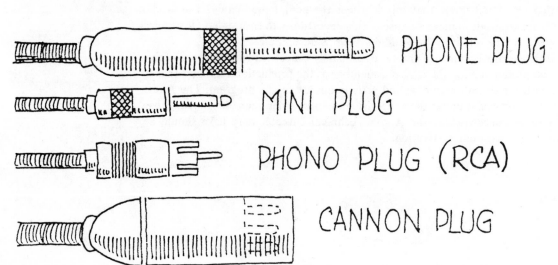

PHONE PLUG

MINI PLUG

PHONO PLUG (RCA)

CANNON PLUG

70

TRANSFERRING RECORDS TO TAPE FOR A PORTAPAK PRODUCTION

First, a word about copyright. Most recorded music is owned by someone else. In some cases there may be a copyright on the words, the music, and even on the arrangement. This copyright is designed to protect the author's property. If you transfer the information on a record to a tape format you are violating the copyright of the people who own the material. If this is the case and you want to use music in your production what are your options? Educational activities tend to fall under what is called fair use. Simplistically this means that if you do not cause the copyright holder to lose money and you do not make money from the process you are not in violation of the copyright. To avoid any problems with copyright you turn to your own resources. Perhaps there is someone in your school who could create a simple melody and someone else who could play it. All you have to do is record it with a tape recorder and you can stop worrying about copyright. Also there are some records such as SOUNDS FOR A PICTURE EVENING that are available from *Popular Photography* that are designed to be used in local production activities. These can be transferred to tape and used without fear of violating someone's copyright.

But how do you go about making these disc to tape transfers? There are two basic systems: (1) through the air duplication and (2) wire duplication. The first is simpler but will not provide the quality. The second is more difficult but will provide a higher quality. These two systems are diagrammed on the opposite page. In the through the air system the equipment is set up as shown. The record player is set up with its speaker system. The mike from the tape recorder is placed fairly close to the speaker. The tape recorder is turned on and the record player is turned on. The sound leaves the speaker of the record player and is picked up by the mike and sent to the tape recorder where it is recorded on audio tape. This needs to be done in a quiet environment as the live mike will pick up sounds of traffic, clocks, airplanes or anything else that is part of that environment. The person doing the recording should wear a pair of headsets to monitor the recording and to identify any extraneous sounds that interfere with the music. Even with this monitoring system you should play the tape back to check the recording and to make sure you have what you want.

For a more polished dubbing from disc to tape, you should consider the wire duplication system. In this case the output of the record player is connected to the input of the tape recorder by wire. Since there is no microphone the speaker of the record player is used only to monitor the recording. The sound from the record player is sent to two different sources. One set of audio signals drives the speaker of the record player for monitoring and the other is sent, by wire, to the tape recorder where it is recorded. In this case, the recording environment may be as noisy as necessary since there is no mike to pick it up. Again a set of headsets should be used to monitor what is being recorded.

Audio equipment may not always have the same input plugs or jacks. This means that you need to know the names of the various audio connectors. On the opposite page, we see the four most common audio plugs. The plug is the male connector and the female connector is called a jack. To complete a connection you need to find out what the output jack looks like and what the input plug or jack looks like and then get a connector that has the right plugs or jacks to interconnect the system. These are often available at your local audio store.

STUDIO:
THE AUDIO SYSTEM (WITH MIXER)

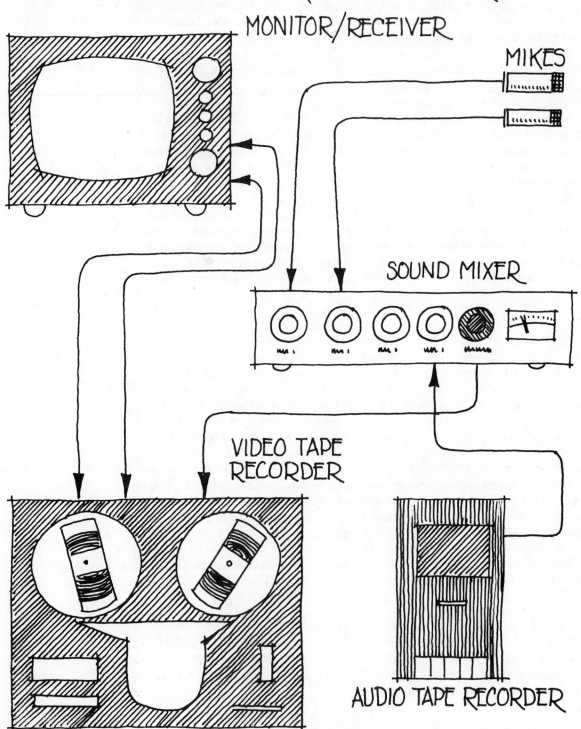

MONITOR/RECEIVER

MIKES

SOUND MIXER

VIDEO TAPE
RECORDER

AUDIO TAPE RECORDER

ASSEMBLY OF THE AUDIO SYSTEM

As we indicated earlier, there are two basic types of audio systems used in a single camera television production unit. First, the single mike is plugged directly into the mike input of the video tape recorder. This means that only a single audio input is being used and this severely limits the flexibility and quality of the audio portion of the television production. If possible you should add a more flexible audio system to the production unit.

The ideal audio system consists of a variety of audio input sources such as microphones and auxiliary tape recorders that are fed into separate channels of a sound mixer. The sound mixer has the ability to control the volume level of each of these input sources and to deliver a composite audio signal to the video tape recorder. The sound mixer is obviously the key component to the audio system so let's look at it in a little detail.

The Sound Mixer

There are a wide variety of sound mixers available that might be used with a single camera studio system. Prices range from $10 to $100. This is no place to skimp on costs. The less expensive sound mixers might work but the quality would leave a lot to be desired. It is better to spend a little more and to get a professional sound mixer. It should have individual "pots" (potentiometers) for each channel. These pots allow you to individually control the volume of the input source that is dedicated to that particular channel. The sound mixer should also have a master pot that controls the volume of the outgoing audio signal. A VU meter is helpful—this is simply a visual display of the quality of the sound level. If it begins to peak in the red area, it means that the sound is being distorted and the master volume level or the individual pots need to be turned down.

Audio Tape Recorder

The audio tape recorder is a sound input that can be fed into the sound mixer. It is best if this is a cassette type of unit and it will be very helpful if it has a digital footage counter. This way the different music and sound effects can be on separate cassettes and quickly inserted and removed as they are needed or used. The footage counter will allow you to accurately cue up the music or sound effects.

The System

The microphones are plugged into the input channels at the rear of the sound mixer. Either purchase your mikes with the right kinds of jacks or purchase adapter cables that will allow them to be plugged into the mixer. The output of the audio tape recorder (usually the earphone jack) is connected to the input channel in the auxiliary pot of the sound mixer. The output of the sound mixer is then plugged into the audio input of the video tape recorder. The audio and video output of the video tape recorder are then plugged into the audio and video input of the monitor/receiver. This interconnection may take many different forms but they all serve the same function.

There is one other component that is not shown on the opposite page that will make your job as Audio Technical Director much easier. A pair of earphones can be an invaluable addition to the system. When these are plugged into the headset jack on the video tape recorder, you will be able to monitor the sound system much more effectively. Without these you will have to rely on the loudspeaker of the monitor/receiver and quite often this must be turned down quite low to eliminate the possibility of feedback through the live microphones.

STUDIO:
MIKES AND MIKE PLACEMENT

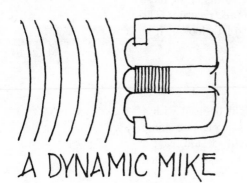

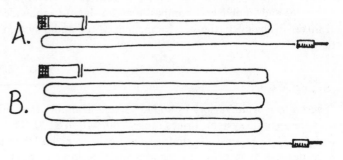

A.

B.

A DYNAMIC MIKE

FIST

—THE LAVALIER MIKE—

FLOOR MIKE

DESK MIKE

MIKES AND MIKE PLACEMENT

Another obvious concern of the Audio Technical Director is with the types of microphones that are used in the production system. These microphones come is a wide range of styles, costs, and functions. Picking the right microphone for a television production system is very important.

Types of Microphones

Basically there are three types of microphones that are commonly used in television production systems. The crystal mike is usually the least expensive but the frequency response leaves a lot to be desired. It is just not normally a professional microphone. Condenser microphones (requiring an auxiliary power source), are much more professional and provide excellent frequency response. The main problem with condenser mikes is simply that they are rather delicate. They normally will not hold up under the type of use that they are given in the public schools. I recommend the dynamic microphone. This type of microphone has an acceptable frequency response and holds up much better under heavy use.

The Impedance of the Microphone

Impedance is basically a measurement of the resistance to the flow of electricity. High impedance microphones (see A on the opposite page) have relatively short mike cables. Low impedance microphones (B) can use much longer mike cables and even extension cables. This is quite important because it allows you to work the Talent further from the equipment and avoid equipment noise.

The Style of the Microphone

The lavalier type of microphone is the most versatile one for television production. The mike can be hung around the Talent's neck or inserted into floor or desk stands for group pickup. Specialty microphones are generally expensive and have relatively limited use in television production situations.

The Placement of the Microphone

Once you have the mikes for your production system the next concern is simply where do you place them. Obviously you need to know how many Talent have speaking parts and what other types of sound input are required for the production. The script/storyboard will give you some insights into this. Also you should check the set or studio diagram that was prepared by the Producer/Director. Let's assume that you need to wire a Talent that will be walking from place to place in the set. The mike is fastened around the Talent's neck. It is adjusted so that it is a fist's length from the Talent's chin and so that it does not hit any hard surfaces (jewelry-buttons-etc). The mike cable is then looped through the belt (or waist band of the skirt) so that it hangs to the side. This will allow the Talent to move without tripping over his/her own mike cord. For an interview situation the mike can be hand held and simply directed to the individual who is doing the talking. In this case it may look rather bad and you will probably want to limit the shots to head and shoulders to avoid seeing the mike and its movement back and forth. When groups are involved you can fasten the lavalier mike into either a floor stand or a desk stand. In these situations you will want to angle the mike toward the talent with the weakest voice.

There is no good rule for mike placement. It will be different for each Talent and each environment. As the Audio Technical Director you should try a placement and then check the quality and level of the sound. This process of trying and checking will result in a mike placement that will improve the audio portion of your program.

STUDIO:
THE ROLE OF THE VIDEO TECH. DIRECTOR

PREPRODUCTION ACTIVITIES

PRODUCTION ACTIVITIES

POST-PRODUCTION ACTIVITIES

THE VIDEO TECHNICAL DIRECTOR: INTRODUCTION

We have arrived at the consideration of the roles and responsibilities of our last crew member, the Video Technical Director. We have looked at the Producer/Director who is in overall charge of the production crew, the Cameraman who assists the Producer/Director and supervises the production crew, and the Audio Technical Director who is responsible for the audio portion of the single camera production. Now we want to explore what the Video Technical Director does.

As with the other crew members the roles and responsibilities of the Video Technical Director vary depending on the production stage. Like most crew members the Video Technical Director appears to be very busy during the preproduction phase and least involved during the post-production activities. Let's look at each of these phases in general terms.

The Preproduction Activities of the Video Technical Director

Given the various design and production documents developed by the Producer/Director and distributed by the Cameraman, the Video Technical Director will be responsible for (1) preparing the studio cards and various graphics for the program, (2) assembling the various instructional aids and modifying them if necessary, (3) assembling the production equipment and checking it out, and (4) operating the video tape recorder during the rehearsal. In some of these activities the Video Technical Director will work closely with other crew members. During the assembly of the production equipment he/she will work closely with the Audio Technical Director and during the rehearsal he/she will work closely with the entire production crew. In other activities the Video Technical Director will operate in isolation. The preparation of the studio cards and the collection and modification of the instructional aids are primarily individual activities.

The Production Activities of the Video Technical Director

During the actual production the Video Technical Director is usually the least involved of the production crew. His/her main role will be to start the video tape recorder, provide the countdown, and then monitor the production. Since there is no great pressure on the Video Technical Director during the production this makes him/her a very important member of the crew. When anything goes wrong or is about to go wrong it will be the Video Technical Director who comes to the rescue. A good Video Technical Director will develop an almost global awareness of everything that is going on and what should be happening. Quite often the Video Technical Director rushes into a breech and solves a problem before it happens.

The Post-Production Acitvities of the Video Technical Director

During the evaluation stage the Video Technical Director will rewind, cue, and playback the production. He/she will also assist the other crew members in providing the Producer/Director with comments and suggestions as to the artistic and technical quality of the production. Often the Video Technical Director can answer the questions as to what can be done to improve a production because he/she was free to see what everyone was doing or wasn't doing. Once the evaluation is completed and the Producer/Director has made the decision to keep the production the Video Technical Director and the Audio Technical Director are free to disassemble the production equipment and return it to its storage area. Also the Video Technical Director will, when possible, assist the other crew member to perform the necessary tasks of putting other things away and preparing for the next production.

STUDIO :
VIDEO T.D., PREPRODUCTION

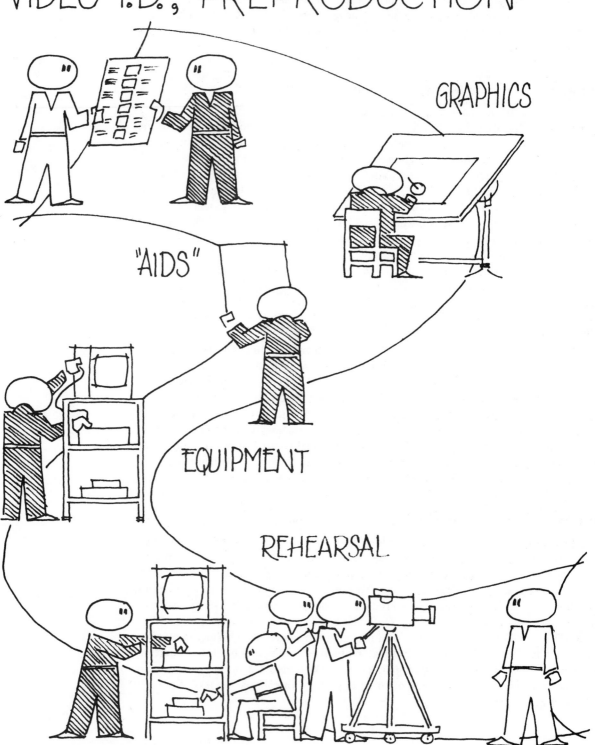

GRAPHICS

"AIDS"

EQUIPMENT

REHEARSAL

VIDEO TECHNICAL DIRECTOR, PREPRODUCTION ACTIVITIES

The preproduction activities of the Video Technical Director begin with the production meeting called by the Producer/Director. At this time the Producer/Director will discuss the assignments and distribute the various design and production documents. Normally the Cameraman will be assigned the task of supervising the Audio and Video Technical Directors and any assistants that they might have. However, the Video Technical Director will utilize these production documents to identify the graphic needs of the production. These studio cards will be used to open or close the program. This is one of the first tasks that the Video Technical Director should perform. The descriptions of these studio cards will be found both in the storyboard/script and the prop and equipment list. The design requirements for these studio cards can be found on the next page and the techniques of mounting, lettering, and illustration that are used to produce them can be found in GRAPHICS: SKILLS, MEDIA, AND MATERIALS, by Les Satterthwaite and published by Kendall/Hunt. Once they are completed they should be approved by either the Cameraman or the Producer/Director.

The next major concern of the Video Technical Director is the various visual aids that are called for in the script. Normally these are used only in instructional and informational programs. They can range from flip charts to projected slides and overhead transparencies. In many cases they will be existing materials and the Video Technical Director will only have to collect them. However, most existing visual aids are not designed for presentation on television. The aspect ratio of the TV screen is 3×4. This means that the display surface is three units high by four units wide. It also means that when you want to show something on that display surface it must conform to that aspect ratio. If your flip chart (an example) is a 2×4 ratio, two units wide by four units high, you will either have to show only a portion of the flip chart or if you show the entire chart there will be empty space on both sides. When necessary visual aids cannot be conformed to the aspect ratio of the television screen it will be the responsibility of the Video Technical Director to either adapt them or to create appropriate visuals.

Once the Video Technical Director has prepared the studio cards and selected and/or modified the visual aids it is time to prepare the equipment. On the day and time listed in the shooting schedule the Video Technical Director will team with the Audio Technical Director to collect and assemble the equipment described in the prop and equipment list. This aspect of the Video Technical Director's responsibility requires that he work closely with another member of the team. Each member will have a special interest (the Video Technical Director will be interested in the video components and the Audio Technical Director will be interested in the audio components) but unless they work closely together they will not be able to assemble a complete system.

Once the system is assembled the Audio and the Video Technical Directors need to check it out. Running a test tape is essential. Check the technical quality of both the audio and the video signal to make sure that you are ready for the rehearsal and the production.

During the rehearsal the Video Technical Director will be responsible for the operation of the video tape recorder, providing the count down to ensure that the sync signal is stabilized, and in monitoring the entire program but especially the video portion. This is the opportunity for the final check on the system and the production before the real thing.

STUDIO:
VIDEO T.D., STUDIO CARDS

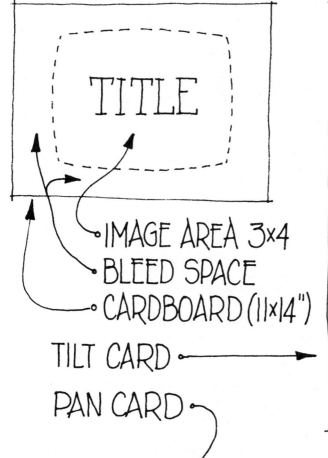

TITLE

→ IMAGE AREA 3×4
→ BLEED SPACE
○ CARDBOARD (11×14")

TILT CARD ——→

PAN CARD

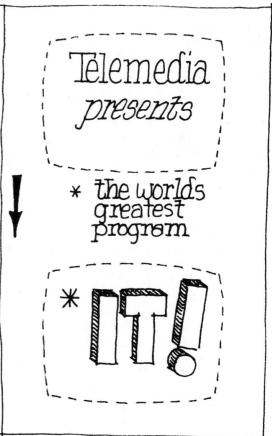

Telemedia
presents

* the world's
greatest
program

* **IT!**

TELEMEDIA
PRESENTS

the
PROGRAM

FEATURING
JOHN

THE VIDEO TECHNICAL DIRECTOR: PRODUCING STUDIO CARDS

One of the first responsibilities of the Video Technical Director is the production of the studio cards called for in the storyboard and the prop and equipment list. These studio cards are primarily used as opening and closing credits for the proposed production, but occasionally they are used for internal information.

There is insufficient space here to go into all of the details on the mounting, lettering and illustration techniques that can be used to produce studio cards. If you feel the need for more information in this area you might consult GRAPHICS: SKILLS, MEDIA AND MATERIALS by Les Satterthwaite published by Kendall/ Hunt. Here we will concentrate on the form and format of these studio cards.

Studio cards should be mounted on railroad board or other medium weight cardboard. Railroad board normally is available in 22 × 28″ format which cuts into quarters that measure 11 × 14″. This is an excellent size for the standard studio card. The first problem is to locate a 3 × 4 area within the railroad board. This 3 × 4 area corresponds to the 3 × 4 ratio of the television screen. In this case a 6 × 8″ visual area (still a 3 × 4 ratio) should be centered as shown on the opposite page. It might be a good idea to draw diagonal lines, locate the center, then measure up and down 3″ and right and left 4″. The result would be the image area. If this were cut out it could serve as a stencil. By simply placing the mask or stencil over other sheets of 11 × 14″ railroad board you could quickly indicate the desired visual area.

We also need to point out the concern for bleed space. The term bleed space is used to describe the space around the visual area that will allow the Cameraman to quickly get a good shot without showing the edge of the studio card. Without the bleed space the effort to fill the screen with the information in the visual area often results in spending an excessive amount of camera time.

A point should be made about the size of the lettering that can be used within the visual area. To ensure that the audience will be able to read this information it should be a minimum of 1/20th the height of the image area. In the case of the 6 × 8″ image area this means that the smallest letter should be a minimum of 1/20th of 6″ or approximately ¼″.

It should also be pointed out that there are variations on the standard studio card. Sets of standard studio cards can be pulled on the air to reveal successive bits of information. If this is not suitable consider the use of pan and tilt studio cards. The tilt studio card, as the name implies, is designed to be used while the camera is tilting up or down across its surface. Note in the example on the opposite page the tilt card is designed for a tilt down. The camera begins with a shot of the top title then tilts down to show the intermediate title and then down again to show the last title. This can be done in one continuous smooth tilt or the tilt can pause at each bit of information. In either case it is essential that the information fall into the same 3 × 4 ratio (or image area) that we discussed before.

The pan title is similar except that the camera will pan across its surface either right to left or left to right. In the example on opposite page the pan card is designed to be use with a left to right pan. The camera sets up the shot on TELEMEDIA PRESENTS. Then it pans left to show THE PROGRAM and continues on to show FEATURING JOHN. Like the tilt studio card the pan movement may be smooth and continuous as it moves across the image or it may pause at each bit of information. Notice that the same 3 × 4 image area is still utilized and that there is still bleed space around the information.

STUDIO:
VIDEO T.D., INTERCONNECTING UNITS

TV CAMERA

MIKES

AUDIO TAPE RECORDER

SOUND MIXER

VIDEO CABLE

AUDIO CABLES

MONITOR/ RECEIVER

AUDIO/VIDEO CABLE

VIDEO TAPE RECORDER

VIDEO CONNECTOR

AUDIO CONNECTOR

AUDIO/ VIDEO CONNECTOR

THE VIDEO TECHNICAL DIRECTOR: INTERCONNECTING THE SYSTEM

When the time for the production has come it is the responsibility of the Video Technical Director working with the Audio Technical Director to collect, deliver, and assemble the production equipment. The prop and equipment list can be used as a check to ensure that you have all of the necessary components. Once the equipment is on hand the next concern is the assembly of the system.

Normally the video tape recorder, the monitor/receiver, and the audio mixer and audio tape recorder are housed on an equipment cart to aid in moving it from place to place. The camera is on the tripod/dolly combination which enables it to be easily moved from place to place. The first thing to do in interconnecting the system is to plug all of the components into an AC power source. There will be five plugs that will need to be inserted into the source and so it is advisable to have a power strip fastened to the equipment cart and a single AC power source going from there to the circuit. You will need to plug in the following pieces of equipment: (1) the monitor/receiver, (2) the audio tape recorder, (3) the sound mixer, (4) the video tape recorder, and (5) the camera. Since you will want the camera to be quite a distance from the other equipment an AC extension cord should be used.

The video out from the camera is connected to the video in on the video tape recorder. A standard video cable with video connectors is used for this. It should be a relatively long cord to allow the camera to be kept away from the rest of the equipment. I would suggest at least a 15 foot video cable with standard video connections on both ends. The audio and video out from the video tape recorder are connected the audio and video in of the monitor receiver. These connections may take many different forms. One type of connector that carries both the audio and video signal is the 8-pin connector shown at the bottom of the opposite page. Another type of connector is an RF line that also carries both audio and video signals between the video tape recorder and the monitor receiver. A third type of connector has separate cables for audio and video. It will be a standard video cable (like the one used to connect the camera and the VTR) and a standard audio cable. The types of connectors you will use depends on the types of inputs and outputs on the VTR and the monitor/receiver. Once you have determined the right ones they should be fastened in and kept in place even when moving the equipment. I might also indicate that these various connectors are a common point for malfunction and it might be wise to have spares on hand.

The audio system may be of two quite different types. In the simpler of the two systems a single mike is plugged directly into the mike input of the video tape recorder. If it is desirable and if you are using a mike with low impedance you may want to use and audio extension cord. In the more complex system the microphones and the auxiliary systems are plugged into the sound mixer and a single audio output is plugged into the mike input on the video tape recorder.

Once you have interconnected all of the systems check to see if you have gone from the output to the input. Just think of where you trying to direct the signal and take the output from the originating source and direct it to the input of the equipment you want it to go to.

Once all of the equipment is checked then run a test tape to make sure that all systems are "go." Be sure to check both the audio and the video signals. During playback evaluate the technical quality of the tape to make sure that everything is ready for the rehearsal and the final production.

STUDIO:
THE VIDEO TAPE RECORDER

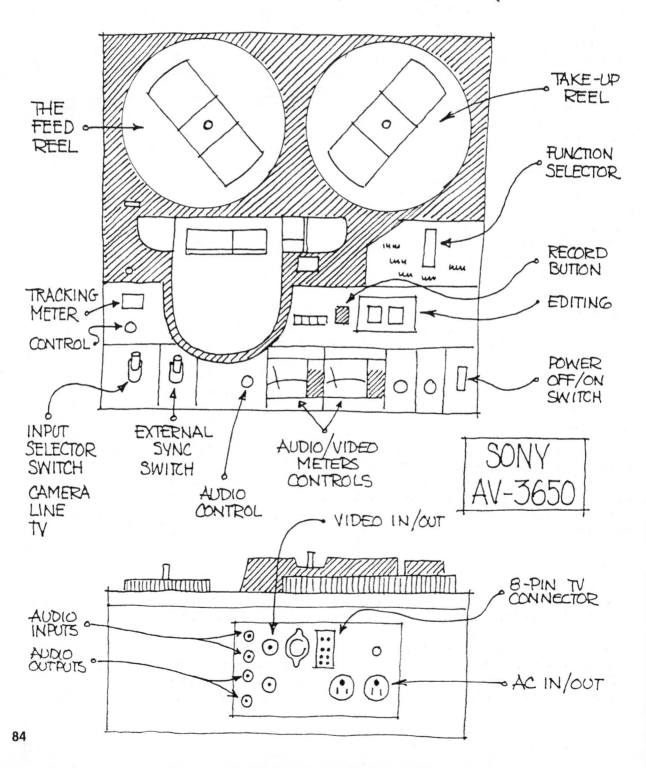

THE
FEED
REEL

TAKE-UP
REEL

FUNCTION
SELECTOR

RECORD
BUTTON

EDITING

TRACKING
METER

CONTROL

POWER
OFF/ON
SWITCH

INPUT
SELECTOR
SWITCH

CAMERA
LINE
TV

EXTERNAL
SYNC
SWITCH

AUDIO
CONTROL

AUDIO/VIDEO
METERS
CONTROLS

SONY
AV-3650

VIDEO IN/OUT

8-PIN TV
CONNECTOR

AUDIO
INPUTS

AUDIO
OUTPUTS

AC IN/OUT

THE VIDEO TECHNICAL DIRECTOR: THE VIDEO TAPE RECORDER

While all components of the single camera production system are important the video tape recorder is a pretty basic piece of equipment. The video tape recorder (VTR) takes the audio and video electronic signals from the cameras and mikes and stores them as magnetic impulses on video tape. Once the signals are stored magnetically they can be played back at a later time.

There are many brands of video tape recorders available but they can be subdivided into two basic categories: (1) reel-to-reel systems, and (2) cassette systems. The Sony AV-3650 shown on the opposite page is a reel to reel system. The blank tape is loaded onto the feed reel threaded through the various recording heads and onto the take-up reel. In the cassette systems this threading is done mechanically. These tapes also come in a variety of tape sizes. Some people may still be using ¼″ video tape but the ½″ format is more common. One inch formats are more commonly found in business and industry and the 2″ formats are for broadcast production units.

One of the primary tasks of the Video Technical Director is the operation of the video tape recorder. In most instances this is a relatively uncomplicated situation. Let's look at some of the common configurations that the Video Technical Director might have to put the VTR into.

The Passive Record Mode

This is the mode that you put the video tape recorder into to allow the system to be checked out without actually recording the information on video tape. In the Sony shown on the opposite page you would just press the record button down. This will open the VTR so that the audio and video signals pass through it and are displayed on the monitor/receiver. Note that in this mode the tape is not moving through the video tape recorder.

The Active Record Mode

This is the mode that you will use when you are actually recording the sights and sounds from the camera and mikes. Hold the record button down and move the function lever to forward (on the Sony on the opposite page) or just press the record and the play switches. The tape will be passing through the VTR in this mode and the images and sounds will be recorded as the image is displayed on the monitor/receiver.

The Rewind Mode

Simply turn the function lever to rewind and keep an eye on the footage counter. When the footage counter approaches the number at the beginning of your production move the function lever to the stop position. This will allow you to get back to the beginning of your production for playback purposes. Note that it is important to keep a record of the numbers from the footage counter for both the beginning and the end of the program.

The Play Mode

When you are ready to view the program make sure that the footage counter is set on the right number. Then simply turn the function lever to play or forward position. Make sure that you do not press the record button or you will erase all of the information.

Each video tape recorder will be slightly different. For the operation of your particular video tape recorder consult the operator's manual that comes with it. Many of the newer models come with a pause control that will allow you to do rough add-on edits for your productions. The best way to learn how your equipment works is to just try it out.

STUDIO:
CLEANING THE VIDEO TAPE RECORDER

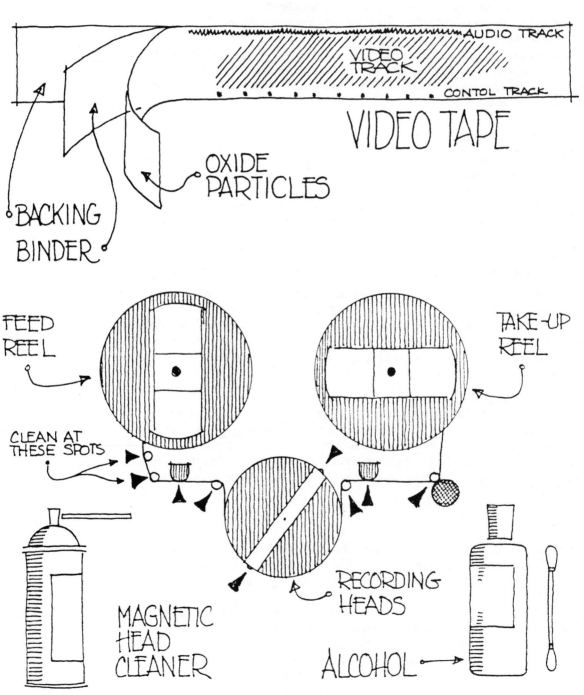

AUDIO TRACK

VIDEO TRACK

CONTOL TRACK

VIDEO TAPE

OXIDE PARTICLES

BACKING

BINDER

FEED REEL

TAKE-UP REEL

CLEAN AT THESE SPOTS

MAGNETIC HEAD CLEANER

RECORDING HEADS

ALCOHOL

VIDEO TECHNICAL DIRECTOR: CLEANING THE VIDEO TAPE RECORDER

Since your major responsibility as Video Technical Director is the operation of the video tape recorder it is essential that you know a little bit about this unit. The video tape recorder accepts incoming audio and video electronic signals and transfers them to magnetic impulses on video tape. In addition to recording signals the video tape recorder stores them and also plays them back. In the playback mode the magnetic signals are translated into electronic signals that are delivered to a television monitor/ receiver and displayed as video images and audio sounds.

What about the nature of this video tape that is used to record these audio and video signals? First, most video tapes are composed of three layers. The base or backing layer is a thin plastic that provides strength for the tape. The second layer is a binder that holds the top and bottom layers together. The third layer actually does all of the work and is composed of oxide particles in an emulsion. These oxide particles are given the magnetic signals during recording and play them back at a later time. The selection of a good quality of recording tape is important. It has often been suggested that you can substitute less expensive computer tape but you will find that this seriously damages the recording heads and ends up costing you more than you save. Try a variety of recording tapes and pick the one that consistently gives you the results you want.

How are these electronic signals transferred to the magnetic video tape? In the diagram on the opposite page you can see how the tape passes through a reel to reel video tape recorder such as the Sony 3650. In this case the video tape comes off the feed reel, around some guide rollers and across the erase head. When the VTR is in record mode this head is activated and erases both the audio and video signals to provide a blank tape for recording. During playback this is inactive to keep from inadvertently erasing materials that you want to keep. From the erase head the tape continues on and is wrapped around the recording head. In this case the recording heads are on either end of the arm that rotates within the entire unit. The tape moves at an angle across the drum and the video signals are laid down diagonally across the tape (see the diagram at the top). From here the tape moves around another guide roller and across the second recording head. This records the audio signal and also lays down the sync track that allows the tape to be played back on other video tape recorders. From here the tape goes around other guide rollers and to the take-up reel.

On the right end of the diagram at the top of the opposite page you can see how the various recording tracks are laid down on the video tape. The audio track runs along the top of the tape. The video track runs diagonally across the center and the sync track is at the bottom. Any damage to the edges of the tape will result in a loss of audio or sync signal.

To clean the video tape recorder use either a spray magnetic head cleaner or an alcohol and Q-tip combination. Cleaning should be done on all of the parts indicated by the dark triangles in the diagram on the opposite page. You should, clean the video tape recorder before every production. Unless there is a cleaning log on your VTR or you are the only one using it you don't want to take a change on dirty heads and thus a loss in the technical quality of the production. To be on the safe side clean all heads and all guide rollers everytime you use the video tape recorder.

CHAPTER III.

THE MULTIPLE CAMERA TELEVISION SYSTEM.........

AN EXAMINATION OF THE EQUIPMENT, PERSONNEL, AND PROCEDURES FOR THE PRODUCTION OF MULTI-CAMERA TELEVISION PROGRAMS.

MULTICAMERA
THE EQUIPMENT, GENERAL

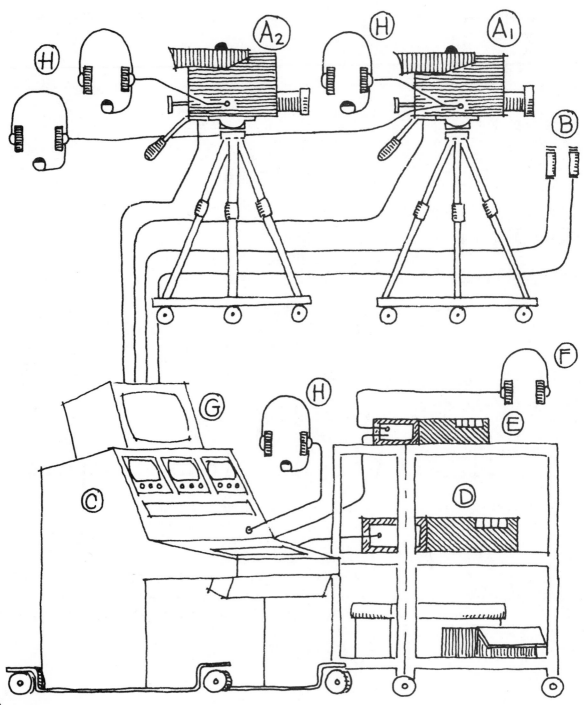

MULTICAMERA EQUIPMENT, GENERAL

The multicamera system is much more complicated that either the portapak or the single camera studio system. The diagram on the opposite page shows the basic equipment.

The Television Cameras   (A1–A2)

These are designed to translate the reflected light from the subject into electronic signals. These electronic signals are sent to the console (C). These cameras need to be the type that can either generate their own sync signal or can accept a sync signal from an external source.

The Microphones   (B)

These are usually the lavalier type of microphone and are designed to translate the sound waves in the studio into electronic signals. These signals are then sent to the console (C). Ideally these will be dynamic low impedance mikes and they should have extension cords to allow them to be used at a distance from the console.

The Console   (C)

The console accepts the audio and video electronic signals and provides a system for displaying these signals. The video signals are displayed on monitors dedicated to each camera. The audio signals are displayed through a visual display (VU meter) and/or a pair of headsets (F) connected to the audio tape recorder (E) or even better the video tape recorder (D). The console also contains the audio and video switchers that allow a single audio and a single video signal to be sent to the video tape recorder (D).

The Video Tape Recorder   (D)

The video tape recorder receives the audio and video signals from the console and transfers then to magnetic signals on video tape. The video tape recorder can also be used to feed a playback signal to the line monitor (G).

The Audio Tape Recorder   (E)

The audio tape recorder is used to play back any music or sound effects that are required for the production. The audio signal is fed into the console (C) and controlled by the sound mixer. A pair of headsets (F) may be used to monitor the audio information and these headsets may be plugged into the audio tape recorder to monitor and cue the audio tapes or into the the video tape recorder.

The Line Monitor   (G)

The audio and video signals from the video tape recorder are sent to the line monitor. This allows the Producer/Director and the other crew members to monitor both the audio and video portions of the program during production.

The Intercom System   (H)

Headsets are necessary for the various crew members so that they may communicate with each other during the actual production. While it is desirable for every crew member to have a headset it is essential that the Cameraman, Floor Director, Switcher, and Director be interconnected through this system.

MULTICAMERA
THE CREW, GENERAL

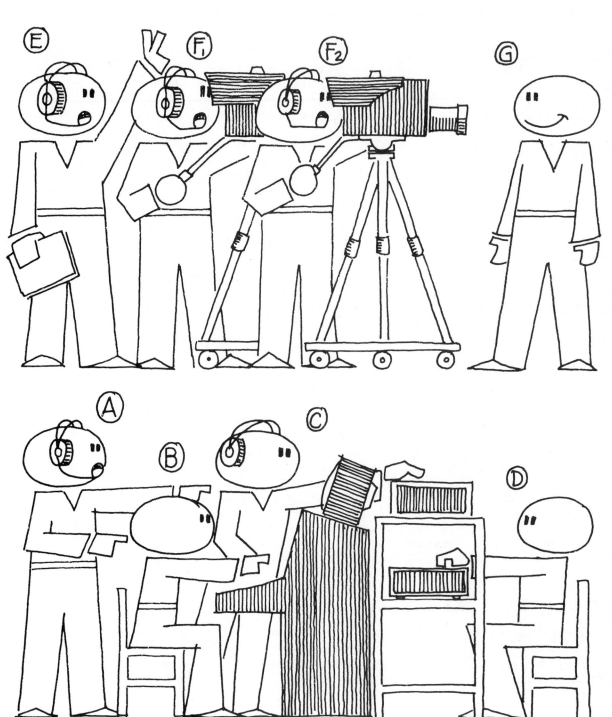

THE CREW FOR A MULTICAMERA SYSTEM, GENERAL

The portapak system was designed to be operated by a single person. The single camera studio system was designed for a small crew of three or four. The multicamera system can effectively utilize a crew of from eight to twelve people. A diagramatic breakdown of the full crew might look like this:

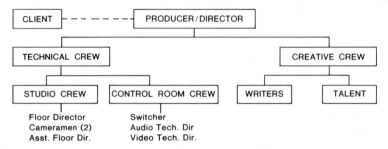

At this point we will only be concerned with the technical crew. The people who actually put the program onto video tape. Let's begin with a general look at the members of the control room crew.

The Producer/Director   (A)

The Producer/Director is the person who is in charge. He/she is the individual who has all of the responsibility for the production and because he/she has all of the responsibility he/she also has all of the authority. The Producer/Director works directly with the client and follows the program from the inception of the idea to the evaluation of the final product.

The Switcher or Assistant Director   (B)

The switcher is in charge of the control room crew and serves as the Producer/Director's direct representative. The Switcher will make sure that the control room crew knows what is expected of them and how to do what is expected of them. In addition, during the actual production the Switcher will operate the video switcher and punch up the shots that the Producer/Director calls for.

The Audio Technical Director   (C)

The Audio Technical Director is responsible for all audio aspects of the production. This includes the selection and placement of the mikes, the preparation of musical audio tapes, and the control of the audio mixer during production. The Audio Technical Director works under the supervision of the Switcher.

The Video Technical Director   (D)

The Video Technical Director is responsible for the production equipment and for the operation of the video tape recorder during the actual production. The Video Technical Director is the individual in the control room with the least amount of responsibility during the actual production and so fills in where needed.

These four people comprise what we normally refer to as the control room crew. The studio crew is the second half of the technical crew in a multicamera production.

The Floor Director   (E)

The Floor Director is in charge of the studio crew. However he/she is also responsible for the preparation of the studio cards and the arrangement of the set elements and the props. Often the Floor Director will be assigned an assistant to help with these responsibilities both before and during the production.

The Cameramen   (F)

The Cameramen assist the Floor Director and are responsible for the operation of the cameras during the production. They operate under the direct supervision of the Floor Director preceeding the production but during the production they execute the commands of the Producer/Director.

DIRECTOR
A GENERAL INTRODUCTION

✳ PREPRODUCTION ACTIVITIES

CLIENT CREW REHERSAL

✳ PRODUCTION ACTIVITIES

✳ POST-PRODUCTION ACTIVITIES

TECHNICAL/ARTISTIC
EVALUATION

INSTRUCTIONAL
EVALUATION

THE PRODUCER/DIRECTOR, A GENERAL INTRODUCTION

The Producer/Director in a multicamera production is the "boss" of production. As the boss the Producer/Director has all of the responsibility for that production. Whatever goes wrong the Producer/Director is the one that is responsible. When anyone is given this total responsibility he/she must also be given total authority—the right to make all of the decisions and support from the crew in these decisions. As with many real life situations there can only be one person in charge of a television production. Television production by committee just will not work. This combination of total responsibility and total authority is difficult for many people to handle. It simply means that not everyone can be a good Producer/Director. The Producer/Director must walk a narrow path between being dictatorial and being liberal. It is necessary to make decisions but you must be sure that these decisions will not alienate your crew. Keeping a good working relationship with the crew while exercising the necessary leadership is not an easy task.

The Producer/Director's involvement with the production begins when a client seeks help in creating a message. This initial client conference seeks to answer the questions "What do you want to say, to whom, with what effect, through what channel or media?" These answers plus research into other sources result in the development of the planning and design documents which are part of the PRODUCTION PROCESS (see Chapter IV for more details). Once the client has approved these documents the Producer/Director then prepares the various design and production documents related to the production. These production and design documents are shared with the crew during the production meeting. At this point the Producer/Director assigns specific roles and responsibilities to the various members of the production crew. Individuals are given supervisory responsibility to oversee the operation of the studio and the control room crews, and other individuals are assigned to perform specific tasks that will be necessary for the smooth production of the program.

While the rest of the production crew are working at their assigned tasks the Producer/Director will be working with the Talent (and often the client) to ensure that the performing members of the creative crew will be ready for the production. Once the materials are prepared and the equipment is set-up and checked-out, the Producer/Director is ready for the walk-through and the rehearsal. During the walk-through the talent performs and the Producer/Director watches to make sure that the shots called for in the storyboard will work. The rehearsal involves the entire production crew and it is actually video taped so that the crew can see any mistakes or problems that need to be corrected. The rehearsal marks the end of the preproduction phase.

During the production phase the Producer/Director will check out the crew and call the shots as the production is transferred to video tape. The Producer/Director is the individual in the crew who can see and hear everything that is going on and the person who knows what is going to happen. Thus the Producer/Director is in full charge during the production. However, the program will be successful only if the entire crew functions in a spirit of teamwork toward a common goal.

Even after the production is on tape the Producer/Director still has certain responsibilities. The production must be evaluated. The technical and artistic quality of the program must be carefully looked at to determine if you will keep the tape or reshoot it. The entire production crew (and even the client) may offer their opinions as to this quality but it is up to the Producer/Director to make the final decision.

DIRECTOR
PREPRODUCTION ACTIVITIES

THE PRODUCER/DIRECTOR: PREPRODUCTION ACTIVITIES

It is during the preproduction phase that the Producer/Director is the busiest. There are six basic steps that the Producer/Director goes through between the inception of the idea and the final rehearsal: (A) the initial client conference, (B) the preparation of the planning and design documents, (C) the client approval meeting, (D) the preparation of the rest of the design and the production documents, (E) the production meeting with the production crew, and (F) the walk-through and rehearsal.

The initial client meeting is normally called at the request of the client for the proposed program. The client has a communication problem and the Producer/Director has the technical skills to help develop and produce the message. During this meeting the Producer/Director will try to get the client's answers to the questions "What do you want to say?" (content), "To whom?" (audience), "With what effect?" (goals and/or objectives), and "Through what channel or medium?" (delivery system). While the client is the primary source for answers to these questions the Producer/Director will also consult other experts and both print and non-print resources to flesh out the client's answers. On the basis of this research the Producer/Director moves to the next phase—preparation of the planning and design documents.

During this time the Producer/Director will correlate the answers from the primary source, the client, and from secondary sources and prepare a polished set of planning documents (content outline, audience analysis, goals/objectives, media selection) and the beginning design document—a treatment. The exact activities involved in the production of these various documents are detailed in Chapter IV THE PRODUCTION PROCESS. Once these documents are prepared you move the next phase—the client approval meeting.

The client approval meeting is just what the name implies, an opportunity for the client to give his/her approval to the various planning and design documents. The client may approve them as submitted, approve them with slight modification, or suggest a major change. Once these documents have been approved the next phase, preparation of the production documents, is ready.

The production documents consist of the shooting schedule, the prop and equipment list, and the set or studio diagram. These documents are intended as communications to the production crew. They are prepared by the Producer/Director on the planning documents approved by the client. Once they are ready we move to the next phase—the production meeting.

The production meeting is a meeting of the various members of the production crew. It is at this point that the Producer/Director will make the crew assignments—which member of the crew will do which task. In addition the Producer/Director will establish the supervisory responsibilities for both the control room crew and the studio crew. The various production documents will be distributed to assist the crew in the performance of their individual and collective responsibilities. The shooting schedule will keep them informed of the where, when, and what of the production. The prop and equipment list will inform the crew of what needs to be collected and taken to the shooting location. The studio or set diagram tells the crew where to put it in the studio or set. Once everything is assembled you are ready for the walk-through and the rehearsal.

During this last phase of the preproduction activities the Producer/Director will walk through the program with the Talent and check to make sure the shots in the storyboard will work. Then the entire crew will be involved in the rehearsal of the proposed program.

DIRECTOR

PRODUCTION ACTIVITIES

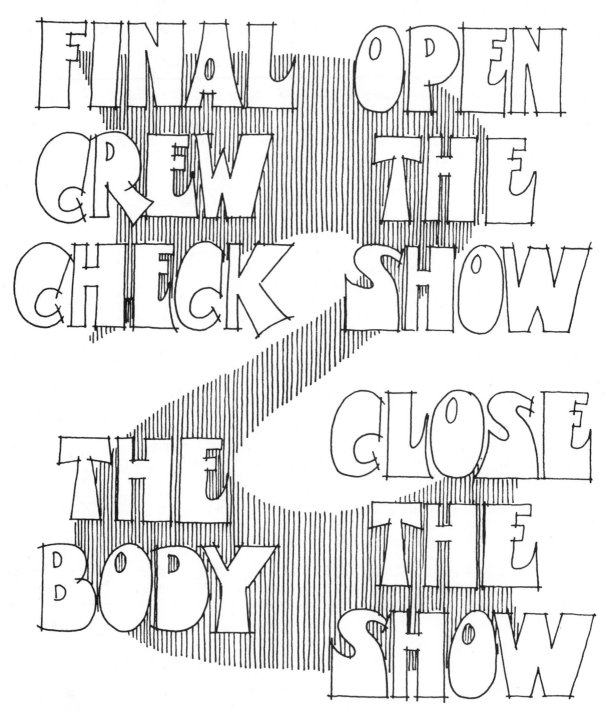

FINAL OPEN

CREW THE

CHECK SHOW

THE CLOSE

THE

BODY SHOW

THE FINAL CREW CHECK

CAM. 1.   CAM. 2.

TELEMEDIA
PRESENTS

DIRECTOR:	CREW MEMBER:
READY ON CAMERA 1.	READY! (I HAVE MY OPENING SHOT AND KNOW THE REST OF MY SHOTS.)
READY ON CAMERA 2.	READY! (I HAVE MY OPENING SHOT AND KNOW THE REST OF MY SHOTS.)
READY ON THE FLOOR.	READY! (I HAVE CHECKED AND EVERYTHING SEEMS TO BE READY.)
READY ON VIDEO.	READY! (I HAVE THE VIDEO TAPE CHECKED AND CUED. I'M READY TO RECORD.)
READY ON AUDIO.	READY! (MY MUSIC IS CUED, MIKES CHECKED, AND I'M READY.)
READY ON CONSOLE.	READY! (THE CONSOLE IS IN BLACK AND I'M READY TO FADE INTO THE FIRST SHOT.)
STANDBY!	(FLOOR DIRECTOR) STAND BY! QUIET IN THE STUDIO. (HAND SIGNAL TO TALENT)
READY TO ROLL VIDEO! ROLL VIDEO!	(THE VIDEO TECHNICAL DIRECTOR PUTS THE VTR INTO ACTIVE RECORD MODE AND GIVES THE COUNTDOWN.) 10-9-8-7-6-5-4-3-2-1.

OPENING THE PROGRAM

TELEMEDIA
PRESENTS

READY TO FADE IN MUSIC AND CAM. 1.	
FADE IN!	AUDIO T.D. FADES IN MUSIC SWITCHER FADES IN CAM. 1.
OPEN TALENTS MIKE!	AUDIO T.D. OPENS THE MIKE.
READY TO CUE TALENT! READY TO FADE MUSIC!	
FADE MUSIC! CUE TALENT	AUDIO T.D. LOWERS VOLUME. FLOOR DIR. CUES TALENT

TALENT DELIVERS LINES.

FADE IN MUSIC!	AUDIO T.D. FADES IN MUSIC AND KILLS TALENTS MIKE.
READY ON CAMERA 2.	CAMERAMAN GETS READY.

(CONTINUED ON THE NEXT PAGE)

TAKE 2.	SWITCHER PUNCHES UP CAM. 2.
NEXT SHOT CAM 1.	CAMERA 1 MOVES TO NEXT SHOT
READY TO PULL CARD	
PULL CARD!	FLOOR DIR. SIGNALS TO HIS ASSISTANT TO PULL THE CARD.
READY TO PULL CARD.	
PULL CARD!	FLOOR DIR. SIGNALS TO HIS ASSISTANT TO PULL THE CARD.
READY ON CAMERA 1. READY TO CUE TALENT OPEN TALENTS MIKE READY TO KILL MUSIC	AUDIO T.D. OPENS TALENTS MIKE

THE BODY OF THE SHOW

TAKE 1.!	SWITCHER PUNCHES UP CAMERA 1.
CUE TALENT!	FLOOR DIR. CUES THE TALENT.
KILL MUSIC!	AUDIO T.D. FADES OUT MUSIC. REWINDS AND RECUES IT.

TALENT INTROS PROGRAM

CAMERA 2 GET YOUR NEXT SHOT. READY ON CAM. 2.	CAMERA 2 MOVES TO THEIR NEXT SHOT --- LONG SHOT.
TAKE 2!	SWITCHER PUNCHES UP CAMERA 2
GET YOUR NEXT SHOT CAMERA 1.	CAMERA 1 MOVES TO THEIR NEXT SHOT --- CLOSE UP.

TALENTS INTRO'S WATER CYCLE

CAM. 2 READY TO PAN WITH THE TALENT	
PAN	CAMERA PANS WITH TALENT
HOLD YOUR SHOT 2	
READY ON CAMERA 1	
TAKE 1!	SWITCHER PUNCHES UP CAMERA 1.

TALENT INTRO'S NEW WORDS

(CONTINUED ON THE NEXT PAGE)

EVAPORATION CONDENSATION PRECIPITATION PERCOLATION		HOLD YOUR SHOT 2 READY ON CAMERA 2
		TAKE 2 — SWITCHER PUNCHES UP CAMERA 2. CAM. 1 GET NEXT SHOT — CAMERA 1 GETS HIS NEXT SHOT. READY ON CAM. 1.
		CAMERA 2 PAN WITH THE TALENT! — CAMERA 2 PANS WITH TALENT READY TO STOP
		STOP! READY ON CAMERA 1. TAKE 1! — SWITCHE PUNCHES UP CAMERA 1.
		HOLD YOUR SHOT 2 READY TO TILT UP 1 TILT UP! — CAMERA 1 TILTS UP.
		READY TO TILT DOWN CAMERA 1. TILT DOWN. — CAMERA 1 TILTS DOWN.
		READY ON CAMERA 2 TAKE TWO! — SWITCHER PUNCHES UP CAMERA 2
A TELEMEDIA PRODUCTION		CAMERA 1 GET THE CLOSING CARD. READY ON MUSIC. — AUDIO T.D. STARB CLOSING MUSIC. READY ON 1.

TALENT CONCLUDES SHOW

CLOSING THE PROGRAM

A TELEMEDIA PRODUCTION		TAKE 1 — SWITCHER PUNCHES UP CAM. 1. ROLL MUSIC — AUDIO T.D. FADES IN MUSIC READY TO FADE OUT
		FADE OUT — SWITCHER FADES TO BLACK AUDIO T.D. FADES OUT MUSIC "CUT" — VIDEO TD. STOPS VTR.

DIRECTOR
POST-PRODUCTION ACTIVITIES

TECHNICAL
AND
ARTISTIC
EVALUATION
WITH THE CREW

EVALUATION

INSTRUCTIONAL EVALUATION WITH THE
AUDIENCE

THE PRODUCER/DIRECTOR: POST-PRODUCTION ACTIVITIES

Even when the program is finally on video tape the role and responsibilities of the Producer/Director are not finished. At this point in time a vital decision must be made and guess who gets to make it—the Producer/Director! What is this vital decision? Do we keep the program we have just completed or shall we shoot it over again? In this evaluation phase there are three aspects that must be considered: (1) the technical quality of the production, (2) the artistic quality of the production, and (3) the instructional/information/entertainment quality of the production.

Evaluating the Technical Quality of the Production

This decision to keep or to reshoot a particular production is a very difficult decision to make. Reshooting will involve more long hard hours of shooting for the talent and the production crew. Reshooting also would involve suggesting what certain members of the crew had done that was not acceptable. It might involve suggesting that the talent modify his/her delivery. These decisions are difficult. But as Producer/Director, as the individual with all of the responsibility and the authority these are the types of decisions you must make. First you must be concerned with technical quality of the production. Is the image clear and distinct? Is the sound quality acceptable in terms of level and clarity? Is the production system putting out the type of signal that creates a program of the appropriate quality? If the answer is no to any of these questions you must then ask if reshooting will improve the poor quality. Is there something that can be done to the equipment to improve the picture quality, the sound quality or is the equipment operating at peak efficiency? Here you, as Producer/Director may need to ask the production crew what they could do to improve the quality. If they have no suggestions and you have no ideas on how the quality can be improved then there is no point in reshooting.

Evaluating the Artistic Quality of the Production

In addition to a concern over the technical quality of the production you must also consider the artistic aspects of the production. These are more difficult to evaluate than the more obvious technical problems. For example, in evaluating the artistic aspects of the camera work you need to consider these questions: (1) are the camera shots well composed? (2) are the moving camera shots (pans, tilts, zooms) smooth and even? (3) is the image in sharp focus? (4) did the Cameraman follow the action properly? (5) did the Cameraman get the shots that were called for in the script? Then you also need to consider the switching from camera to camera: (1) were the cuts (or other transitions) done at the proper time in the show? (2) were the transitions used appropriate for the program content? (3) were these transitions timed properly? What about delivery of the Talent: (1) did it appear that the Talent was at ease? (2) was the delivery accurate? (3) did the Talent appear knowledgable about the topic and well organized? These are just a few of the questions that need to be asked (and answered) to determine the artistic evaluation of the production.

Evaluating the Instructional/Informational/Entertainment Quality

Programs can be classified as instructional, informational, and entertainment. To evaluate these aspects of the program we go back to the goals and/or objectives developed as part of the planning documents. Here the client can "guestimate" about these aspects but to really determine how sucessful the program is in achieving these goals and/or objectives it would be essential to try it out on a sample audience and actually measure its effectiveness. In this case it becomes the client's responsibility.

FLOOR DIRECTOR

A GENERAL INTRODUCTION

PREPRODUCTION ACTIVITIES

PRODUCTION ACTIVITIES

POST-PRODUCTION ACTIVITIES

THE FLOOR DIRECTOR: A GENERAL INTRODUCTION

The Floor Director is the individual in a multicamera crew who is responsible for that portion of the technical crew that is usually called the studio crew. This includes the Cameramen and any assistants that the Floor Director might need. The Floor Director is responsible *to* the Producer/Director and *for* what goes on in the studio. In general the roles of the Floor Director fall into two areas; (1) supervisory roles in which he/she prepares the studio crew, and (2) direct activities for which he/she is individually responsible.

Supervisory Responsibilities of the Floor Director

Before the production begins the Producer/Director will meet with the production crew and assign the various roles they will play and the responsibilities they will have. At this time the Producer/Director will indicate that the Floor Director has the responsibility for the studio production crew. The various design and production documents will be distributed and you, as Floor Director, will be ready for your first meeting with your studio crew.

First, make sure that they understand what their individual responsibilities will be during the preproduction, production, and post-production phases. Secondly, make sure that each crew member you are responsible for knows how to do the assigned jobs. This obviously means that you have to know how to do all of their jobs so that you can provide the training if they need it.

Direct Activities of the Floor Director (and Assistants)

During the preproduction phase of the process the Floor Director is responsible for the production of the studio cards, the assembly of the props and set elements, the development of the set and the arrangement of the props for the production. Also the Floor Director is responsible for locating where the cameras, mikes, and lights should be during the production.

The storyboard and the prop/equipment list that the Producer/Director distributes during the production meeting will tell you what studio cards are needed for the beginning, middle, and end of the production. The Floor Director may assign an assistant to this role but the Floor Director must approve and get the approval of the Producer/Director for any graphics. The specifics of producing these studio cards is described in detail in just a few pages.

Another direct responsibility of the Floor Director is the assembly of the props and set elements for the production. The prop and equipment list provided by the Producer/Director during the production meeting will be your guide as to what is necessary. The set or studio diagram distributed at the same time is the blueprint of where the materials will go.

During the rehearsal and the production the Floor Director will be responsible for transferring the Producer/Director's signals to the Talent. Hand signals will be used since voice signals might be picked up by the live mikes in the studio.

Once the production is over the Floor Director, with the other crew members, will assist the Producer/Director in the evaluation of the technical and artistic qualities of the production. Once the Producer/Director has made the decision to keep the program the Floor Director will supervise the dismantling of the set and the transporting of the set elements and props back to storage.

FLOOR DIRECTOR
PREPRODUCTION ACTIVITIES

THE FLOOR DIRECTOR: PREPRODUCTION ACTIVITIES

The preproduction phase of the program is a very busy time for the Floor Director. It all begins with the production meeting called by the Producer/Director. At his point of series of production documents and some design documents are distributed to the crew. The shooting schedule tells the crew the where, when, what, and why of the production. The prop and equipment list tell the crew what needs to be collected or produced and then delivered to the set and assembled. The set diagram is a blueprint of where each item should be placed. The storyboard script (a design document) gives people in the crew a better idea of what the proposed program will look and sound like.

Production of Graphics and Studio Cards

One of the first responsibilities the Floor Director must tackle is the design and production of the studio cards that are used to open and/or close the program. The mounting, lettering, and even illustration techniques that are necessary for this production are too numerous to cover here. For more information on graphics production consult GRAPHICS: SKILLS, MEDIA AND MATERIALS by Les Satterthwaite and published by Kendall/Hunt. The prop and equipment list will provide a rough idea of what graphics are required and the storyboard/script will provide the necessary detail.

Collection, Transportation and Assembly of the Props

The term "props" is an abreviation for properties and these are the items that the Talent will manipulate during the program or those things that will be used to dress up the set. The prop and equipment list indicates the props that are required, but you should also check the script/storyboard to make sure that the Producer/Director has not missed anything that is important.

Preparing the Setting for the Program

Another of the direct responsibilities of the Floor Director and his assistants is the development of the setting for the production. This setting may be one of three types: (1) using an existing set (doing the chemistry program in the chem lab), (2) using an existing set but modifying it (making the chem lab look like the laboratory of a mad scientist), or (3) creating a totally new set. Obviously there will be quite a difference in the lead time necessary to prepare these three different sets. Using an existing set requires little or no time but modifying or creating a set may require days or even weeks. Again it will be your responsibility as Floor Director to get this all done in time for the production.

Checking Out the Studio and the System

Since part of the responsibility of the Floor Director is a supervisory responsibility you need to take some time out to check on the people for whom you are responsible. Check the Cameramen, your assistants and then also check to make sure that the audio and the video systems are working. This is normally the responsibility of the Switcher but it never hurts to double check the system.

The Walk-through and the Rehearsal

The last preproduction activity of the Floor Director is his/her participation in the walk-through and the rehearsal for the production. During the walk-through your role will be observer—watching what the Talent is going to do. During the rehearsal yours will be an active role—just what you will do during the regular production.

FLOOR DIRECTOR
GRAPHICS, STUDIO CARDS-VISUALS

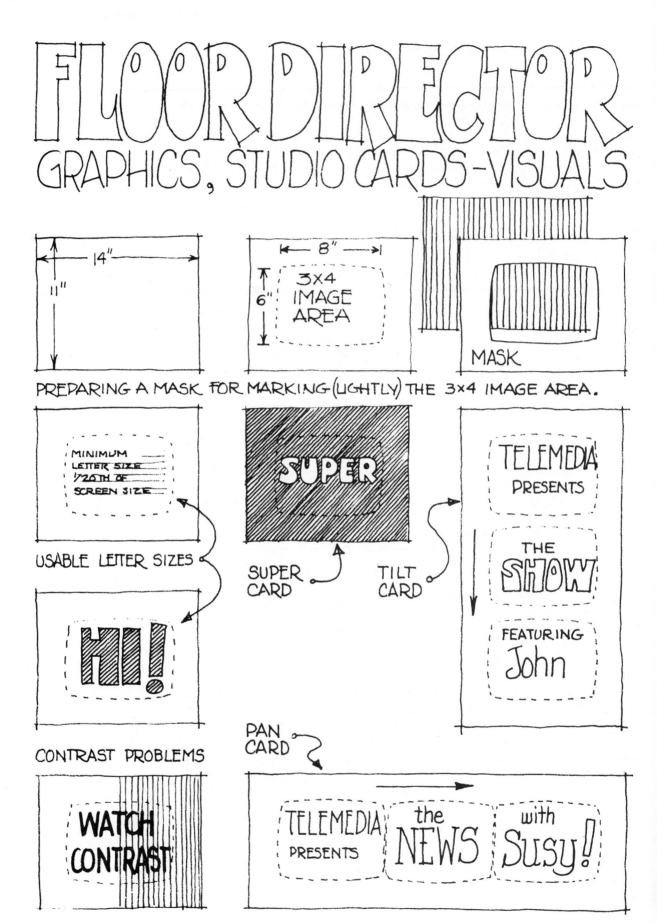

14"

11"

8"

6"

3×4 IMAGE AREA

MASK

PREPARING A MASK FOR MARKING (LIGHTLY) THE 3×4 IMAGE AREA.

MINIMUM LETTER SIZE 1/20TH OF SCREEN SIZE

SUPER

TELEMEDIA
PRESENTS

THE SHOW

FEATURING John

USABLE LETTER SIZES

SUPER CARD

TILT CARD

HI!

CONTRAST PROBLEMS

PAN CARD

WATCH CONTRAST

TELEMEDIA PRESENTS   the NEWS   with Susy!

THE FLOOR DIRECTOR: PRODUCING STUDIO CARDS

One of the first responsibilities of the Floor Director is the production of the studio cards called for in the storyboard and the prop and equipment list. These studio cards are primarily used as opening and closing credits for the proposed production, but occasionally they are used for internal information.

There is insufficient space here to go into all of the details on the mounting, lettering and illustration techniques that can be used to produce studio cards. If you feel the need for more information in this area you might consult GRAPHICS: SKILLS, MEDIA AND MATERIALS by Les Satterthwaite published by Kendall/Hunt. Here we will concentrate on the form and format of these studio cards.

Studio cards should be mounted on railroad board or other medium weight cardboard. Railroad board normally is available in a 22 × 28″ format which cuts into quarters that measure 11 × 14″. This is an excellent size for the standard studio card. The first problem is to locate a 3 × 4 area within the railroad board. This 3 × 4 area corresponds to the 3 × 4 ratio of the television screen. In this case a 6 × 8″ visual area (still a 3 × 4 ratio) should be centered as shown on the opposite page. It might be a good idea to draw diagonal lines, locate the center, then measure up and down 3″ and right and left 4″. The result would be the image area. If this were cutout it could serve as a mask. By simply placing the mask or stencil over other sheets of 11 × 14″ railroad board you could quickly indicate the desired visual area.

We also need to point out the concern for bleed space. The term bleed space is used to describe the space around the visual area that will allow the cameraman to quickly get a good shot without showing the edge of the studio card.

A point should be made about the size of the lettering that can be used within the visual area. To ensure that the audience will be able to read this information it should be a minimum of 1/20th the height of the image area. In the case of the 6 × 8″ image area this means that the smallest letter should be a minimum of 1/20th of 6″ or approximately ¼″.

It should also be pointed out that there are variations on the standard studio card. Sets of standard studio cards can be pulled on the air to reveal sucessive bits of information. If this is not suitable consider the use of pan and tilt studio cards. The tilt studio card, as the name implies, is designed to be used while the camera is tilting up or down across its surface. Note in the example on the opposite page the tilt card is designed for a tilt down. The camera begins with a shot of the top title then tilts down to show the intermediate title and then down again to show the last title. This can be done in one continuous smooth tilt or the tilt can pause at each bit of information. In either case it is essential that the information fall into the same 3 × 4 ratio (or image area) that we discussed before.

The pan title is similar except that the camera will pan across its surface either right to left or left to right. In the example on opposite page the pan card is designed to be use with a left to right pan. The camera sets up the shot on TELEMEDIA PRESENTS. Then it pans left to show THE NEWS and continues on to show WITH SUSY. Like the tilt studio card the pan movement may be smooth and continuous as it moves across the image or it may pause at each bit of information. Notice that the same 3 × 4 image area is still utilized and that there is still bleed space around the information.

FLOOR DIRECTOR
SETS, PROPS AND OTHER ITEMS

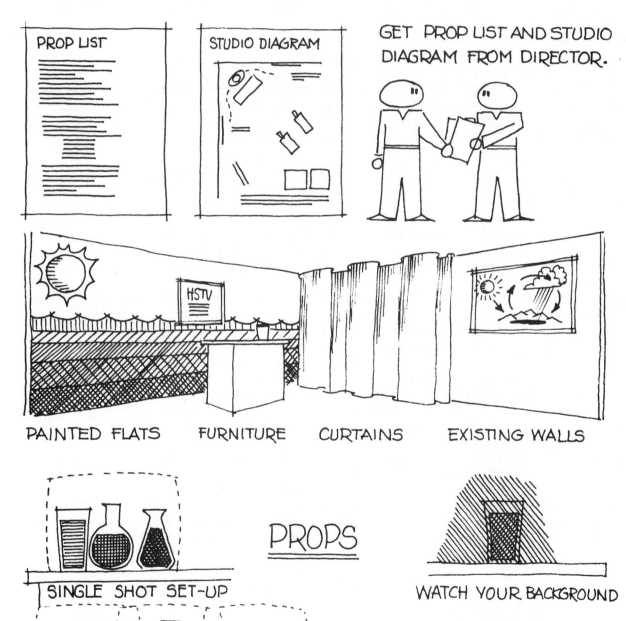

PROP LIST

STUDIO DIAGRAM

GET PROP LIST AND STUDIO DIAGRAM FROM DIRECTOR.

HSTV

PAINTED FLATS   FURNITURE   CURTAINS   EXISTING WALLS

SINGLE SHOT SET-UP

PROPS

WATCH YOUR BACKGROUND

PAN SHOT SET-UP

DON'T CLUTTER

FLOOR DIRECTOR: SETS, PROPS, AND OTHER ITEMS

As Floor Director you are responsible for everything that goes on in the studio and this includes the setting in which the production takes place and the props or set elements that create the desired effect. Since all of these materials must be ready for the production by the date specified in the shooting schedule it is essential that this activity be given a high priority.

The prop list and the studio diagram will be your guides in completing this assignment. The prop list will indicate what items need to be collected and delivered to the studio. The studio diagram will indicate where these elements will be placed for the production. In addition you will want to read the script/storyboard carefully to get a feeling for the atmosphere that the Producer/Director wants to create and to identify any props or set elements that might have been left off of the prop list or omitted from the studio diagram.

The actual set will fall into one of three different categories. First there is the existing set. If your multicamera system is portable you may move to an area that already looks like the setting called for in the script and storyboard. If you are doing a sports show perhaps the locker room, the gym, or even the football field might be appropriate. Secondly, it might require a set in which you could use an existing area with some modification. Certain props might change the principal's office into a board room or a corporation office or even a news room. Third, there are times when you will have to build a set from scratch. This latter is a very expensive and time consuming process and here is where you might want to draw upon the expertise of the drama department in your school. These constructed sets may be relatively simple like those on the opposite page. You might use some attractive curtains for a backdrop or a blank wall on which you can hang appropriate props. Or you could produce a set from a sheet of muslin stretched over a wooden frame and painted. These "flats" can become a setting for a musical, the interior of a submarine, or even a Hobbit's home. Needless to say it is vital that programs calling for special settings require a lot of lead time. Often you, as Floor Director, will need to meet with the Producer/Director well in advance of the production crew meeting to give you the needed time to prepare these various sets and to collect special set elements.

You are also concerned with the various props that the talent will either manipulate or show during the program. One of your major concerns will need to be with the kinds of shots that the Cameramen can get of these various props. At the bottom of the opposite page there are some basic things to consider. First you need to refer to the storyboard/script to determine how these props are to be displayed. If they are to be presented as a group you need to cluster them so that the camera can get them all in a single shot. If the props are to be shown one at a time they need to be arranged so that the camera can pan from one to another and show each in isolation. When you set these shots up you also need to be aware of the backgrounds and how well the props will separate. Also consider how background elements might detract from the items to be shown.

In the case of props that are to be displayed or demonstrated by the Talent you will need time to work with them on the proper way to show the props to the best advantage. For example a common problem that untrained Talent have is simply that they don't hold the props still and this creates major problems when a Cameraman is trying to get a close-up. Another problem is that they wrap their hands around the props and then on the close up all you see is knuckles and the props are hidden.

FLOOR DIRECTOR
LIGHTING FOR TELEVISION

NORMAL ROOM
LIGHT IS FLAT.
MAY CAUSE
SHADOWS.
COMPENSATE WITH
REFLECTOR PANELS.

PORTRAIT LIGHTING

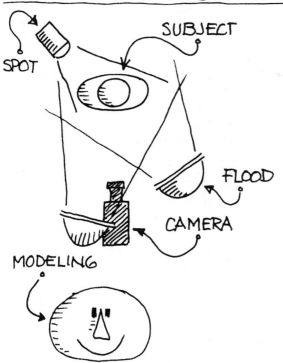

SPOT

SUBJECT

FLOOD

CAMERA

MODELING

POOL LIGHTING

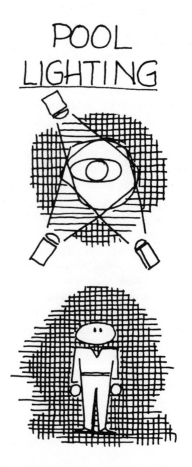

FLOOR DIRECTOR: LIGHTING FOR TELEVISION

All television cameras require light—reflected light from the subject is focused by the camera lens onto the vidicon tube that translates the light into an electronic signal. Different cameras require different amounts of light. Color cameras require the most light to get a good picture and low light level black and white cameras require the least amount of light. While I recommend the low light level black and white cameras even these may occasionally require some degree of auxiliary light.

A common problem that faces a television production unit that is shooting in a less than perfect light condition (on location) is that there is minimal light available. Often this is sufficient to get an adequate picture but perhaps the Talent have, as a result, deep shadows under their eyes or chins. This can also happen when you are shooting outside in direct sunlight. A simple compensatory technique is to put some sort of reflector in position so that some of the light will be reflected up under the Talent's faces and fill in the shadows. While you can purchase these from a TV supply house you can often get by with sheets of cardboard that are covered with aluminum foil or cardboard that has foil mounted to one side (available from art supply houses).

But there are other situations in which auxiliary lighting is required for a special effect. Normally auxiliary lighting is used in a studio situation where a lighting grid can be hung from the ceiling and spot lights and floodlamps can be attached to the grid. However, there are also portable light packages available that have the fixtures mounted on stands. These can be used when you are shooting on location.

One major disadvantage of lighting for television is the simple fact that with a limited number of lights it is difficult, at best, to light large areas. This forces your lighting and your action into certain limited areas of the production set. The most common type of lighting is what is normally referred to as portrait lighting. This is designed to provide modeling for the subject—a roundness that will make it more lifelike and help the subject to separate from the environment. Unfortunately this drastically limits the subject's mobility. In this case three lamps are used. The key (to the right of the camera) provides modeling to the features but also creates deep shadows. The fill light (over or to the left of the camera) fills in these dark shadows but maintains the modeling. The third lamp, the backlight, throws a rim of light around the head and shoulders and helps it to separate from the background. The problem with this, or any other specific lighting for television, is that it is best accomplished when the talent is stationary.

Another common specialized lighting situation is what is normally referred to as pool lighting. This is a situation in which you want the Talent to appear in a limbo type of environment. The Talent is lit but the background is in black. This is especially appropriate when you are dealing with musical subjects—instrumental and/or vocal. The black background allows you to do slow dissolves, supers and other special effects that look really great on video tape. This effect is achieved by using three (and only three) light sources. The lamps are positioned in sort of a Y shape. Two from the front that act like key and fill lights and one from the rear that acts as a back light. However the lights are placed high so that they do not hit the background. When all of the other lights in the room are turned off the Talent is alone in a pool of light and the effect can be very dramatic.

Again we need to point out that lighting creates special problems and that under normal situations it is not necessary for black and white television. But when it is needed it can make a very real difference.

FLOOR DIRECTOR
HAND SIGNALS

STAND BY

YOU'R ON

SPEED UP

SLOW DOWN

CUT

30 SEC.

15 SEC.

WIND IT UP

TWO MINUTES

FLOOR DIRECTOR: HAND SIGNALS

One of the responsibilities of the Floor Director during both the rehearsal and the actual program is to transfer the commands of the Producer/Director to those crew members who are not hooked into the intercom system. This would include the Talent and any assistants that the Floor Director might have. These commands cannot be transferred audibly since the sound might be picked up by a "live" mike. Therefore the Floor Director must resort to hand signals to provide this essential communication between the Producer/Director and the crew members. On the opposite page are some of the common hand signals that the Floor Director might use for this purpose.

The one in the upper left hand corner is the "standby" signal. After the final check of the crew members the Producer/Director will say "Stand by!" On this command the Floor Director will give the standby signal and say "Standby, Quiet in the studio!" This is the last oral command that the Floor Director will use until the end of the program.

Another common command that the Producer/Director might give is "Cue the Talent!" This tells the Floor Director to indicate to the Talent that he/she is to begin his/her delivery. This is accomplished by sweeping the hand from the standby position to a finger pointing at the Talent. This same cue is often used to tell other crew members to begin what they are supposed to do. For example it may also cue the assistant Floor Director to pull the cards for the studio opening and/or closing.

Sometimes the Producer/Director may want to adjust the pace at which the Talent is delivering the information. In a portion of the program where it appears to be dragging the Producer/Director might give the command "Speed the Talent up." In this situation the Floor Director would give the speed up signal shown on the opposite page. This is a simple movement of one hand around the other. In other situations the Producer/Director might give the command "Slow the Talent down." Here the hand signal given by the Floor Director is like pulling taffy.

Another common set of signals are the time cues. While these are normally only used for programs that must be a specific length (to fit into a program schedule) you, as Floor Director should be aware of them and their meaning. Minutes remaining are indicated by extended fingers. One finger, one minute—two fingers, two minutes—five fingers, five minutes, etc. Thirty seconds is indicated by bending the finger at the second knuckle. Fifteen seconds is indicated by a closed fist.

Two signals that are commonly used toward the end of the program are "wind it up" and "cut." The Producer/Director determines that the program should come to a close and calls for the end with the command "Wind it up!" This command is translated by the Floor Director into a sweeping hand movement and the Talent knows that the Producer/Director wants him/her to complete the concept and say good by. The cut signal is used to indicate the end of the program. The Producer/Director calls "Cut!" and the Floor Director passes his hand across his throat in a cutting motion. The reason for using a silent signal is quite simple—it allows the Video Technical Director to turn off the VTR without picking up a shout of relief or the word cut from a live mike in the studio.

The above represents common hand signals. However one of the roles of the Floor Director is to translate other commands from the Producer/Director into signals that may not be in a common vocabulary. If the Producer/Director want the Talent to sit, stand or move to the right or left the Floor Director must make up a signal and get it to the Talent so that he/she will do what the Producer/Director wants.

FLOOR DIRECTOR

PRODUCTION POST-PRODUCTION

WATCH THE ACTION

ANTICIPATE

EVALUATE

CUE THE TALENT

A CHECKLIST FOR THE FLOOR DIRECTOR

Preproduction Activities

_____ 1. Attend the production meeting and pick up the following documents: shooting schedule, prop and equipment list, studio or set diagram, and script/storyboard.

_____ 2. Identify the studio crew: cameramen, assistant floor directors, etc., and check to see if they know what their jobs are and how to do them.

_____ 3. Provide in-service training for the studio crew as necessary.

_____ 4. Identify and produce the studio cards described in the prop and equipment list and the storyboard/script.

_____ 5. Identify, evaluate, and modify (if necessary) or create any instructional materials to be used in the program.

_____ 6. Identify props and set elements required for the program and assemble and deliver them to the shooting area.

_____ 7. Identify any sets that need to be constructed for the production and build them.

_____ 8. Assemble the set, the set elements, and props on the site of the proposed production.

_____ 9. Check the positioning of the cameras and other studio equipment using the studio or set diagram.

_____ 10. Check the operation of all production equipment (with the switcher).

_____ 11. Check to make sure your studio crew know what is expected of them.

_____ 12. Observe the walk-through and note modifications that are suggested by the Producer/Director.

_____ 13. Inform the studio crew of the above changes (if any).

_____ 14. Check to make sure that the Talent knows and understands the basic hand signals to be used during the rehearsal and the production.

_____ 15. Take a last look around the studio to make sure that everything is where it should be and ready for the rehearsal.

_____ 16. Provide the appropriate hand signals during the rehearsal.

_____ 17. Assist the producer/director to identify and correct any problems seen on the rehearsal tape.

_____ 18. Inform the studio crew of any changes brought about by the rehearsal.

_____ 19. Prepare the studio crew for the production.

Production Activities

_____ 1. Make a last minute check of the studio and respond "ready" to the Producer/Director's question "ready in the studio."

_____ 2. On the Producer/Directors command "standby" give the standby hand signal and say (loudly) "Standby, quiet in the studio."

_____ 3. Provide the appropriate hand signals during the production.

_____ 4. Keep your eyes open during the production and anticipate problems that might occur.

Post-Production Activities

_____ 1. Assist the Producer/Director in the evaluation of the production.

_____ 2. Supervise the collection of props, set elements, studio cards, etc., and their return to their original locations.

CAMERAMAN
A GENERAL INTRODUCTION

PRE-PRODUCTION ACTIVITIES

✳ PRODUCTION ACTIVITIES

✳ POST-PRODUCTION ACTIVITIES

CAMERAMEN, A GENERAL INTRODUCTION

The Cameramen in a multicamera production system are part of the studio crew. They are immediately responsible to the Floor Director. While the main responsibility of the Cameramen is the operation of the television cameras during both the rehearsal and the actual production they also have other responsibilities as part of the studio crew. Like all members of the production crew their activities are organized into the preproduction, production and post-production phases of the actual program.

Preproduction Activities of the Cameramen

During the preproduction phase there are four basic activities that the Cameramen are concerned with: (1) assisting the Floor Director in the collection, transportation and assembly of the props and set elements, (2) setting up the cameras and checking their operation, (3) memorizing and practicing the shots called for in the storyboard, and (4) operating the cameras during the rehearsal.

Before the props and equipment are delivered to the shooting area on the scheduled date someone has to check the prop list and make sure what needs to be collected. This is the responsibility of the Floor Director, but he can't do it all himself, and the Cameramen and any assistant Floor Directors help in this task. Once they are collected and delivered the Cameramen will also assist in the assembly and placement of these materials.

Once the equipment is all set up the Cameramen then need to check their cameras. The first thing to check is the location. Can they get the shots called for in the storyboard? Secondly, the cameras need to be balanced. This simply means that the cameras are adjusted so that they are sending the same quality of picture to the console. The Switcher will assist in this balancing and will tell the Cameramen the proper setting for the cameras.

Once the cameras are operating properly and well-balanced the next task of the Cameramen is to practice the shots called for in the storyboard. This design document will be distributed during the production meeting and the Cameramen should have had time to memorize their shots. Then of course the Cameramen follow the Producer/ Director's commands during the rehearsal. Note that during this rehearsal or as a result of it, the Producer/Director may change some of the shots called for in the original storyboard. This means that as Cameramen you will have to be on your toes and adapt your shots as required.

Production Activities of the Cameramen

During the actual production the Cameramen will operate their cameras and follow the directions of the Producer/Director. This will involve anticipating the upcoming shots but not taking them before the Producer/Director calls for them. It will involve holding the camera steady on static shots and making smooth transitional shots. It is a high pressure moment but all of the previous activities are preparing you for this activity.

Post-Production Activities of the Cameramen

Once the production is over the next role of the Cameramen is to assist the Producer/Director in the evaluation of the product. As Cameramen you may be asked if certain shots or transition can be improved. Or if there are things that you as Cameramen could do to improve the program. You will assist in the evaluation of both the technical and the artistic quality of the program. Note that the key word is assist. The Producer/Director will make the final decision to keep or to reshoot the program but your input will assist in this decision. Once the program is in the can you will assist the Floor Director in returning the props and set elements to their proper places.

CAMERAMAN
PREPRODUCTION ACTIVITIES

CAMERAMAN: PREPRODUCTION ACTIVITIES

The preproduction phase of the project is the busiest time for the Cameraman (or any crew member). There is much to be done and no matter how far ahead of the scheduled shooting date you begin there just never seems to be enough time. These busy activities seem to fall into two general categories: (1) those in which you provide assistance to the Floor Director, and (2) those in which you are concerned with activities that are specifically oriented to the camera.

Assisting the Floor Director

The responsibilities of the Floor Director described in the preceeding pages are numerous and varied. In most instance they are just too much for a single individual. In some cases the Floor Director may have a crew member assigned specifically as his assistant but it is more common for the Cameramen to fill in. In this latter case your tasks as Cameraman will possibly include (1) preparation of the studio cards, (2) collection of the props and set elements, and (3) assembly of the set elements and the setting for the production. These are described in the section dealing with the roles and responsibilities of the Floor Director so we will concentrate here on those preproduction activities that are specific to the operation of the camera.

Activities Related to Camera Operation

The assembly and basic checking of the production equipment are the responsibility of the Assistant Director (Switcher) and the control room crew. However there are certain activities related particularly to the cameras that are the particular responsibilities of the Cameramen. These include (1) placement of the cameras, (2) checking the cameras, (3) balancing the cameras, and (4) working out your camera shots.

The studio diagram developed by the Producer/Director and distributed during the production meeting will suggest the approximate position of the cameras in the studio area. However, in most cases there will need to be slight adjustments to ensure that you can get the shots called for in the storyboard. As Cameraman, you will be responsible for making these slight adjustments to ensure that you can get the shots that you are required to get. Once the cameras are positioned you need to check their operation. Check not only the camera itself but also the tripod and dolly to ensure that everything is OK. Check the intercom system to ensure that you will be able to communicate with the Producer/Director. Also check out the talley lights to make sure that they are on when your camera is punched up on the switcher. In most of these situations you will need the assistance of the Switcher to ensure that your cameras are operative. However also check the zoom, pan, and tilt controls to make sure they are working properly.

The one step that requires both Cameramen and the Switcher is the balancing of the cameras. This is the process of ensuring that the cameras are sending similar video signals to the switcher—that their pictures will be compatable. Each camera gets the same shot and the f-stops are adjusted on the Switcher's command to ensure this. This will make sure that cuts between cameras result in similar picture quality.

The last part of the preproduction phase is both the simplest and the most important. This is the process whereby you memorize the various shots that you are responsible for during the production. Initially the storyboard is your guide. However the Producer/Director may make some changes as a result of the walk-through with the Talent. There may be even more changes as a result of the rehearsal. In short you must be flexible enough to change your shots when modifications are suggested by the Producer/Director. Now you are ready for the production.

CAMERAMAN

THE TELEVISION CAMERA

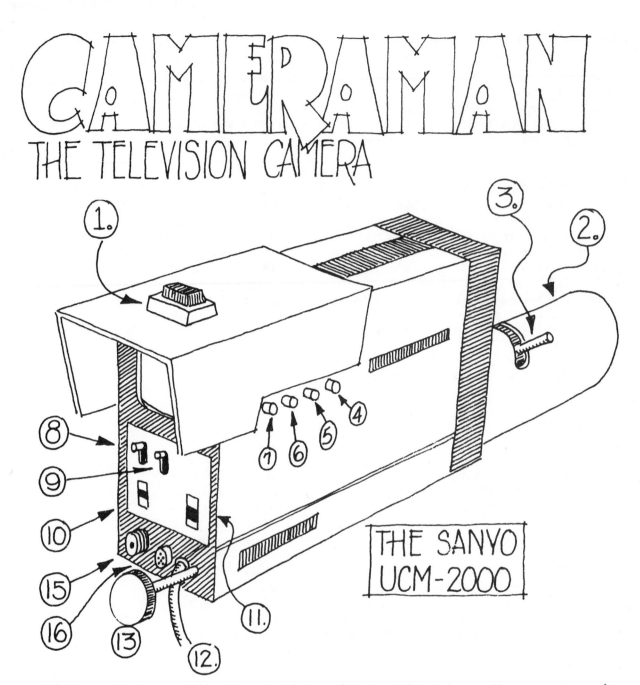

THE SANYO
UCM-2000

SCANNING SYSTEM: EIA STANDARD (525 LINES; 30 FRAMES, 60 FIELDS)

ILLUMINATION REQUIRED: 1.0 FOOT CANDLE (F 1.6 LENS)

SYNCHRONIZATION: INTERNAL: CRYSTAL CONTROLLED 2:1 INTERLACE
EXTERNAL: EIA 2:1 HORIZ. AND VERT. DRIVE

ACCESSORIES: SANYO REAR CONTROL ZOOM LENS
(RCL-2000)

CAMERAMEN: YOUR EQUIPMENT, THE CAMERA

There are many cameras that can be used in a multicamera system. The one on the opposite page is the Sanyo UCM-2000. This camera is one that I personally have had a great deal of sucess with. First it is a simple camera—simple to operate and simple to maintain. Secondly it is a low light level camera that will function in almost every light situation you will find in the public schools. I am sure that there are other cameras that meet these characteristics but we will use this one to acquaint you with the nomenclature of cameras in general.

The talley light (1) is a display signal for the Talent. When your camera is in the "on-the-air" mode the talley light will be on. It tells the Talent which camera he/she should be talking to. The zoom lens (2) allows the Cameraman to enlarge or reduce the picture size without physically moving the camera. You can get close-ups or long shots from the same camera position. Some zoom lenses are operated from in front of the camera (on the lens itself) but it is better is the zoom and focus control can be remoted and operated from the rear of the camera (13). In the rod control shown, pushing the rod in zooms the lens in and pulling it out zooms the lens out (making the picture bigger). Focus is controlled by rotating the disc on the end of the rod. There are other types of remote zoom controls but I find that this type is easiest to learn to operate. There is still one control at the front of the zoom lens—the aperture or f-stop (3). This controls the amount of light that is entering the camera and is used to balance the camera during the preproduction phase.

The viewfinder of the camera is designed to provide the Cameraman with an image of what the camera is seeing. This viewfinder has a separate set of controls (4–7) that allow you to adjust the contrast, brightness, and vertical and horizontal aspects of the image. These control only the image on the viewfinder and do not affect the image that is going to the console.

There are always some type of controls on the camera that do control either the outgoing electronic signal or the incoming signal. One reason that I like this camera is the fact that there are relatively few of these controls. On the back of this camera there is a camera/monitor switch (8) that allows the viewfinder to either monitor the camera signal or a signal from the video tape recorder. Next to it is ALC defeat switch (9) which allows you to use the automatic light control built into the camera or to turn it off as desired. The sync selector switch (10) allows you to select the source of the sync—either from the camera or from a sync generator in the console. In multicamera operation it is in external position and in single camera production it is in internal position. To the right of this is the power switch (11) which simply turns the camera on and off as needed. There are two types of video output jacks on this camera. One is for a straight video out (15) which takes a straight video cable. The other is a multicable connector (16) that is commonly used in a multicamera system and carries video, intercom, talley light and other signals. Just below this is the AC power cable (12) which carries the AC power to the camera.

Some television cameras will have more controls and some will have fewer. There is a wide range of options available on the market today. While this will introduce you to the basic nomenclature of all television cameras you need to use the operator's manual for your specific brand and model of camera. Each camera is different in some particulars but all cameras have a high degree of similarity.

CAMERAMAN
CAMERA ACCESSORIES

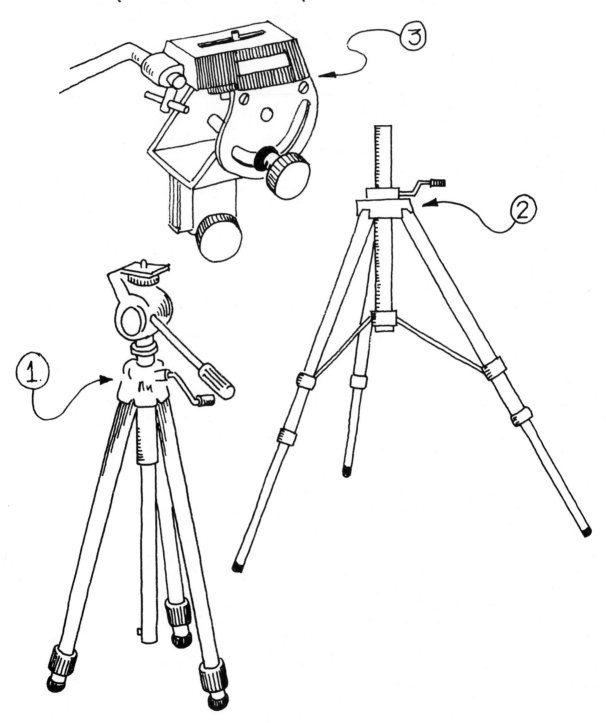

CAMERA ACCESSORIES

The camera in the multicamera studio system, unlike the portapak camera, cannot be hand held. It requires some sort of support system that will provide both stability and mobility to the camera. There are actually three different components in this support system: the pan head, the tripod, and the dolly. Each of these three elements serves a specific function and comes in a wide range of quality. Again we are faced with the situation of cost. You can buy inexpensive support systems but you have to remember that they are supporting a very expensive piece of equipment. In many instances it is not cost effective to settle for the least expensive item.

The Pan Head

The pan head (3) is designed to be the connection between the camera and the tripod. The camera is bolted to the pan head and the pan head is bolted to the tripod. The function of the pan head is to provide the Cameraman with the ability to smoothly pan and/or tilt the camera as desired. The handle for the camera extends from the pan head and lock nuts are loosened on the sides to allow the desired freedom of movement. Basically there are three types of pan heads available for the support of television cameras. The least expensive is the friction pan head in which the camera is held steady by the friction of the lock nuts on the side of the pan head. There are also gear pan heads in which the tilt mode can be controlled by a gear mechanism. While this will smooth out any tilts that are required for the program they do not aid the pans or combinations of pans and tilts. The cam-link pan head shown on the opposite page (3) provides smooth pans and tilts and prevents the possibility of the camera nose-diving.

The Tripod

The tripod is the basic support system for the camera. Make sure that you get a tripod that will support the weight of the camera, lens, and pan head. Like the pan heads the tripods come in a wide range of quality and cost. The Quick-Set tripod shown on the opposite page (1) is an example of one of the least expensive tripods. Note that it also has a built-in pan head. Heavy duty tripods like the one shown on the opposite page (2) have lateral supports from the elevator column to the individual legs. The third type of tripod is the pedestal tripod (not shown) which looks like the professional support system found in broadcast studios. The tripod should have legs that are adjustable in length and it should also have a elevator or pedestal that will allow you to raise or lower the height of the camera. This is generally called "booming"—you boom up or boom down.

The Dolly

The dolly is a three-wheeled support system that provides the entire camera assembly with mobility. It allows you to move the camera from position to position either before the production or even during the production. A dolly is essential in a multicamera system but not in a single camera system. The physical movement of the camera during an actual production is commonly called trucking or dollying. You truck to the right or left and dolly in or out. It is difficult to control these shots and they are not commonly used on the air. However, it is common to reposition the camera that is off the air during a multicamera production. In a single camera system the only real purpose of the dolly is to move the camera to and from the shooting area.

These three elements, the pan head, the tripod, and the dolly are common accessories that you will find with the television camera. They add to the cost but the smoothness that they provide is well worth it.

CAMERAMAN
STATIC SHOTS

LONG SHOT

MEDIUM SHOT

CLOSE-UP

LONG SHOT

MEDIUM SHOT

CLOSE-UP

TWO SHOTS

"TALKING ROOM"

HEAD ROOM

CAMERAMEN: KNOW YOUR STATIC SHOTS

What do you do, as Cameraman, when the Producer/Director call for a long shot, a close-up or a two-shot? Obviously the first thing you must do is to understand what the Producer/Director is asking for—you need to know what these shots are. The diagrams on the opposite page will introduce you to the basic static shots (the next few pages will cover transitional or action shots).

The long shot is sometimes called the establishing shot. It is intended to show the subject and the environment in which the subject exists. In the case of the visual on the opposite page we have a long shot of a Talent in an office setting and a long shot of a goldfish in his environment. In both cases these are long shots—they show the subjects in their environments. But the sizes of the shots are different. Thus a long shot of an ant may be different in size from a long shot of an elephant but they are both long shots—they show the subject in its environment.

The medium shot moves in slightly to put the emphasis on the subject and eliminate much of the environment. In this case portions of the environment may still be in the picture but the subject is much more prominent. Note the difference in size between the medium shot of the Talent and the medium shot of the goldfish. In some instances the medium shot may be called a head and shoulders shot. This would mean that it was slightly tighter than the medium shot of the Talent shown on the opposite page.

The close up moves in even tighter and eliminates almost all of the environment. The Talent or subject almost fills the screen. Like in the previous shots it is not the size of the shot that counts but the amount of the subject that it shows. The long shot, medium shot, and close-up are basic shots and while there are variations within all of them the basic concept deals with the amount of subject and the amount of environment that is shown.

Occasionally the Producer/Director may call for a two shot. In the diagram on the opposite page there are two examples of the two shot. In the top one the two shot shows quite a bit of the environment and all of the Talent. This might be referred to as a long two-shot. The one on the bottom is much tighter and might be referred to as a medium two shot. However the key phrase in both is "two-shot." The Producer/Director might call for a "two-shot of a boy and his dog," a "two shot of the pitcher and glass," or a "two-shot of the people who are talking." It will be your job, as cameraman, to translate these commands into action—to get the appropriate picture on your camera.

Another common command that the Producer/Director might use is "Give the Talent room to talk." Translated into action this simply means that rather than center the subject you move them off-center so that there is more room in the direction of the action than there is away from the action. In the example on the opposite page you can see how a cameraman might adjust a shot to provide the required room. This "action" room holds for people talking, walking, or making any type of movement.

Another common correction that the Producer/Director might ask for is "Give the Talent more headroom." In this case the Producer/Director is simply asking the Cameraman to make sure that there is space between the top of the Talent's head and the frame. It should be pointed out that in most cases there will be slight differences between the picture on your viewfinder and the picture on the line monitor. Since the line monitor is the "accurate" image you must follow the Producer/Director's instructions.

CAMERAMAN
MOVING CAMERA SHOTS

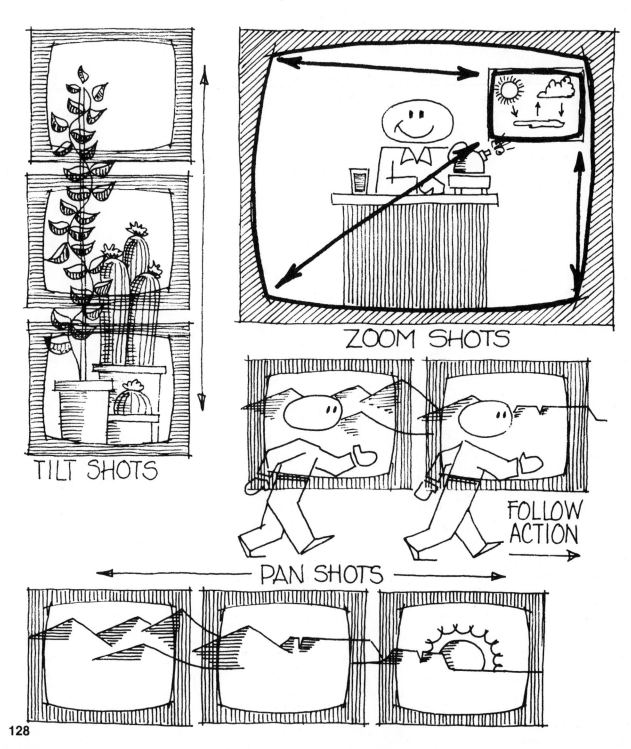

TILT SHOTS

ZOOM SHOTS

FOLLOW ACTION

PAN SHOTS

CAMERAMEN: KNOW YOUR MOTION (TRANSITIONAL) SHOTS

These motion or transitional shots are more difficult since they involve the physical movement of the camera. Basically there are three shots: (1) the zoom (in or out), (2) the tilt (up or down), and (3) the pan (right or left).

The zoom is normally used to change from one shot to another when your camera is off-the-air. However, in a few instances the Producer/Director may call for a zoom on the air. In the example on the opposite page the commands (and actions) might be like this:

DIRECTOR	CAMERAMAN
Ready to zoom in on the visual.	The cameraman gets ready to zoom in.
Zoom in!	The Cameraman zooms in slowly and smoothly to the visual.
Ready to zoom back out.	The Cameraman gets ready.
Zoom out!	The Cameraman zooms out slowly and smoothly to the original shot.

Note that because the visual is off-center, this is not only a zoom but it also requires that the Cameraman tilt and pan at the same time. A straight zoom in is relatively uncommon since most of the time you will zoom in (or out) off-center.

The tilt is another action movement. In this case the camera moves up or down as the picture also moves up and down. In the example on the opposite page the Producer/Director's commands might go like this:

DIRECTOR	CAMERAMAN
Ready to tilt up.	The Cameraman gets ready to tilt up.
Tilt up!	The Cameraman pushes the handle down and the image moves up on the screen.
Ready to stop.	The Cameraman begins to slow down.
Stop!	The Cameraman stops the tilt up.
Ready to tilt down	The cameraman gets ready.
Tilt down!	The Cameraman lifts the camera handle and the image moves down on the screen.

Note that to do a tilt you move the camera handle in the direction that is opposite of the desired camera movement. For a tilt up you push the camera handle down—for a tilt down you lift the camera handle up.

The third common action movement is the pan, shown at the bottom of the opposite page. The pan is a horizontal motion either to the left or to the right. The commands and actions might look like this:

DIRECTOR	CAMERAMAN
Ready to pan right.	The Cameraman gets ready.
Pan right!	The Cameraman moves the handle left as the image moves to the right.
Ready to stop	The Cameraman slows down.
Stop!	The Cameraman stops the pan.

This horizontal camera movement may also be used to "follow action." In the case of a moving talent, subject, or even prop the Cameraman is asked, by the Producer/Director, to "follow action." In this case they are simply asking you to keep the moving subject in the viewfinder of the camera—and if possible to give it room to move (see the preceding page).

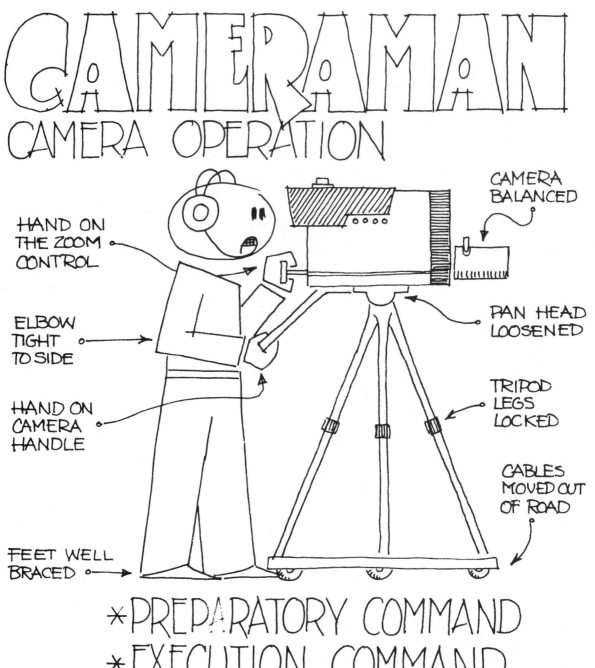

CAMERAMAN
CAMERA OPERATION

HAND ON THE ZOOM CONTROL

ELBOW TIGHT TO SIDE

HAND ON CAMERA HANDLE

FEET WELL BRACED

CAMERA BALANCED

PAN HEAD LOOSENED

TRIPOD LEGS LOCKED

CABLES MOVED OUT OF ROAD

* PREPARATORY COMMAND
* EXECUTION COMMAND

KNOW YOUR SHOTS

CAMERAMAN: OPERATING THE TELEVISION CAMERA

Once you have become familiar with the various parts of your camera and once you know the various static and action camera shots that the Producer/Director might call for, you are ready to deal with the actual operation of the camera during rehearsals and production. In this case the operation of the camera does not include the activities of setting up and balancing the cameras—it is the process of getting the shots called for by the Producer/Director and the steps necessary to get these shots.

Let's begin by looking at the steps of preparing your camera. First it must be the right height for you to operate. This is accomplished by raising or lowering the center column of the tripod. This process is called booming. You boom the camera up (raise it) or boom it down (lower it) until it is a comfortable height for the operator. The next step is to unlock the pan head. There are normally two knobs that are loosened to allow the pan head to move horizonatlly or vertically. These should be loosened but then readjusted until they are finger tight. Just enough tension should be used to allow the camera to pan and tilt and yet to hold it steady for the static shots.

You also want to check the locks on the dolly. Normally the dolly has at least two wheels that are locked. However, if it will be necessary to reposition the camera during the production by dollying in closer or dollying out—or by trucking to the right or the left then you will want to unlock the wheels of your dolly.

The next concern is you—the operator. Most people run into problems when they try to operate a camera with arms extended. This puts quite a strain on the arm and makes it very difficult to hold the camera steady during the static shots. I suggest a different approach. First position yourself comfortably behind the camera. Your feet should be about 12–18″ apart and parallel to the set. Take the handle of the camera in one hand and the zoom control in the other. Now keep your elbows tight against your side and use your whole body for the camera movements. This position usually forms a solid brace for the common static shots and when a pan or tilt is required it will be much smoother if you move with your lower body than if you try to do it with your wrist or arm. However, the key is smoothness and if you can develop a system that is better for you and still gives steady static shots and smooth transitional shots then use it.

Another concern for the operation of your camera is the commands that the Producer/Director gives over the intercom system and your response to them. Basically the Producer/Director will give two types of commands, first a preparatory command followed by an execution command. The preparatory command tells you to prepare—to get ready. The execution command tells you to do it. For example "Ready to pan right." (preparatory), "Pan right!" (execution.). There will be times during the production where preparatory commands are not necessary or where there simply will not be sufficient time. This means that as the Cameraman you need to know the program, know your shots, and be on your toes at all times.

This process of actually operating the camera during either the rehearsal or the production will be some of the most intense moments in your life. The preparation for this activity is essential. The process of learning the camera parts, learning the shots, learning the activities of the other crew members all contribute to your ability to handle the roles and responsibilities of the Cameraman during production.

CAMERAMAN
PRODUCTION – POST-PRODUCTION

FOLLOW
DIRECTIONS

DIRECTOR

ANTICIPATE

GET YOUR
SHOTS

THEN HOLD

STORE THE
EQUIPMENT

EVALUATE

A CHECKLIST FOR THE CAMERAMAN

Preproduction

_____ 1. Attend the production meeting and pick up the following documents: shooting schedule, prop and equipment list, set or studio diagram, and script/storyboard.

_____ 2. Check with the Floor Director for your specific assignments.

_____ 3. If there are some tasks that you are not sure of seek out the Floor Director for additional training or information.

_____ 4. Assist the Floor Director in collecting, transporting, and arranging the props, set elements and graphics for the production.

_____ 5. Assist the Floor Director in the preparation of studio cards and other graphics for the production.

_____ 6. Check your camera position to make sure that you can get all of the shots that are required in the storyboard.

_____ 7. Balance your camera with the Switcher and the other cameramen.

_____ 8. Practice the shots that you are expected to get during the rehearsal and the production.

_____ 9. Check your intercom to ensure that you can communicate with the Producer/Director and the rest of the crew.

_____ 10. Operate your camera during the rehearsal following the Producer/Director's commands.

_____ 11. View the playback of the rehearsal and note how you can improve your camera work.

_____ 12. Listen to the Producer/Director's comments and adjust your camera shots as required.

_____ 13. Prepare yourself for the production.

Production

_____ 1. Check the operation of your camera.

_____ 2. Think about the camera shots you will be getting.

_____ 3. When the Producer/Director says "ready on camera" respond "ready." (You should be on your first shot.)

_____ 4. Listen carefully to the preparatory and execution commands of the Producer/Director.

_____ 5. Hold your static shots steady.

_____ 6. Do your motion shots smoothly.

Post-Production

_____ 1. Assist the Producer/Director in the evaluation of the production.

_____ 2. Assist the Floor Director in collecting and returning the props, set elements and other materials to their rightful place.

SWITCHER

A GENERAL INTRODUCTION

 PREPRODUCTION ACTIVITIES

PRODUCTION ACTIVITIES

POST-PRODUCTION ACTIVITIES

134

THE SWITCHER: A GENERAL INTRODUCTION

Just as the Floor Director is in charge of and responsible for the studio crew the Switcher is in charge of and responsible for the crew who works in the control room of a multicamera production unit. This means that part of the responsibilities of the Switcher are supervisory. He/she supervises the activities of the Audio Technical Director and the Video Technical Director during the preproduction, production, and post-production phases of the project. In addition to these supervisory roles the Switcher also has some of these roles and responsibilities in general.

Preproduction Activities

Like all other members of the production crew the Switcher seems to be the busiest during the preproduction activities. The main role of the Switcher and his/her crew during this phase of the project is the collection, assembly, and checking of the production equipment. This process begins with the prop and equipment list that is distributed by the Producer/Director during the production meeting. This list indicates all of the equipment and materials that will be required. In a normal situation you will already know most of the equipment and the set-up. However, when there are special requirements that need special pieces of equipment you will need to talk this over with the Producer/Director. Once you have the prop and equipment list you and your crew begin the process of collecting, assembling, and checking the equipment.

In a fixed studio situation this is simply the checking of the equipment since it is already there and assembled. However, if you are using the portable type of studio systsm and are shooting on location, the equipment will all have to be moved to the location, interconnected, and checked to make sure that it is functioning properly.

Once everything is checked out you will then do the necessary switching during the rehearsal. Since you are closest to the Producer/Director during the rehearsal and the production in many ways you are the Assistant Director. This also means that you should make yourself as familiar with the production as possible. In addition to reading all of the design and production documents as closely as possible you need to be with the Producer/Director during the walk-through and be especially observant during the rehearsal. In the rotation of personnel through the responsibilities of the production crew the role of Switcher leads directly to that of Producer/Director.

Production Activities

During the phase of the production you will be primarily responsible for the operation of the video console. However, you will also be expected to make sure that the control room crew knows what their jobs are and how to do them. These responsibilities require that you be totally familiar with all of the production equipment and particularly the operation of the video switcher for your particular system. You need to know how to do the simple cuts and fades that are common parts of the program, but you also need to know how to create any special effects that are indicated in the script/storyboard.

Post-Production Activities

When the production is finally on video tape your role as Switcher is still not over. During this phase you have two major responsibilities: (1) you will assist the Producer/Director in evaluating the product, and (2) you will supervise the control room crew in the dismantling and storage of the production equipment.

SWITCHER
PREPRODUCTION ACTIVITIES

THE SWITCHER: PREPRODUCTION ACTIVITIES

As with any crew position the preproduction activities, those that occur before the actual production of the message, are normally the busiest time. As Switcher your responsibilities will include (1) supervisory activities and (2) operation of the video console. This process begins when the Producer/Director distributes the various design and production documents at the production meeting. As Switcher you will want copies of (1) the storyboard/script, (2) the shooting schedule, (3) the prop and equipment list, and (4) the studio or set diagram.

The prop and equipment list will tell you and the rest of the control room crew what pieces of equipment are needed for the production. It will be your responsibility, as Switcher, to supervise the collection, transportation and assembly of that equipment. This activity will vary depending on whether you are shooting in a studio or whether your equipment is portable and is being used on location. In a fixed studio situation the equipment will already be there and hooked up. This limits your responsibility to simply turning it on and ensuring that it is operating properly. If, on the other hand, you are on location the equipment will have to be collected, moved to the location, set-up, and checked out. The other members of the control room crew will assist in this but it is your responsibility to make sure that everything is working properly and if it is not to make simple repairs if necessary.

Checking the equipment is a relatively complicated process. It is not enough that the equipment is on and apparently working. You will need to ensure that the incoming audio and video signals are set at appropriate levels. This will involve working with the Cameramen in the studio in balancing the video signals from the cameras and working with the Audio Technical Director in setting the appropriate levels for the mikes in the studio. Once the levels are set you will want to run a test tape to ensure that the program is recording well. This test recording should include video signals from both cameras, special effects, sound inputs from all audio sources and anything else that might be used in the program. Play back the entire test tape and have your crew evaluate the technical quality of the recording. Discuss anything that can be done to improve the production.

You need to know as much about the upcoming production as possible. You must read and memorize the script and the storyboard. You must be ready to anticipate those areas that are likely to cause difficulty for either you or your control room crew. For example, are there points in the script where quick transitions from scene to scene are called for? Are there complex audio requirements that might confuse the Audio Technical Director? The ability to anticipate these potential trouble spots usually means that they will not occur.

In addition to these supervisory activities you also have to prepare for your particular responsibilities. You will be operating the video switcher and this requires a lot of homework on your part. You need to know how to respond to the various commands of the Producer/Director. What do you do when the Producer/Director says "Ready on camera one—take one!" or "Ready to dissolve to two—dissolve to two!" There must be a common understanding between you and the Producer/Director as to the meaning of these commands and the actions that you will take. This also implies that you have totally mastered the operation of your particular video switcher.

During the rehearsal you will operate the video switcher but you also need to keep track of what your crew is doing.

SWITCHER
THE SYSTEM, GENERAL

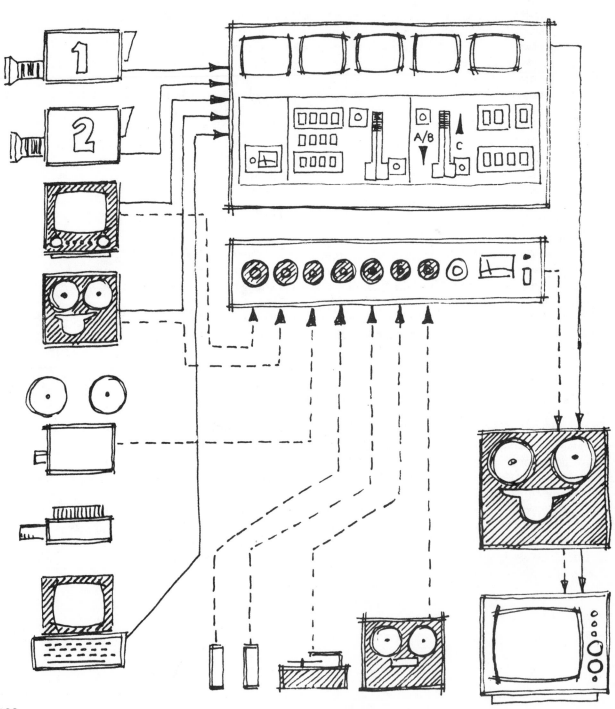

THE SWITCHER: THE TELEVISION SYSTEM, GENERAL

Since one of your major responsibilities, as Switcher, is the supervision of the assembly of the components of the multicamera system you need to have an idea of how it goes together. While each system will be slightly different, there are some common characteristics of all systems.

First, each system is composed of (1) audio and video inputs, (2) audio and video control centers, (3) the recording system, and (4) a line monitor that displays the signal being recorded. There are a number of different video inputs that can be fed into a multicamera system. Obviously there are the cameras, camera cables connect these to the camera monitors and the video switcher. In a multicamera system these cables not only carry the video signals they also carry sync signals, intercom signals, and even talley light signals. Other video sources that can be provided with a common sync signal can also feed the system. These might include off-the-air signals from a monitor/receiver or even video signals from an auxiliary video tape recorder. In each case both audio and video signals are fed into the console. In some situations a film chain or a slide chain will allow motion pictures or slides to be inserted into the production. In this case the images are shown on the projector and focused into a separate television camera. The camera signal is then sent to the console. In the case of the motion picture it may also require an audio output that is fed into the audio input of the console. You could even add a character generator to your system. The character generator will allow the superimposition of words or even lines of lettering across the existing pictures from other sources.

In addition to the variety of video input sources that are available there are also a number of possible audio input sources. Microphones, record players, audio tape recorders as well as the audio from television monitor/receivers, video tape recorders, and even a motion picture projector can be fed into the console.

The console usually consists of three parts: (1) a set of camera monitors used to view incoming video signals, (2) a video switcher that permits the selection of a video signal (or combination of signals) to be sent to the video tape recorder, and (3) an audio mixer that serves the same purpose for incoming audio signals. The camera monitors display each camera's picture and other video sources as required. These monitors allow the Producer/Director and the Switcher to see what is ready to be punched up on the line monitor. The console also includes the video switcher that will allow you to cut and dissolve between video signals or to fade them in or out and activate other special effects. The audio mixer will allow you to select the audio source that will be sent to the video tape recorder or to mix a variety of sources and send a composite signal to the VTR.

The audio and video output from the console is sent to the video tape recorder where the electronic signals are transferred to video tape. These recorded signals can be played back immediately or they can be stored for future playback. The video tape recorder is the storage and playback part of the multicamera system.

The signal from the master video tape recorder is then sent to the monitor/receiver—often called the line monitor. With the video tape recorder in passive record mode the signal passes directly through the VTR without being recorded and is displayed on the monitor. With the VTR in active record mode the picture is being recorded but the line monitor is also displaying the signal that is being recorded.

SWITCHER

THE CONSOLE, GENERAL

Portable

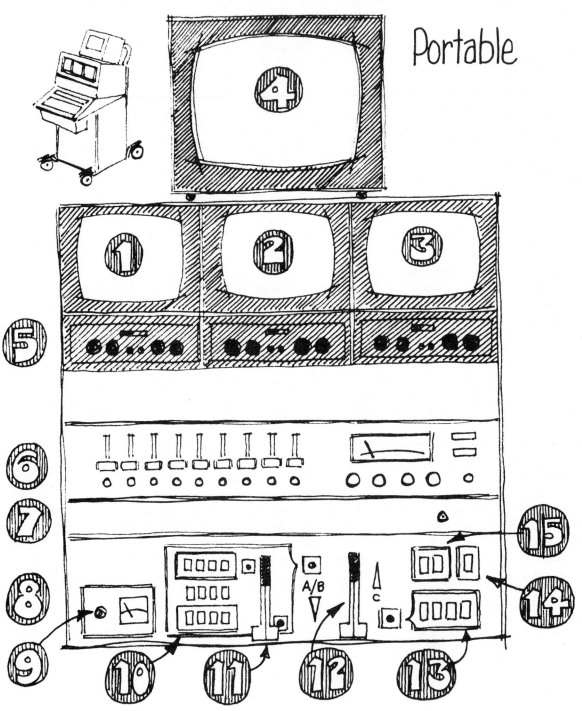

THE SWITCHER: THE PORTABLE CONSOLE, INTRODUCTION

Consoles are generally of two types: (1) the fixed console that is usually located in the control room of a studio and (2) the portable console that is mounted on wheels and can be moved from place to place. One definite advantage of the portable console is that it allows you to do multicamera productions on location. While it is limited to areas where AC power is available it is much more flexible than the studio console. However, there are disadvantages. In the studio console the audio and video switchers are usually side by side allowing for easier operation by two people while with the portable console the audio and video switchers are usually mounted over each other which makes it more difficult for two people to operate. I have used the portable console in the TELEMEDIA Project for the past five years and found that it can be used sucessfully by students from the third grade through graduate school. It has allowed me to take the television experience to the students at their school rather than having the students come to a central location.

This section is intended to familiarize you with the basic components of this portable console. While your console may vary in form and format from the one shown on the opposite page the functions of the various components are the same.

Beginning at the top of the console we find the line monitor (4). This is fed with the audio and video signal from the master video tape recorder. It is used to tell the Producer/Director and the Switcher what the image (and sound) being recorded looks (and sounds) like.

Immediately below the line monitor in the diagram are the camera and preview monitors. The camera monitors (1–2) are use to display the images from the two cameras. Monitor one always shows the picture from camera one and monitor two always shows the image from camera two. Monitor three (3) is the preview monitor and used to preview any desired special effects or auxiliary video input signals before they go on the air. Immediately below these monitors are the monitor controls (5). These controls affect only the images on the monitor and do not have any affect on the outgoing video signal.

Below the camera monitors is the audio mixer (6). Incoming audio signals are fed into the individual controls and a composite audio signal is sent from here to the video tape recorder. This is covered in more detail in the section dealing with the Audio Technical Director.

Below the audio mixer is the power unit for the systems intercom (7). The headset that the Producer/Director will wear to communicate with the rest of the production crew plugs into this section. Just below this is the video switcher. The video switcher (8) accepts the video input signals from the various video sources and selects which signal, or combination of signals, will be sent to the video tape recorder. In this case the video switcher consists of a genlock or sync selector switch (9) which allows you to determine the source of the sync signal tht will be used and a series of video controls. These video controls include a special effects component (10) complete with an effects lever (11) and to the right of that a dissolve lever (12) and buttons (13) that select the image. That will go to the video tape recorder. Just above these buttons are buttons (15) that control the image shown on the preview monitor (3) so the Producer/Director can easily see what camera shot is coming next. Button number 14 is the on/off button for the console.

While there will be variations in the form and format of these units the functions of the various components will be the same and each brand and model of console will at least contain these components.

SWITCHER

THE 361 SHINTRON VIDEO SWITCHER

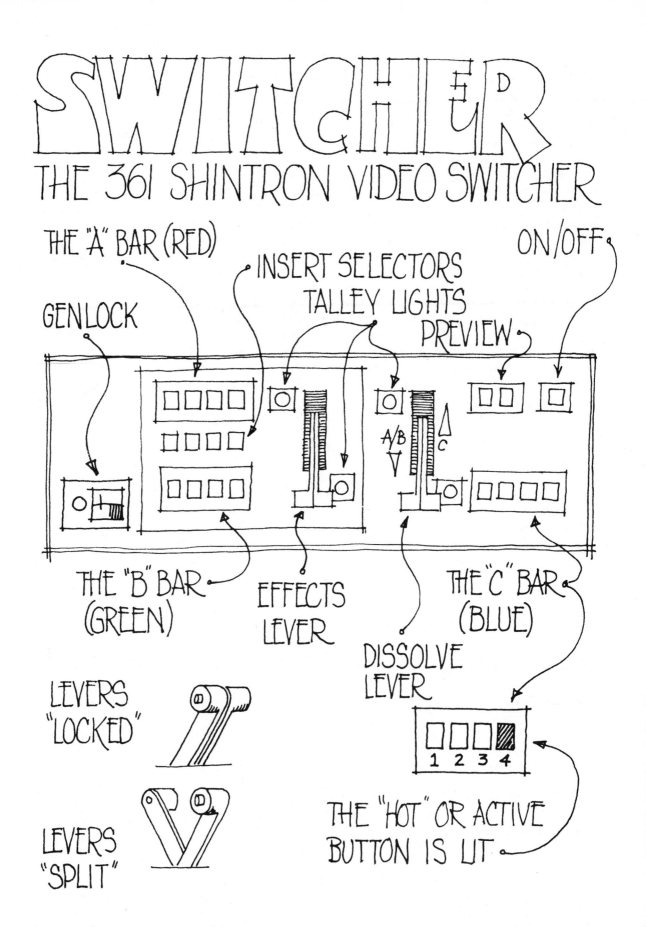

THE "A" BAR (RED)

INSERT SELECTORS
TALLEY LIGHTS
PREVIEW

ON/OFF

GENLOCK

A/B   C

THE "B" BAR
(GREEN)

EFFECTS
LEVER

THE "C" BAR
(BLUE)

DISSOLVE
LEVER

LEVERS
"LOCKED"

LEVERS
"SPLIT"

1 2 3 4

THE "HOT" OR ACTIVE
BUTTON IS LIT

OPERATING THE SHINTRON SWITCHER

CAMERA ONE   CAMERA TWO   CAMERA THREE   LINE MONITOR

READY ON THE CONSOLE.

- POWER SWITCH ON
- CAMERA THREE ON
- DISSOLVE LEVER SPLIT AND THE CONSOLE (LINE MONITOR) IS IN BLACK.

READY TO FADE IN THREE.
FADE IN CAMERA THREE!

- MOVE THE DISSOLVE LEVER (THE RIGHT SIDE) TO THE DOWN POSITION.
- LINE MONITOR NOW SHOWS THE PICTURE FROM CAMERA THREE.

READY ON CAMERA TWO.

- POSITION FINGER OVER THE CAMERA TWO BUTTON ON THE BLUE BAR.

TAKE TWO!

- PRESS CAMERA TWO BUTTON ON THE BLUE BAR
- LINE MONITOR NOW SHOWS THE PICTURE FROM CAMERA TWO.

READY ON CAMERA ONE.

- POSITION FINGER OVER THE CAMERA ONE BUTTON ON THE BLUE BAR.

TAKE ONE!

- PRESS CAMERA ONE BUTTON ON THE BLUE BAR.
- LINE MONITOR NOW SHOWS THE PICTURE FROM CAMERA ONE.

READY TO DISSOLVE TO 2.

- PRESS CAMERA TWO BUTTON ON THE GREEN BAR---INACTIVE-- GRASP THE DISSOLVE LEVER.

▲(2)   ▲(1)

DISSOLVE TO TWO!

- MOVE THE ENTIRE DISSOLVE LEVER INTO THE UP POSITION.

- LINE MONITOR NOW SHOWS THE PICTURE FROM CAMERA TWO.

  * NOTE THAT THE TALLEY LIGHTS NOW INDICATE THAT THE GREEN BAR AND THE SPECIAL EFFECTS SECTION IS "HOT".

READY ON CAMERA ONE.

- POSITION FINGER OVER THE CAMERA ONE BUTTON ON THE GREEN BAR.

TAKE ONE!

- PRESS THE CAMERA ONE BUTTON ON THE GREEN BAR.

- LINE MONITOR NOW SHOWS THE PICTURE FROM CAMERA ONE.

READY TO DISSOLVE TO TWO.

- GRASP THE DISSOLVE LEVER AND PRESS THE CAMERA TWO BUTTON ON THE BLUE BAR.

DISSOLVE TO TWO!

- MOVE BOTH HALVES OF THE DISSOLVE LEVER INTO THE DOWN POSITION.

- LINE MONITOR NOW SHOWS THE PICTURE FROM CAMERA TWO.

  * NOTE THE TALLEY LIGHTS NOW INDICATE THAT THE BLUE BAR IS HOT.

READY ON CAMERA ONE.

- POSITION FINGER OVER CAMERA ONE BUTTON ON THE BLUE BAR.

TAKE ONE!

- PRESS THE CAMERA ONE BUTTON ON THE BLUE BAR.

- LINE MONITOR NOW SHOWS THE PICTURE FROM CAMERA ONE.

READY ON CAMERA THREE.

- POSITION FINGER OVER THE CAMERA THREE BUTTON ON THE BLUE BAR.

CAMERA ONE CAMERA TWO CAMERA THREE LINE MONITOR

TAKE THREE!

- PRESS THE CAMERA THREE BUTTON ON THE BLUE BAR.
- LINE MONITOR NOW SHOWS THE PICTURE FROM CAMERA THREE.

READY TO FADE TO BLACK

- GRASP THE RIGHT HALF OF THE DISSOLVE LEVER.

FADE TO BLACK!

- MOVE RIGHT HALF OF DISSOLVE LEVER INTO THE UP POSITION.
- THE LINE MONITOR NOW SHOWS NO IMAGE.
  - * NOTE THAT ALL OF THE TALLEY LIGHTS ARE OFF.

TO TURN THE CONSOLE OFF PRESS THE ON/OFF BUTTON AND ALL MONITORS WILL GO BLANK.

AS SWITCHER THIS IS YOUR MAIN TOOL---LEARN IT. NOT ONLY THE SIMPLE CUTS, FADES, AND DISSOLVES BUT ALSO THE UNUSUAL SPECIAL EFFECTS.

CAMERA ONE	CAMERA TWO	CAMERA THREE	LINE MONITOR

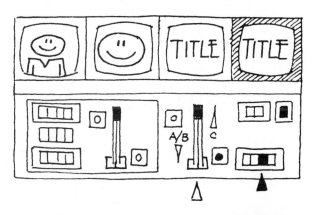

SWITCHER

TRANSITIONS & SPECIAL EFFECTS

FADE IN/OUT

SIMPLE CUTS

DISSOLVES

WIPES
HORIZONTAL
VERTICAL

INSERTS

SPLIT SCREEN

SUPERS

SWITCHER: TRANSITIONS AND SPECIAL EFFECTS

As Switcher one of your responsibilities will be to punch up the transition and/ or special effect that the Producer/Director calls for. To do this you need to know how to manipulate the controls on the video switcher but you also need to know what these effects look like and what they might be used for. In some cases the Producer/Director may even ask you before the program for suggestions about the most appropriate special effect to use. During the rehearsal or the production you have to know what the effect is and how to create it.

The fade in and fade out are common effects used to open and close a television program. The effect on the line monitor will be to have the image gradually fade in to full intensity or to fade out to black. The term fade to black is often used at the end of a program but you really just fade out the picture—the line monitor will not turn a total black.

The cuts are the most common type of transition from one shot to another. The cut is an abrupt change from one scene to the next scene. Usually the Producer/ Director's commands will be "Ready on one," "Take one!" On the command "Take one!" you punch up the appropriate shot on the line monitor.

Dissolves are not as commonly used as cuts yet they too are a means of creating a transition between scenes. In this case rather than an abrupt change the dissolve is a slow disappearance of one image and the gradual replacement with the other. At one point both images are on the screen. The speed of the dissolve may be varied depending on the effect the Producer/Director desires. This type of transition is commonly used in programs that are more artistic than instructional.

The wipe can be used as either a transition or in setting up what is referred to as a split screen. Though it is not often appropriate a wipe can be used as a transition. In this case once scene is replaced by another by a line moving either vertically or horizontally across the screen. This transition is quite unusual and will often call attention to itself. For this reason it is not often used.

In addition to these transitions there are also special effects that the Producer/ Director might call for. The technique for setting up these special effects will vary depending on the video switcher you are using. Make sure you consult the operator's manual that came with your switcher and practice with the equipment.

The term insert is used to describe a situation in which you have a major image with a minor image built into the corner of it. These corner inserts are very useful when you want to show an entire action or scene and still be able to see a close-up of a part of that action or scene. However it does tie up both cameras and requires that you have some time to practice the shot before the production.

The split screen is similar except that instead of inserting the second image in a corner it appears as either vertical or horizontal part of the screen. A common use of the split screen is to insert a title or other information at the bottom of the main picture (see the example on the opposite page).

One of the most popular special effects is the super or superimposition. In this case words or pictures are literally superimposed over the main picture. To do this the words or pictures to be supered must be printed on black railroad board using white ink or paint, or dry transfer letters. Then with the super on the second camera you do the reverse of a fade out and the result is that the super image will appear superimposed over the master image. This can be very effective.

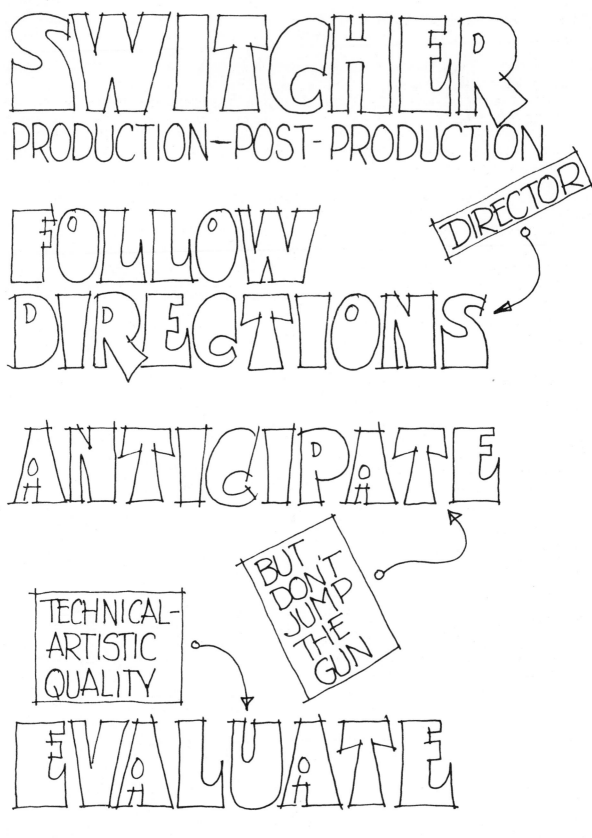

SWITCHER

PRODUCTION—POST-PRODUCTION

FOLLOW DIRECTIONS

DIRECTOR

ANTICIPATE

BUT DON'T JUMP THE GUN

TECHNICAL-ARTISTIC QUALITY

EVALUATE

SUPERVISE EQUIPMENT STORAGE.

A CHECKLIST FOR THE VIDEO SWITCHER

Preproduction

_____ 1. Attend the production meeting and pick up the following documents: the shooting schedule, the prop and equipment list and the storyboard/script.

_____ 2. Identify the people assigned as the control room crew and determine if they know their jobs and how to do them.

_____ 3. Provide in-service training for those crew members who feel unsure of their roles or their skills.

_____ 4. Using the prop and equipment list as a guide supervise the control room crew in the identification, transport, and assembly of the production equipment.

_____ 5. Run a test tape to check out the production system.

_____ 6. Balance the studio cameras.

_____ 7. Set levels for audio inputs.

_____ 8. Familiarize yourself with the script and the storyboard with special emphasis on transitions and special effects that are called for in these documents.

_____ 9. Observe the Producer/Director and the Talent during the walk-through of the program—identify any changes that the Producer/Director wants to make in the script/storyboard.

_____ 10. Inform the control room crew of any of these changes that affect their responsibilities.

_____ 11. Check out the control room crew before the rehearsal.

_____ 12. Operate the video switcher during the rehearsal.

_____ 13. Monitor the rehearsal tape and identify any changes that are suggested by the Producer/Director.

_____ 14. Inform the control room crew of changes suggested by the rehearsal of the program.

Production

_____ 1. Check out the control room before the production.

_____ 2. Place the console in black.

_____ 3. Listen carefully to the Producer/Director.

_____ 4. Follow the commands of the Producer/Director.

_____ 5. Operate the video switcher.

_____ 6. Monitor the activities of the other members of the control room crew.

Post-Production

_____ 1. Assist the Producer/Director in the evaluation of the video tape.

_____ 2. Once the video tape is approved supervise the control room crew in the dismantling and return of the production equipment.

VIDEO T.D.
A GENERAL INTRODUCTION

✳ PREPRODUCTION ACTIVITIES

 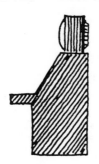 

✳ PRODUCTION ACTIVITIES

✳ POST-PRODUCTION ACTIVITIES

VIDEO TECHNICAL DIRECTOR: A GENERAL INTRODUCTION

The Video Technical Director is often called Video TD or just Video. The Video TD works under the direction of the Switcher as part of the control room crew. Basically the Video TD is responsible for the care of the video production equipment and assisting the Audio TD with the audio production equipment. Lets look at these roles and responsibilities of the Video TD during the preproduction, production, and post-production phases.

Preproduction Activities of the Video TD

One you have been assigned the role of Video TD by the shooting schedule you need to check with the Switcher and acquire a copy of the prop and equipment list to make sure what is required in the way of equipment for the production. Your main responsibility will then be to (1) locate, collect, transport the production equipment to the shooting location; (2) set the production system up and check it out; and (3) to load, check, and cue the video tape recorder. In this process you will be assisted by the Audio TD. While you are primarily responsible for the video system and the Audio TD is primarily responsible for the audio system it is essential that you work together since both audio and video are part of the overall production system.

If the production system is a fixed studio system your job is quite simple since all of the equipment is stored in the same place and it is already interconnected. In this case all you have to do is to turn it on and check it out. However, if the system is a portable production unit and you are shooting on location you need to make arrangements to get the equipment together, transport it to the shooting location that is indicated on the shooting schedule, arrange it according to the set or studio diagram and then check it out to make sure that everything is operational.

Once the entire system has been checked you need to go back over the video tape recorder which is your primary responsibility. Load it and check its operation. It is a good idea to run a practice tape including all of the audio and video sources and then play it back and critique the technical quality.

When the system is completely operational you are ready for the rehearsal. You will be responsible for taping the production and for monitoring the program on the line monitor. During either the program or its rehearsal you have relatively little to do so spend the time assisting others and observing to better prepare yourself for other production responsibilities.

Production Activities of the Video Technical Director

During the actual production you, as Video Technical Director, will be responsible for operating the VTR and monitoring the production. You will need to check the tape to ensure that you are not erasing any important information. You will need to record the beginning and ending numbers of the production (from the footage counter on the VTR). You will also give the Producer/Director a 10-second countdown at the beginning of the production (when he says Roll Video) to ensure that all sync is locked into the VTR.

Post-Production Activities of the Video Technical Director

Once the production is on video tape you, as Video TD, will rewind the tape, cue it up to the beginning, and play it back for the technical and artistic evaluation. You will also assist the Producer/Director in the critique of the production. Once the production is accepted you will work with the Audio Technical Director and the Switcher to turn off the equipment and put it away for another day.

VIDEO T.D.
PREPRODUCTION ACTIVITY

THE VIDEO TECHNICAL DIRECTOR: PREPRODUCTION ACTIVITIES

While the preproduction activities for a television program begin with the initial conference between the client and the Producer/Director the production crew does not generally become involved until the production meeting called by the Producer/Director. At this time the various crew positions are assigned and if you are selected as the Video Technical Director you will have a number of responsibilities during the preproduction phase.

Your first set of responsibilities will center around the production equipment. Working with the Audio Technical Director and under the supervision of the Switcher you will be responsible for the location, collection, transportation, assembly and checking of the production equipment. If you are working with a fixed studio system this will be relatively simple. The equipment will already be located, collected and assembled. It will be in the studio area. All you will have to do is turn it on and check it out. On the other hand if you are working with a portable multicamera system you have to get it to the location where the production will take place. If it is in the school proper it is simply a matter of wheeling it from the storage area to the production area. If you are really going on remote you need to acquire transportation that will get the equipment there. Check the prop and equipment list to make sure that just the standard equipment is necessary or if there are special production items needed.

Once you get it to the location then you need to put the system together and check it out. In the next few pages you will see how a basic system is wired. Checking simply means that you will run a test tape utilizing all of the video input and audio input sources. Play back this test tape and evaluate the technical quality of the production. The Switcher will make the final decision about the acceptability of the quality.

Once the system has been checked you can begin to work on your specific tasks. Since you are the Video Technical Director the main piece of equipment you will be working with is the video tape recorder. Since there is a wide variation in the form and format of video tape recorders the best we can do here is to speak in generalities. In actual practice you will need to read the operator's manual that comes with the particular VTR that is part of your system. However, there are some common activities that are needed regardless of the brand or model of video tape recorder.

First you need to clean your VTR. Specifics about cleaning are covered a little later in this section but it might be worthwhile to point out that you should clean your video tape recorder before every use. This is the only way you can be sure that your video tape recorder is ready to give you the best possible quality. Once you have checked the video tape recorder and cleaned it you will want to run it back to the beginning of the tape (making sure that there is nothing on the tape you want to save) and then log the footage counter numbers to make sure you can find the beginning at a later time.

When all the equipment, including the VTR, is ready you need to be concerned with the upcoming rehearsal. The preceeding walk-through is not normally video taped but the rehearsal is. When the Producer/Director says "Roll video!" you will put the VTR into active record mode and give the 10-second count down. This countdown will allow all of the video sources to be locked together with the sync signal. Once you have completed the countdown you really have very little to do. As you monitor the production you should also keep your eyes and ears open. Look for ways in which you can help others in the production crew.

VIDEO T.D.
WIRING THE BASIC SYSTEM

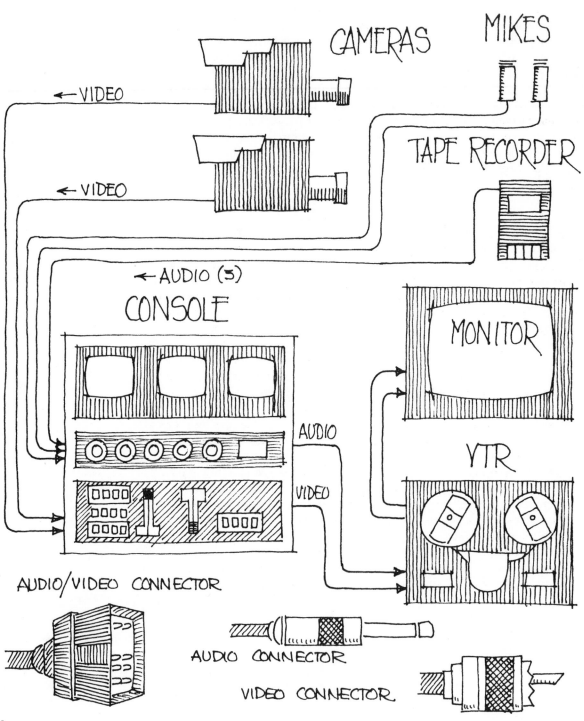

CAMERAS

MIKES

TAPE RECORDER

← VIDEO

← VIDEO

← AUDIO (3)

CONSOLE

MONITOR

AUDIO

VIDEO

VTR

AUDIO/VIDEO CONNECTOR

AUDIO CONNECTOR

VIDEO CONNECTOR

VIDEO TECHNICAL DIRECTOR: WIRING THE BASIC SYSTEM

Since one of your major responsibilities, as Video Technical Director, will be the collection, assembly, and checking of the production system you need to know the basics of wiring it. In the diagram on the opposite page there are two video input sources (the cameras) and three audio input sources (two mikes and an auxiliary audio tape recorder). These input sources feed their audio and video signals into the console which contains the camera monitors, the audio mixer, and the video switcher. The outputs from the console (composite audio and composite video) are fed into the video tape recorder. The audio and video signals from the video tape recorder are fed into the line monitor where the image being recorded is displayed. Now, how are these system components interconnected?

The connection between the cameras and the video switcher are multiwire camera cables. These cables carry the video signal from the camera to the video switcher. The also carry the same signal to the camera monitors on top of the console. However, they carry a variety of other important signals. The intercom signal is also carried over this camera cable allowing the Producer/Director to communicate directly with the Cameramen and the Floor Director. These camera cables also carry the talley light signals from the video switcher to each camera. And they also carry the sync signal between the sync generator and the various video sources. The camera cable is normally attached to the camera and the back of the console where it branches to the camera monitors.

The audio inputs are connected to the audio jacks in the console. These audio jacks are dedicated to various channels in the audio mixer. The connections are straight audio lines either using the audio connectors shown on the opposite page or cannon connectors. Occasionally you may need to use audio extension cords to get the mikes into areas of the set that are quite a distance from the console.

The audio mixer and the video switcher take the incoming audio and video signals and either select a specific signal as output or mix a combination of signals as output. These outputs from the audio mixer are sent through straight audio lines to the audio input of the video tape recorder. The outputs from the video switcher are sent by a straight video line (see the video connector) to the video input of the video tape recorder.

The video tape recorder not only records these audio and video signals, it also allows them to be played back. This requires a line monitor which is connected to the video tape recorder. This interconnection between the video tape recorder and the line monitor may take many different forms depending on the types of inputs that are available on the line monitor and the type of outputs on the video tape recorder. In one format separate audio and video signals will be sent from the video tape recorder to the line monitor. In another format these separate audio and video signals are combined into a multiwire cable (see audio/video connector on the opposite page). The third format that is becomming increasingly popular is the RF signal. In this case the video tape recorder internally combines the audio and video signal into what is called an RF output. This RF output is then connected to the antenna leads of the line monitor (or any televison set).

It will be your responsibility as the Video Technical Director to play a major part in the setting up, checking, and operating this production system. You will be working closely with the Audio Technical Director and under the supervision of the Switcher. Learn the system and the basic problems that you might encounter.

VIDEO T.D.
CLEANING THE VTR

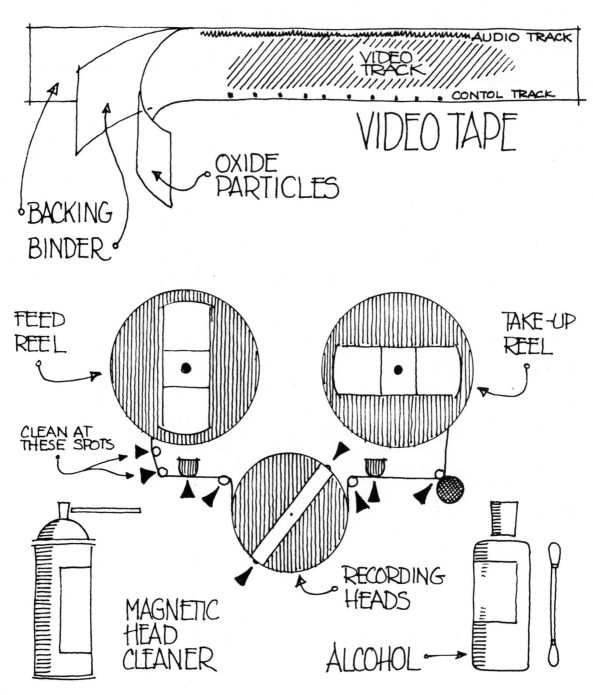

VIDEO TAPE

AUDIO TRACK

VIDEO TRACK

CONTOL TRACK

OXIDE PARTICLES

BACKING BINDER

FEED REEL

TAKE-UP REEL

CLEAN AT THESE SPOTS

MAGNETIC HEAD CLEANER

RECORDING HEADS

ALCOHOL

VIDEO TECHNICAL DIRECTOR: CLEANING THE VIDEO TAPE RECORDER

Since your major responsibility as Video Technical Director is the operation of the video tape recorder it is essential that you know a little bit about this unit. The video tape recorder accepts incoming audio and video electronic signals and transfers them to magnetic impulses on video tape. In addition to recording signals the video tape recorder stores them and also plays them back. In the playback mode the magnetic signals are translated into electronic signals that are delivered to a television monitor/ receiver and displayed as video images and audio sounds.

What about the nature of this video tape that is used to record these audio and video signals? First, most video tapes are composed of three layers. The base or backing layer is a thin plastic that provides strength for the tape. The second layer is a binder that holds the top and bottom layers together. The third layer actually does all of the work and is composed of oxide particles in an emulsion. These oxide particles are given the magnetic signals during recording and play them back at a later time. The selection of a good quality of recording tape is important. It has often been suggested that you can substitute less expensive computer tape but you will find that this seriously damages the recording heads and ends up costing more than you save. Try a variety of recording tapes and pick the one that consistently gives you the results you want.

How are these electronic signals transferred to the magnetic video tape? In the diagram on the opposite page you can see how the tape passes through a reel to reel video tape recorder such as the Sony 3650. In this case the video tape comes off the feed reel, around some guide rollers and across the erase head. When the VTR is in record mode this head is activated and erases both the audio and video signals to provide a blank tape for recording. During playback this is inactive to keep from inadvertently erasing materials that you want to keep. From the erase head the tape continues on and is wrapped around the recording head. In this case the recording heads are on either end of the arm that rotates within the entire unit. The tape moves at an angle across the drum and the video signals are laid down diagonally across the tape (see the diagram at the top). From here the tape moves around another guide roller and across the second recording head. This records the audio signal and also lays down the sync track that allows the tape to be played back on other video tape recorders. From here the tape goes around other guide rollers and to the take-up reel.

On the right end of the diagram at the top of the opposite page you can see how the various recording tracks are laid down on the video tape. The audio tracks runs along the top of the tape. The video track is diagonally across the center and the sync track is at the bottom. Any damage to the edges of the tape will result in a loss of audio or sync signal.

To clean the video tape recorder use either a spray magnetic head cleaner or an alcohol and Q-tip combination. Cleaning should be done on all of the parts indicated by the dark triangles in the diagram on the opposite page. You should, clean the video tape recorder before every production. Unless there is a cleaning log on your VTR or you are the only one using it you don't want to take a chance on dirty heads and thus a loss in the technical quality of the production. To be on the safe side clean all heads and all guide rollers every time you use the video tape recorder.

VIDEO T.D.
THE VIDEO TAPE RECORDER

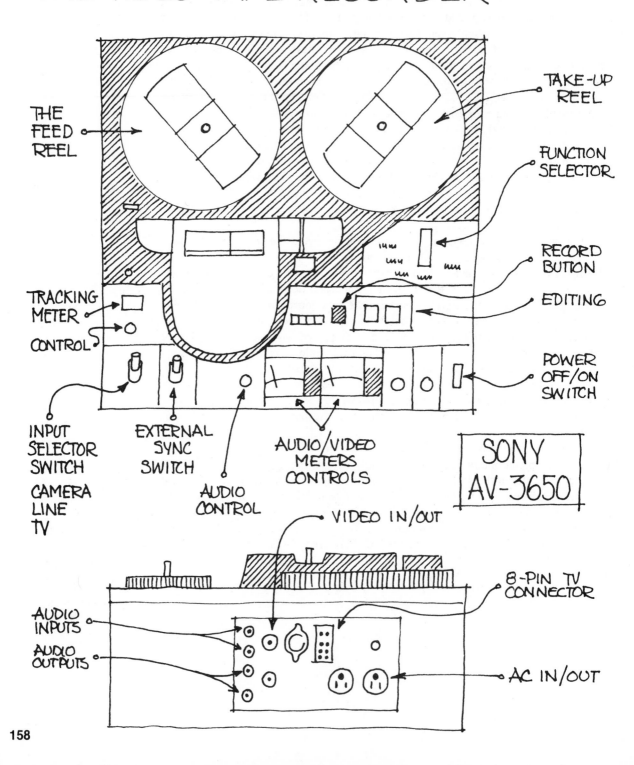

THE FEED REEL

TAKE-UP REEL

FUNCTION SELECTOR

RECORD BUTTON

EDITING

POWER OFF/ON SWITCH

TRACKING METER

CONTROL

INPUT SELECTOR SWITCH

CAMERA LINE TV

EXTERNAL SYNC SWITCH

AUDIO CONTROL

AUDIO/VIDEO METERS CONTROLS

SONY AV-3650

VIDEO IN/OUT

8-PIN TV CONNECTOR

AUDIO INPUTS

AUDIO OUTPUTS

AC IN/OUT

VIDEO T.D.
THE VIDEO TAPE RECORDER
SONY VP-1000

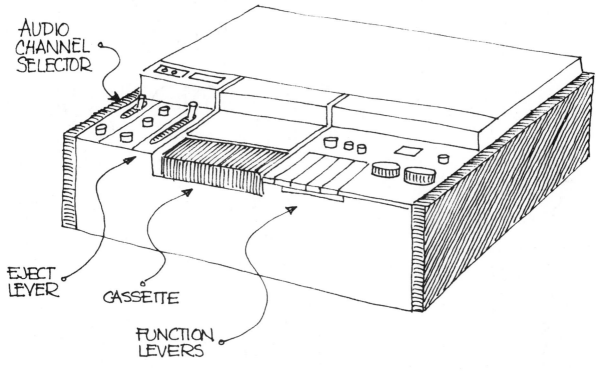

AUDIO
CHANNEL
SELECTOR

EJECT
LEVER

CASSETTE

FUNCTION
LEVERS

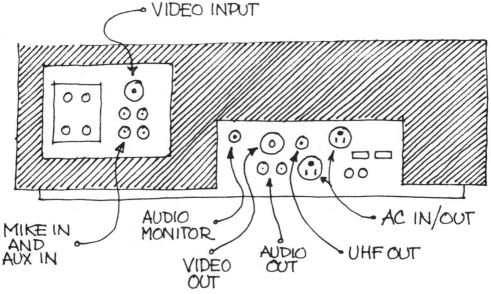

VIDEO INPUT

MIKE IN
AND
AUX IN

AUDIO
MONITOR

VIDEO
OUT

AUDIO
OUT

UHF OUT

AC IN/OUT

VIDEO T.D.

PRODUCTION-POST-PRODUCTION

COUNTDOWN 10-9-8-7-6-5-4

MONITOR

STOP
REWIND
CUE
PLAYBACK

EVALUATE

LOG THE NUMBERS

* STORAGE

CHECKLIST FOR THE VIDEO TECHNICAL DIRECTOR

Preproduction

_____ 1. Attend the production meeting and get a copy of the prop and equipment list.

_____ 2. Check with the Switcher to find out what assignments you have.

_____ 3. If you have any doubts about what your responsibilities are or your skills to do them check with the Switcher for information and/or instruction.

_____ 4. Assist the Audio Technical Director in the collection, transportation, assembly, and checking of the production equipment.

_____ 5. Run a test tape and have it approved by the Switcher.

_____ 6. Clean your video tape recorder.

_____ 7. Cue up your video tape.

_____ 8. Record the rehearsal and log the beginning and end numbers.

_____ 9. Rewind and playback the rehearsal for evaluation.

Production

_____ 1. Rewind the tape, cue it and log the numbers.

_____ 2. Stand by for the program.

_____ 3. Roll the tape on the Producer/Director's command.

_____ 4. Give the 10-second countdown.

_____ 5. Monitor the production and look for ways to help.

Post-Production

_____ 1. Rewind the tape to the beginning of the program.

_____ 2. Play back the tape for evaluation.

_____ 3. Assist in the technical and artistic evaluation of the program.

_____ 4. Once the program is accepted help the Audio Technical Director to put the equipment away.

AUDIO T.D.
A GENERAL INTRODUCTION

 **PREPRODUCTION ACTIVITIES**

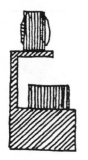  

PRODUCTION ACTIVITIES

POST-PRODUCTION ACTIVITIES

THE AUDIO TECHNICAL DIRECTOR: A GENERAL INTRODUCTION

The Audio Technical Director is the third member of the control room crew in a multicamera production. The Audio Technical Director, sometimes referred to as Audio or Audio TD, works directly under the supervision of the Switcher. The Audio Technical Director and the Video Technical Director have some responsibilities that they share but there are also some production responsibilities that are unique to the Audio Technical Director. Like all crew members the preproduction phase is normally the busiest but the Audio Technical Director is also heavily involved in the production and post-production phases.

Preproduction Activities of the Audio Technical Director

Your activities begin with the production meeting called by the Producer/Director. At this point the shooting schedule will indicate the various roles that the crew members will play and if you are appointed the Audio Technical Director you have your job cut out for you. As Audio Technical Director you have two types of duties: (1) those which you share with the Video Technical Director involving the collection, transportation, assembly, and checking of the production equipment, and (2) those which specifically involve the audio components of the proposed program.

When you are appointed as the Audio Technical Director you need to pick up most of the production and design documents. The shooting schedule will provide you with a deadline for all of your activities and the prop and equipment list will tell you what is needed. The set or studio diagram will tell you where the equipment is to be placed during the rehearsal and production phases. The script and storyboard are necessary so that you can identify the type of music that is needed for the opening and closing of the production and for the number of mikes that will have to be set up to service the various talent who have speaking parts on the program.

Your first activity is the preparation of the various audio tapes that are required. While these are normally music which is used with the studio cards opening and closing the program they can also include sound effects, off camera narration, and other audio information. Check the finished product with the Switcher before you get to the production date.

Then assist the Video Technical Director is collecting, transporting, assembling, and checking the production equipment in general. You will then need to pay particular attention to the audio systems. This will include placing the mikes, checking the sound levels, and running a test video tape to ensure that you are getting the best possible technical quality.

Production Activities of the Audio Technical Director

During the actual production of the proposed program you will put to use all of the information gained in the rehearsal. You may have to relocate microphones or reset sound levels. You may have to work out any drastic changes with the Producer/Director. You must do everything you can to ensure the best possible professional production. You also need to monitor the audio portion of the production. While you can do this through the speaker in the line monitor it is much better if you have a set of earphones that you can plug directly into the VTR.

Post-Production Activities of the Audio Technical Director

Once the production is over you will assist the Producer/Director in the evaluation of the technical and artistic qualities of the production. Once the production is approved then you will assist the Video Technical Director in the dismantling of the production equipment and returning it to storage.

AUDIO T.D.
PREPRODUCTION ACTIVITIES

SCRIPT

AUDIO

SET-UP

WIRE THE TALENT

REHEARSAL

AUDIO TECHNICAL DIRECTOR: PREPRODUCTION ACTIVITIES

The preproduction activities of the Audio Technical Director begin with the production meeting called by the Producer/Director. At this time in the production process the individual is assigned the role of Audio Technical Director and assigned as a member of the control room crew under the supervision of the Switcher. Once the Switcher has checked you out in terms of your various roles and responsibilities he/she will give you copies of the production documents and the script/storyboard to assist you in your various activities.

Your first responsibility concerns the production of all audio tapes that are needed for the production. The most common of these will be musical tapes that are played as the opening and closing studio cards are shown. However, they might also include sound effects, background or mood music, and even off-camera narration. As the Audio Technical Director you will identify appropriate information, usually on disc recordings, and transfer it to the appropriate audio format for your audio system. The disc-to-tape transfer methods are described in more detail on the next set of pages. Once you have checked the script and the storyboard to make sure what is needed and transferred then to audio tape your next step is to check the tapes with the Switcher and the Producer/Director to make sure that they are acceptable.

Your next assignment is to work with the Video Technical Director under the supervision of the Switcher to collect, transport, assemble and check out the production equipment. The prop and equipment list will be a major guide in this activity. While you will be concerned primarily with the audio components of the system and the Video Technical Director will be primarily responsible for the video components of the production system you will need to work closely together to make sure that the entire system is operational. Once the system is completely assembled you will want to run a test tape utilizing all of the audio and video input signals. Play back the test tape and check the technical quality of the various signals—modify as necessary to give maximum signal quality.

Once the entire system has been checked you now need to concentrate on the audio components. Gather the Talent together in the studio and with the help of the Floor Director position them where they will be during the rehearsal and production. Place your microphones in the best positions and wire the Talent for sound. Run sound levels on your mikes and on the auxiliary audio tape recorder. Remember that the Talent will generally speak louder during the actual production than they will when they are checking out the mikes for the appropriate levels. It is also a good idea to label the controls on the sound mixer when you are using a variety of sound sources. Now you are ready for the last phase of the preproduction activity—the rehearsal. During the rehearsal you will be responsible for the operation of the various components of the audio system under the direct command of the Producer/Director. In working with the Producer/Director you can expect two types of commands: (1) the preparatory command, and (2) the execution command. The preparatory command will tell you to get ready to do something and the execution command will tell you to do it. For example, "Ready to roll music." is a preparatory command and "Roll music!" is the execution command. However, there will be some situations in which you will have to anticipate the commands. For example, in the opening of the program you will probably want to open the Talent's mike while the music is still on. This will ensure that the Talent's first words are heard. Check these anticipatory actions out with the Producer/Director before the rehearsal.

AUDIO T.D.
RECORD TO TAPE TRANSFER

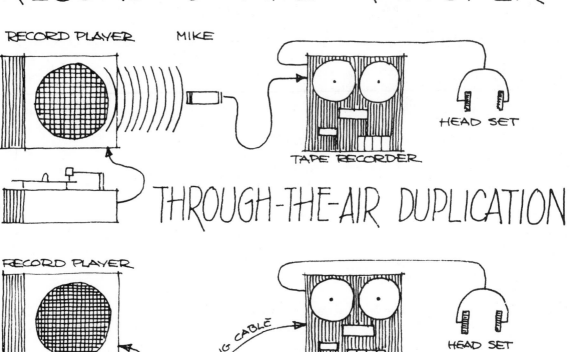

RECORD PLAYER   MIKE

HEAD SET

TAPE RECORDER

THROUGH-THE-AIR DUPLICATION

RECORD PLAYER

CONNECTING CABLE

HEAD SET

TAPE RECORDER

WIRE DUPLICATION

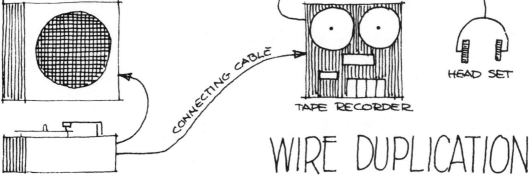

PHONE PLUG

MINI PLUG

PHONO PLUG (RCA)

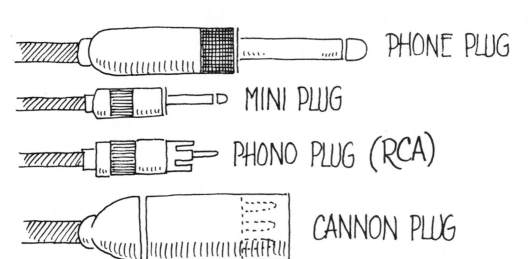

CANNON PLUG

AUDIO TECHNICAL DIRECTOR: THE RECORD-TO-TAPE TRANSFER PROCESS

One of the first responsibilities of the Audio Technical Director is the preparation of audio tapes of music, sound effects, and narration for the proposed production. To do this effectively you need to know (1) the techniques for preparing these audio tapes, and (2) the problems you are faced when you prepare these tapes—copyright.

To prepare materials for use in a television program you are normally faced with the problem of transfering this information from a disc or record format to a tape format that is compatible with the audio tape recorder in your TV production system. There are two techniques for making this transfer: (1) through-the-air duplication, and (2) wire duplication. The through-the-air duplication system is the least professional of the two but if you do not have the necessary cables to interconnect the record player and the tape recorder you may have to use it. In this system you need four pieces of equipment: (1) the record player to play the selected disc recordings, (2) the audio tape recorder to record this information onto the same format as is used in the audio tape recorder in the TV system, (3) a microphone plugged into the audio tape recorder, and (4) a head set to monitor the recording. The selected record is loaded onto the record player. The microphone from the audio tape recorder is placed close to the speaker and rested on a piece of foam rubber or folded toweling. The record player is turned on, then the tape recorder is turned into the record mode, and the level set for the recording. The tape is backed up and the record recued and the transfer completed.

The wire duplication system produces a much higher quality recording since there is no chance of extraneous sound being picked up by the "live" mike. In this case the output of the record player is plugged into the input of the tape recorder. The record is played and a test tape recorded to check the appropriate level. Then the materials are recued and the final transfer made.

You can see that the process of transferring audio information from record to tape is not difficult but there is a major problem—copyright. The term copyright refers to the fact that the information on most records and commercial tapes is owned by someone else. If you copy the material into another format such as audio tape you are breaking the copyright law. However, there is a part of the copyright law called the "fair use doctrine" which relates to education. In this case it says that if you do not cause the copyright owner to lose money, and if you do not make money from the process, then you have not infringed the owner's copyright. There are some records that are designed for these specific purposes—sound effects records and even music that is intended to be used as audio information for home movies, slide tape programs, and television programs. The copyright problem is amplified when you intend to distribute your video tapes—to send copies to other people. How do you overcome these problems? The best way is to produce your own audio materials. Rather than transfer materials from existing sources, make your own music and sound effects. This is not as difficult as it sounds. Every school has some people who are quite good in the musical area. They can actually write some music for your production and then others can perform it. With this approach you will find that you can get some excellent music to go over the studio cards for your opening and closing or even background music without any fear of violating someone else's copyright. This audio information can add a real professional touch to your production, so take care in the selection, recording, and playback of the information.

AUDIO T.D.

MIKES AND MIKE PLACEMENT

A DYNAMIC MIKE

A.

B.

FIST

THE LAVALIER MIKE

FLOOR MIKE

DESK MIKE

MIKES AND MIKE PLACEMENT

Another obvious concern of the Audio Technical Director is with the type of microphones that are used in the production system. These microphones come in a wide range of styles, costs and functions. Picking the right microphone for a television production system is very important.

The Type of Microphone

Basically there are three types of microphones that are commonly used in television production systems. The crystal mike is usually the least expensive but the frequency response leaves a lot to be desired. It is just not normally a professional microphone. Condenser microphones (requiring an auxiliary power source), are much more professional and provide excellent frequency response. The main problem with condenser mikes is simply that they are rather delicate. They normally will not hold up under the type of use that they are given in the public schools. I recommend the dynamic microphone. This type of microphone has an acceptable frequency response and holds up much better under heavy use.

The Impedance of the Microphone

Impedance is basically a measurement of resistance to the flow of electricity. High impedance microphones (see A on the opposite page) have relatively short mike cables. Low impedance microphones (B) can use much longer mike cables and even extension cables. This is quite important because it allows you to work the Talent further from the equipment and to avoid equipment noise.

The Style of the Microphone

The lavalier type of microphone is the most versatile one for television production. The mike can be hung around the talent's neck or inserted into floor or desk stands for group pick up. Specialty microphones are generally expensive and have relatively limited use in television production situations.

The Placement of the Microphone

Once you have the mikes for your production system the next concern is simply where do you place them. Obviously you need to know how many Talent have speaking parts and what other types of sound input are required for the production. The script/storyboard will give you some insights into this. Also you should check the set or studio diagram that was prepared by the Producer/Director. Let's assume that you need to wire a Talent that will be walking from place to place in the set. The mike is fastened around the Talent's neck. It is adjusted so that it is a fist's length from the Talent's chin and so that it does not hit any hard surfaces (jewelry-buttons-etc). The mike cable is then looped through the belt (or waist band of the skirt) so that it hangs to the side. This will allow the Talent to move without tripping over his/her own mike cord. For an interview situation the mike can be hand held and simply directed to the individual who is doing the talking. In this case it may look rather bad and you will probably want to limit the shots to head and shoulders to avoid seeing the mike and its movement back and forth. When groups are involved you can fasten the lavalier mike into either a floor stand or a desk stand. In these situations you will want to angle the mike toward the Talent with the weakest voice.

There is no good rule for mike placement. It will be different for each Talent and each environment. As the Audio Technical Director you should try a placement and then check the quality and level of the sound. This process of trying and checking will result in mike placement that will improve the audio portion of your program.

AUDIO T.D.
PRODUCTION — POST-PRODUCTION

CONTROL MIKES
[OFF/ON AND VOLUME]

[AUDIO TAPES] CUE/PLAY

✳ MONITOR THE AUDIO

CHECK THE EQUIPMENT AND STORE IT.

Evaluate!

CHECKLIST FOR THE AUDIO TECHNICAL DIRECTOR

Preproduction

_____ 1. Attend the production meeting and get copies of the following documents: prop and equipment list, shooting schedule, set or studio diagram, and script/storyboard.

_____ 2. Check with the Switcher to find out what assignments you have.

_____ 3. If you have any doubts about what your responsibilities are or your skills to do them, check with the Switcher for information and/or instruction.

_____ 4. Prepare the audio tapes called for in the prop and equipment list and script/storyboard.

_____ 5. Check these tapes with the Switcher and Producer/Director.

_____ 6. Assist the Video Technical Director in the collection, transportation, assembly, and checking of the production equipment.

_____ 7. Run a test video tape and have it approved by the Switcher.

_____ 8. Determine the placement for your mikes using the set or studio diagram and the script/storyboard.

_____ 9. Run sound levels on all microphones and the auxiliary audio system.

_____ 10. Mark levels on the audio mixer.

_____ 11. Cue up the audio tapes and prepare for the rehearsal.

_____ 12. Operate the audio mixer during the rehearsal.

_____ 13. Watch and listen to the rehearsal tape and assist the Producer/Director identify positive changes that might be necessary.

_____ 14. Make changes that are suggested by the rehearsal tape.

Production

_____ 1. Recue your music and reset your sound levels as suggested by the rehearsal.

_____ 2. Stand by for the program.

_____ 3. Attend to the Producer/Director and follow his/her preparatory and execution commands.

_____ 4. Operate the audio mixer during the production.

Post-Production

_____ 1. Assist the Producer/Director in the artistic and technical evaluation of the program.

_____ 2. Assist the Video Technical Director in dismantling and storing the production equipment.

TALENT

A GENERAL INTRODUCTION

PREPRODUCTION ACTIVITIES

PRODUCTION ACTIVITIES

POST-PRODUCTION ACTIVITIES

TALENT: A GENERAL INTRODUCTION

So far we have dealt with the roles and responsibilities of the people behind the camera. At this point it might be wise to offer some assistance to those who will appear in front of the camera—the Talent. Like the rest of the production crew the Talent is also involved in all three phases of production: (1) preproduction activities, (2) production activities, and (3) post-production activities.

Preproduction Activities of the Talent

As Talent you will first become involved with the production process at one of two stages. If you are also the client (and this is quite common), then your involvement begins with the Producer/Director during the first client conference at the very beginning of the production process. If you are Talent but not client then your involvement begins at the production meeting. At this point the Producer/Director will supply you with the script and the storyboard. The script will either be an outline script or a verbatim script. If it is an outline script then the assumption is that you know enough about the content to be able to ad-lib around the topics indicated in the outline. If it is a verbatim script than the first job you have is to memorize the script.

During this time you will be working closely with the Producer/Director. Not only will the Producer/Director be concerned with your delivery of the verbal information but he/she will also be concerned with your movement patterns and the way in which you handle the various props and materials in the set.

When you are feeling pretty good about your delivery and your movements then you are ready for the walk-through. The walk-through is the opportunity for the Producer/Director to see what changes may be needed in the original storyboard/script. During the walk-through the cameras will not be operative and the Producer/Director may want to accelerate the process. The next step in the preproduction phase is the rehearsal.

The rehearsal begins with the Producer/Director informing the crew of changes (if there are any) that were identified in the walk-through. The rehearsal will involve the entire crew and will be video taped. As Talent you should react as if this was the final production. You will be getting last minute instructions from the Producer/Director, and the Floor Director will explain the hand signals to you. When the rehearsal is complete you then go through the production.

Production Activities of Talent

Just before the production phase begins the Producer/Director will cover any changes identified during the playback of the rehearsal tape. Then, when the Floor Director gives you the cue you are on the air for the final production. Play it cool. Just follow the instructions of the Producer/Director and deliver the information to the best of your ability. If you need them there will be a number of different types of cues or prompts that can be used to assist you in your delivery.

Post-Production Activities of the Talent

Even when the program is over you still have some responsibilities. You will want to view the playback of the production to assist the Producer/Director in the evaluation of the artistic and technical quality of the production. You need to concentrate on your delivery and your accuracy. One question the Producer/Director may well ask you is "If we reshoot what could you do to improve the production?" While you will have input into the decision about whether to keep or reshoot the production, the Producer/Director makes the final decision.

TALENT
CUE CARDS AND OTHER IDEAS

MEMORIZE

CUE CARDS

USE THE PROPS

CUES

A PROMPTER

TALENT: CUE CARDS AND OTHER IDEAS

Since the most important part of your responsibility is the delivery of information in front of a live camera, let's talk about some of the things that can be done to aid in this delivery. As we indicated on the preceeding pages there are two kinds of scripts: (1) the outline script, and (2) the verbatim script. The outline script is used primarily when the Talent is also the client. In this case you already are quite familiar with the content of the message. You will be able to ad-lib around the content that is indicated in the outline. The term ad-lib simply means that you will be able to take the bones of the outline and flesh it out verbally—talk about it. The verbatim script is normally used with professional performers who are used to memorizing lines and delivering them sucessfully to an audience. In either case you have something to memorize—the points in the outline script or all of the verbatim script. If you have difficulty with memorization there are some aids or prompts that can be used.

Cue cards are the most common type of memorization aid in a TV production system. These cue cards may be just that—cards—with the necessary information printed on them, or in the more professional situations they may be on rollers, mechanized and automated. In either case they contain either the outline script or the verbatim script. To use these it is necessary that they be placed as close to the camera lens as possible. It is also necessary that they be divided into segments according to which camera will be used at any given time. They also have to be rigid enough (if you are using cards) so that the assistant Floor Director will be able to hold them up without their folding over. Also make sure that the printing on these cue cards is sufficiently large so that you can read it from where you will be delivering the information.

Another approach to cue cards is simply to use the props. Quite often it is possible to break the program up into basic segments that fit the script. These segments are then isolated in terms of individual set areas. If you have four basic ideas there may be four basic set areas. Within each area you place the props and set elements relevant to that topic. In the illustration on the opposite page there are three set areas. The Talent might begin in the center set then walk to the left hand area to use the poster. Then he/she may return to the base (the center area) for a few seconds and then to the third area—the feltboard. In each of the areas would be the props or instructional materials that would be used. These serve as reminders and all you would have to do is walk to the appropriate set at the appropriate time.

Last but not least there are other sneaky tricks that can be used to help you remember the material you are to deliver. If you have items to show, then the things you want to say about them can be taped to the back. Typewritten script hints can be hidden all over the set as you feel you need them.

The bottom line is that you will have to do some degree of memory work. You will have to become familiar with the order and sequence of the materials as well as the content. To the degree that you feel uncomfortable you will have to provide cues and prompts to aid you in the delivery of this information. Remember, the entire production crew will do their best to make you look as good as possible. They will provide every aid and assistance that is available; but you will be the one out there in front of the camera—and the Talent will make or break a television program.

TALENT
CLOTHING AND MOVEMENT

WEAR
NORMAL
CLOTHES

FACE
THE
AUDIENCE

MOVE
PREDICTABLY

TALENT: CLOTHING AND MOVEMENT HINTS

One of your concerns as Talent will be "How will I look on TV?" This is best answered by simply getting in front of a TV camera and looking at yourself on the monitor. You will probably be suprised since even our image in the mirror isn't quite the same as it is on the television screen. However, there are some hints that you might want to consider to help you present a better appearance. These first few are what we might call technical considerations.

Note the illustrations on the opposite page. The clothes that you wear when you are making your television presentation can make a major difference. Notice that our man at the top of the opposite page is wearing a combination of checks and stripes. Both of these are bad. Both checks and stripes will set up pattern disturbances in the television picture. This simply means that the horizontal scanning of the TV screen is disrupted by the vertical patterns in stripes and checks. Generally plain colors are preferred. The same type of thing holds for the young ladies' floral patterns. These create perceptual pattern problems and should be used only for specific effects. The key is simply that you should wear normal clothes—those that you would wear if you were making the presentation live—without the TV cameras.

Also avoid jewelry. Jewelry can create two types of problems. First, it may catch the light and flash calling attention to itself and away from you. Secondly, if it is around your neck it may bump against the microphone and create audio disturbances.

Another concern is how you move during the program. It is normal to turn our back on the audience when we point to something that is slightly behind us. This creates two problems. First, the audience cannot see your expression and this removes a vital communication tool. Secondly, this puts a hard surface right in front of you and the sound will bounce off it creating an audio distortion. It is better if you can change your habits and learn to stand facing the audience as you point. You also need to be aware of how you handle the props that are part of the production. If possible you should not pick up something that you want to show—rather you should point to it where it rests. This will allow the cameraman to get the close-up shot ahead of time. It will also ensure that the object is still so that the cameraman does not have to move back and forth trying to keep the object centered in the screen. If you do have to pick up the prop you need to be concerned with how you hold it and how you show it. First make sure that your hand does not block the audience's ability to see what you are showing. Secondly make sure that you hold it steady so that the Cameraman can get a good close up. Third make sure that it is pointed toward the camera that will get the close up.

Another concern over Talent movements is how they "announce" their intention to move. Consider the situation shown at the bottom of the opposite page. An individual is seated and then simply stands up. If the camera is on a long shot this poses no problem. However if the camera is on a medium shot or a close-up then the Talent will suddenly just disapear. You can, of course, use a verbal cue to announce your intentions but it becomes rather obvious when the Talent says, "I'm going to stand up now!" It is better if you identify a common habit pattern and inform the Cameraman and the Producer/Director of it. For example, it is common for someone to lean forward slightly when they are getting ready to stand up. Don't exaggerate—be natural.

TALENT
PRODUCTION & POST-PRODUCTION

STAY AWARE OF THE CAMERA AND THE FLOOR DIRECTOR

BE NATURAL IN YOUR ACTIONS IN YOUR DELIVERY

FOLLOW THE SCRIPT

RELAX

HONESTLY EVALUATE

* YOUR PERFORMANCE

A CHECKLIST FOR THE TALENT

Preproduction

_____ 1. Acquire the script/storyboard from the Producer/Director.

_____ 2. Memorize your narration.

_____ 3. Work with the Producer/Director on your delivery.

_____ 4. Prepare any prompts and/or cues that you need to aid in your delivery.

_____ 5. Walk-through the program with the Producer/Director.

_____ 6. Make any modifications suggested by the walk-through.

_____ 7. Prepare for the rehearsal.

_____ 8. Rehearse the program with the entire production crew.

_____ 9. View the production tape and evaluate for any possible positive changes.

Production

_____ 1. Prepare for the production.

_____ 2. Present the information during the production.

Post-Production

_____ 1. View the production and assist the Producer/Director in the technical and artistic evaluation.

CHAPTER IV.

THE PRODUCTION PROCESS

THE PROCESS FOR THE PLANNING AND DESIGN OF TELEVISION PROGRAMS. AN EXAMINATION OF THE STAGES FROM THE IDEA FOR THE PROGRAM TO ITS EVALUATION.

AN OVERVIEW

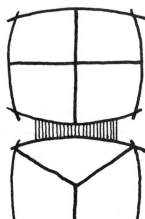

PLANNING

- ● CONTENT OUTLINE
- ● AUDIENCE ANALYSIS
- ● GOALS / OBJECTIVES
- ● MEDIA SELECTION

DESIGN

- ● TREATMENT
- ○ STORYBOARD
- ○ SCRIPT

PRODUCTION

- ○ PRODUCTION DOCUMENTS
- ○ COMPONENT PRODUCTION
- ○ COMPONENT ASSEMBLY

EVALUATION

- ○ TECHNICAL QUALITY
- ○ ARTISTIC QUALITY
- ○ INSTRUCTIONAL QUALITY

THE MESSAGE

PLANNING
DESIGN
PRODUCTION
EVALUATION

THE PRODUCTION PROCESS: AN OVERVIEW

The production process is a procedure that will assist you in making your own production everything that you want it to be. This process is simply a series of stages or steps that any good producer goes through in the design and production of a mediated message. It takes you from the idea for the program to the finished product—the program itself. You might think of the production process as an iceberg. Just as there is a part of the iceberg that we can see, we can also see the product—the message. But for an iceberg to be stable and stay afloat there must be a much larger invisible mass below the surface. The same thing is true when you are creating a predictable message. There is an invisible portion that keeps the message professional and predictable. This is the production process. This unseen portion of production makes the difference between an amateur and a professional production.

The production process has four basic steps or stages: (1) the planning stage, (2) the design stage, (3) the production stage, and (4) the evaluation stage. Each of these stages has a number of sub-stages. For example, in the planning stage we are concerned with the production of various documents such as the content outline, the audience analysis, the goals or objectives, and the media selection rationale. In the design stage the sub-stages include the preparation of the treatment, the visual storyboard, and the script. Even in the production stage there are the various production documents, the production of the components of the message, and finally the assembly of the components into the finished product. Even with the production completed there is still one last stage—evaluation—and the sub-stages of technical evaluation, artistic evaluation, and the evaluation of the effectiveness of the production. These four stages and their sub-stages are the cornerstone upon which you construct a predictable and professional production.

These documents in the production process are important for another reason. Every message begins with a need. Someone has a need to say something to someone else. If you are a Producer you may have a need to say something. This is an example of an *internal* need. It is internal to you the Producer. You are both the Producer and the client. As the Producer you have the necessary communication skills. As the client you have the need for a message—something you want to say. In this case some of the documents in the production process (those with the black dots on the opposite page) may not be essential since they are designed to be communications between the client and the Producer.

However, when you are operating from an *external* need all these documents are vital. An external need is one that a client, the person with the communication problem, brings to you the Producer, the person with the communication skills. Operating from an external need means that there are at least two people involved in the production process. These two people are the client and the Producer. In this situation the various documents in the production process ensure that you the producer will meet the needs of the client. These documents allow both you and the client to have the same "picture" of what will be communicated and the way in which it will be communicated. Since the client provides the funds for production it is necessary to meet his/her needs if you wish to continue in this career.

PLANNING THE MESSAGE AN OVERVIEW:

WHAT DO YOU WANT TO SAY, TO WHOM, WITH WHAT EFFECT, THROUGH WHAT CHANNEL?

THE PLANNING STAGE: AN OVERVIEW

The planning stage is the beginning of the production process. Let's assume that a client has contacted you and asked for your assistance in the design and production of a message. How do you go about helping this client? Your first step will be to take the client through the planning stage of the production process.

This planning stage is composed of four sub-stages: (1) the preparation of the content outline, (2) the analysis of the intended audience, (3) the formation of the goals or objectives of the message, and (4) the decision as to what media will be the best delivery system for the message. Since you are working for a client, someone with a need to say something to someone else, you need to go through the entire set of planning documents to ensure that both you and the client understand WHAT YOU WANT TO SAY, TO WHOM, WITH WHAT EFFECT, THROUGH WHAT CHANNEL OR MEDIUM? This question can be divided into four parts and each part represents one of the planning documents. WHAT DO YOU WANT TO SAY? This represents the development of the content outline. TO WHOM? This represents the analysis of the intended audience for the message. WITH WHAT EFFECT? This represents the goal statement or the instructional objectives that you need to develop for the proposed message. THROUGH WHAT CHANNEL OR MEDIUM? This is the document in which you select and justify the media that will be used to deliver the message to the intended audience.

How do we, as Producers, go about finding the answers to these four questions? The client is the person with the communication problem and is that likely person to ask. Actually you will find that just asking "WHAT DO YOU WANT TO SAY?" is not enough. You will have to dig a little deeper than this single question to elicit all of the information you need to answer these concerns. You may need to consult some secondary sources. These might include other "experts," books and other print resources, and even some non-print resources such as films, filmstrips, etc.

Once you have collected the information from the client and any other useful secondary resources, you then need to pull it all together and produce a polished set of planning documents. This set of planning documents is then shared with the client. At this point one of three things will happen. First, the client may accept the documents as you have ~~propared~~ prepared them. Second, the client may make some moderate suggestions for changes in the documents. Third, the client may feel that somehow the documents are way off base. The client/producer interaction at this point is very important. It is your job as producer to make sure that the client understands and agrees with these planning documents.

The process that we have just described is appropriate in those situations where you are working for a client—operating from an external need. In situations where you are both the client and the producer it may not always be necessary to go through the entire planning process. Productions originating from an internal need often short-circuit many of these stages and sub-stages.

An overview of this stage of the production process is just that, an overview. To develop the skills that are necessary to make this procedure a part of your production skills it is essential to delve a little deeper into each sub-stage of the planning stage. For the next few pages we will explore the dos and don'ts of the content outline, the audience analysis, the goals and objectives, and the media selection rationale.

CONTENT OUTLINE
WHAT DO YOU WANT TO SAY ?

EXPERTS.

PRINT SOURCES.

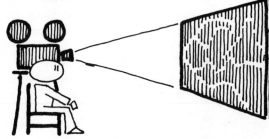

NON-PRINT SOURCES.

CONTENT OUTLINE

THE WATER CYCLE

I.   INTRODUCTION TO THE WATER CYCLE

II. PHASES OF THE WATER CYCLE

III. THE EVAPORATION PHASE

IV. THE CONDENSATION PHASE

V.   THE PRECIPITATION PHASE

VI. THE PERCOLATION PHASE

VII. SUMMARY CLOSING

CONTENT OUTLINE

THE WATER CYCLE

I.   INTRODUCTION TO THE WATER CYCLE

   A. MILLION YEAR OLD WATER

   B. STILL USABLE (DRINKABLE)

II. PHASES OF THE WATER CYCLE

   A. EVAPORATION

   B. CONDENSATION

   C. PRECIPITATION

   D. PERCOLATION

III. THE EVAPORATION PHASE

IV. THE CONDENSATION PHASE

V.   THE PRECIPITATION PHASE

VI. THE PERCOLATION PHASE

VII. SUMMARY, CLOSING

   A. WHAT IT DOES

   B. THE NAMES (PHASES)

CONTENT OUTLINE

THE WATER CYCLE

I.   INTRODUCTION TO THE WATER CYCLE

   A. THERE IS NO NEW WATER IN THE WORLD.

   B. ALL THE WATER WE HAVE, AND USE, IS MILLIONS OF YEARS OLD.

   C. THE WATER CYCLE IS NATURES WAY OF CONTINUALLY PURIFYING IT.

II. THERE ARE FOUR BASIC PHASES IN THE WATER CYCLE

   A. THE EVAPORATION PHASE

   B. THE CONDENSATION PHASE

   C. THE PRECIPITATION PHASE

   D. THE PERCOLATION PHASE

III. THE EVAPORATION PHASE OF THE WATER CYCLE

   A. A CHANGE FROM LIQUID TO VAPOR THROUGH A HEAT PROCESS.

   B. EXAMPLE, THE TEAKETTLE CHANGING WATER TO STEAM.

   C. IN THE WATER CYCLE THE HEAT IS THE POWER FROM THE SUN.

IV. THE CONDENSATION PHASE OF THE WATER CYCLE

   A. A CHANGE FROM VAPOR TO LIQUID OR SOLIDS.

   B. A COOLING PROCESS AS THE VAPOR RISES OR TEMPERATURE LOWERS.

   C. EXAMPLE, MIRROR IN A SHOWER ROOM, THE STEAM CONDENSES.

V.   THE PRECIPITATION PHASE OF THE WATER CYCLE

   A. THE LIQUID OR SOLID IS TOO HEAVY TO STAY ALOFT.

   B. FALLS AS A LIQUID***(SHOWERS, RAIN, DRIZZLE).

   C. FALLS AS A SOLID***(SNOW, HAIL).

VI. THE PERCOLATION PHASE OF THE WATER CYCLE

   A. SURFACE RUN OFF (STREAMS, RIVERS, ETC.).

   B. SURFACE STORAGE (LAKES, OCEANS, ETC.).

   C. UNDERGROUND PERCOLATION.

VII. SUMMARY OF THE WATER CYCLE

   A. NATURES PURIFICATION SYSTEM.

   B. RENEWS THE WORLDS EXISTING WATER SUPPLY.

   C. REVIEW THE NEW VOCABULARY.

      1. EVAPORATION, DEFINITION/PRONUNCIATION/SPELLING

      2. CONDENSATION, DEFINITION/PRONUNCIATION/SPELLING

      3. PRECIPITATION, DEFINITION/PRONUNCIATION/SPELLING

      4. PERCOLATION, DEFINITION/PRONUNCIATION/SPELLING

THE CONTENT OUTLINE

This will begin our examination of the various documents that are part of the production process. To organize this discussion we will look first at the function of the document, secondly at the form the document should take, and finally at the procedure for the development of the document and its utilization.

The Function of the Content Outline

The content outline is designed to answer the simple question WHAT DO YOU WANT TO SAY? It is a document that spells out in some detail the content that is to be delivered in the proposed message. Not only will it be concerned with what is to be included but it should also indicate, by omission, the content that is not necessary. This content outline, once approved by the client, will set the content and eliminate those last minute changes which are so expensive in the production process.

The Form of the Content Outline

As the name implies the content outline is simply that—an outline of the content to be communicated. There are three major reasons for the outline format. First, an outline is easier to read than a paragraph. Since the main function of the content outline is to provide a communication between the client and the producer this ease of reading is essential. Second, the outline format also shows the sequence in which the information is to be presented in the message. Quite often the sequencing of information is as important and the information that is being communicated. The third reason for using an outline format is that it is easily modified during the approval meeting between the client and the Producer. These three reasons—readability, organization, and ease of manipulation— are why the outline format is the most appropriate for the content outline.

Developing the Content Outline

The content outline is one of the first documents that you, as the Producer, will develop. The major question that needs to be answered is simply WHAT DO YOU WANT TO SAY? Where can we find this information? Since the client is the person with the communication problem that started the process it is logical that we begin there. The client is a primary source of information about the content. Naturally you will need to go beyond the original question WHAT DO YOU WANT TO SAY? and pull out that information which makes the content clear to you. You will also find that you may have to go to secondary sources for some additional information on the content. The client may suggest other "experts" that you can consult. The client may also suggest some print materials (books and magazines) that you can examine to fill out this content outline. The client may also suggest non-print media such as films or filmstrips that may be used in this process. Once you have gathered all of the information your next step as the producer is to organize this information into an appropriate order and sequence. Again the client is a primary source for this organization. You also can examine print and non-print resources to develop the best possible sequence. After you have collected all of the necessary information you then need to polish the content outline for approval by the client.

The client may do any of three different things with your content outline. First, he/she may accept your content outline as is, without any changes. Second, he/she may suggest minor changes in the document. Third, and this is uncommon, he/she may reject the entire thing. In any case, the process is completed when the client gives his/her stamp of approval to this planning document. It now becomes a basis for the development of other documents and the final production.

AUDIENCE ANALYSIS

TO WHOM ?

EXPERTS.　　OBSERVATION.　　SCHOOL RECORDS.

```
AUDIENCE ANALYSIS

THE WATER CYCLE

PRIMARY AUDIENCE:

          THIRD GRADE STUDENTS IN MRS. JONES CLASS,

          GREENFIELD SCHOOL, GILBERT, ARIZONA.

          THE CLASS IS A MIXED ETHNIC GROUP WITH A

          FEW STUDENTS FOR WHOM ENGLISH IS A

          SECOND LANGUAGE.

          WHILE IT IS PRIMARILY A RURAL AREA MANY

          OF THE CHILDREN LIVE IN THE EXPENSIVE

          "RANCHETTES" THAT ARE ONE OR TWO ACRES IN

          SIZE.

          THE MAJORITY OF STUDENTS READ AT GRADE

          LEVEL BUT THE RANGE IS FROM FIRST GRADE

          THROUGH THE EIGHTH GRADE.

SECONDARY AUDIENCE:

          OTHER THIRD GRADE CLASSES AT GREENFIELD.

          OTHER THIRD GRADE CLASSES IN ARIZONA.

          OTHER THIRD GRADE CLASSES.
```

THE AUDIENCE ANALYSIS

The Function

The audience analysis is intended to provide the producer with a description of the intended audience. It will concentrate on those characteristics of the audience that may have some influence on how the message is designed and/or received. While it is used primarily by the Producer it is also approved by the client to ensure that both the client and the Producer are putting together a message for the same audience.

The Form

The audience analysis is probably most appropriate as a listing. First, it is easier to read and secondly it is easier to concentrate on those characteristics which are deemed important for the production.

Developing the Content Outline

Like the content outline the audience description begins with a few questions to the client. The client may be your primary source but there are many other sources that you may need to consider before you complete the audience description. Naturally there are "experts" other than the client who may be able to bring you up to date on the characteristics of the audience. It is hard to beat direct observation: the opportunity to watch the audience and identify for yourself those characteristics that might affect either the design of the message or their reception of the message. In some cases it may be helpful to consult the school records to gather information.

At this point we need to make a distinction between a general audience and a specific audience. The general audience means that you intend the message for *all* third graders. The specific audience means that the intended audience is third graders in Mrs. Jones' class at the Greenfield School in Gilbert, Arizona. For the general audience we must develop a general message. For the specific audience we can develop a message that is both task-specific and audience-specific and is more likely to affect that audience.

What characteristics do we look for in the audience analysis? Will age make a difference in how they react to a message? There is an obvious time limit imposed on the message by the age of the audience. The vocabulary level is different at different ages and this too will affect their reception of the message as well as its design. What about the socio-economic background of the audience? Will an audience that is primarily rural react differently to a message than an audience that is primarily urban? There is a definite difference in these background experiences. This difference will result in different perception of the same message. There are many other characteristics which may also affect the audiences reception or your design of the message. It is a truism that the more you know about an audience the more effective your message to them will be.

Investigate your primary source, the client, and any secondary sources that are appropriate to collect information on those audience characteristics that might influence your design or their reception of the proposed message. Prepare a listing of these characteristics and then share it with the client for approval. Then, as Producer, use these audience characteristics to assist you in the design of the proposed production.

GOALS/OBJECTIVES
WITH WHAT EFFECT (ON THE AUDIENCE)?

- FOR INSTRUCTIONAL PROGRAMS:

 { PREPARE INSTRUCTIONAL OBJECTIVES.

- FOR INFORMATIONAL PROGRAMS:

 { INSTRUCTIONAL OBJECTIVES OR GOALS.

- FOR ENTERTAINMENT PROGRAMS:

 { GOAL STATEMENTS.

INSTRUCTIONAL OBJECTIVES:

1. LEARNER ORIENTED,
2. BEHAVIORALLY STATED,
3. WITH CONDITIONS, AND
4. STANDARDS.

GOALS AND OBJECTIVES

The preparation of goals and/or objectives is perhaps the most difficult of all the documents to produce. The type of document that you will need is determined by the type of program that you are producing. There are three types of programs: (1) instructional programs that are designed to teach a body of information, (2) informational programs that are disigned to inform the audience about a specific topic, and (3) entertainment programs that are designed strictly for amusement. Naturally there are also combinations since it is to be desired that even instructional programs be entertaining, but these are the three basic types.

Instructional programs require instructional objectives. Informational programs may require either instructional objectives or goal statements. Entertainment programs utilize the goal statements to answer the question WITH WHAT EFFECT? Precision and orientation are the main differences between instructional objectives and goal statements. The goal statement is presentor-oriented—something that the producer will do—while the instructional objective is learner-oriented—something the learners will do. Goal statements are rather general statements while instructional objectives are very precise. Since instructional objectives are the most difficult to master we will concentrate on them.

The Function

The function of instructional objectives (and the goal statement) is to answer the basic question WITH WHAT EFFECT? It should be a clear and concise statement of what you (and the client) expect the viewer to be able to do after viewing the program that he or she could not do before.

The Form of the Instructional Objective

There are four basic elements in a well stated instructional objective. First, it should be learner-oriented—something the *learner* is expected to do. Second, it should be behaviorally stated. It should describe something the learner will *do* in terms of observable, measurable behaviors. Third, it may contain a statement of the *conditions* under which the behavior will occur. Last but not least a well stated instructional objective may contain a statement of *standards* that describe the acceptable performance of the learners. Two of these characteristics—learner orientation and behaviorally stated—must be present in any well-stated instructional objective. The conditions and standards are often present but they are not always essential.

Developing Goals and Objectives

The development of this document is a little different than those we have previously discussed. You begin by asking the client the important question, WHAT EFFECT DO YOU WANT THIS PRODUCT TO HAVE, WHAT DO YOU WANT THESE LEARNERS TO BE ABLE TO DO? With this as a beginning point you will have to pin the client down to specifics. The client may respond to the question with a statement like, THE STUDENTS WILL UNDERSTAND. . . . In this case the word "understand" has multiple meanings and needs to be clarified. Ask the client what the learners will be able to do that tells you they understand. Look for words like write, describe, name, identify, list, etc. to develop the necessary precision for the instructional objective.

Once you have mastered this planning document you will find that you are better able to develop the instruction and perhaps even more importantly to evaluate the instructional quality of the program. Do not become frustrated, because this is the most difficult of all of the documents to develop. Now we are ready to move to the last sub-stage of the planning stage of the production process.

MEDIA SELECTION
THROUGH WHAT CHANNEL OR MEDIA ?

- ○ MEDIA CHARACTERISTICS.

- ○ MEDIA UTILIZATION.

- ○ MEDIA COSTS.

- ○ MEDIA AVAILABILITY.

MEDIA SELECTION

This last phase of the planning stage deals with the selection and justification of both the production and the delivery system that will be used to create the message and deliver it to the audience. This decision is normally made by the producer since he/she is supposedly the expert in the area of media. However, it is not uncommon for a client to express a strong preference for a particular medium. Since this is a book dealing with television production we hope that all the messages that you plan are appropriate for television as both a production and a delivery system.

Let's look first at the general problem. How do you deal with the selection of the most appropriate medium for a particular message. There are four major characteristics that you should consider in making this decision: (1) the characteristics of the particular media that are under consideration, (2) the utilization strategies that are appropriate for the media, (3) the costs that are associated with the production of the materials in those particular media, (4) the availability of the media for both production and delivery, and naturally the availability of the expertise to produce messages in those particular media.

These are some of the things that you need to take into consideration when you are selecting an appropriate medium. Since television is the medium that we are working with we will look at these characteristics as they relate to the television medium. First, let's examine the various characteristics of television. Television is a motion medium, it can effectively present real motion cues. If these cues are essential to an understanding of the message then only film and television will fill the bill. Television is also a medium that utilizes sync sound. This means that the sound can be syncronized with the lip movements of the talent. Only 16mm sync sound production and television do this. The ability of immediate playback of materials is unique to television and is an important factor in production. These and other characteristics may make television the most appropriate medium for your production.

We also have to consider the utilization of the completed message. Television is probably best when it is used as a presentation device. It can deliver information to small, medium and large groups of learners. It can also be used for independent study but in this mode requires a special message design treatment. Television can be a great stimulus for interaction; however it is not normally suitable during the program. Even drill and practice can be an effective utilization strategy for this versatile medium. But when we think of television we most normally think of the presentation of information.

The costs that are associated with television are medium to high. The cost of the production equipment is high. The cost of materials such as video tape is medium to high. Even the delivery systems are expensive. However, the more use you make of the equipment the less expensive the costs.

A major concern is the availability of both the production equipment and the delivery system. There is no point in producing materials that will never reach the intended audience. You must also be concerned with the availability of production expertise. Do you have the necessary production skills to make a production of reasonable technical and artistic quality? After this course you will.

These are the concerns that you must deal with as you select the most appropriate medium for the proposed message.—Television.

DESIGNING THE MESSAGE AN OVERVIEW.

PLANNING

TREATMENT (WRITTEN)

STORYBOARD (VISUAL)

DESIGN

SCRIPT (WRITTEN)

VERBAL AND VISUAL DESCRIPTIONS OF WHAT THE PROGRAM WILL BE LIKE.

THE DESIGNING STAGE: AN OVERVIEW

Where are we in the production process? Our client has contacted us with a problem (THE WATER CYCLE). We have had our original meeting and asked the appropriate questions WHAT DO YOU WANT TO SAY, TO WHOM, WITH WHAT EFFECT, THROUGH WHAT CHANNEL OR MEDIUM? Then consulting other sources (experts, print, non-print) we prepared a rough set of planning documents. These rough planning documents were then polished and presented to the client for approval. We now have a set of planning documents that can form the basis for the next step in the production process—the design stage.

The design stage of the production process is primarily a producer-oriented activity. Utilizing the planning documents the producer is now faced with the task of making the pictures in his mind—what the program should look like—visible to the client and the production crew. There are three sub-stages in this design stage: (1) the treatment, (2) the story board, and (3) the script.

The treatment is simply a written description of what the proposed program will look like. Normally the producer will create a single treatment and share it with the client. The client then has the opportunity to accept, reject, or suggest modifications in the treatment. Once the treatment is accepted the direct interaction of the client with the production process ceases.

The storyboard may take two quite different forms. You may have a developmental storyboard in which a group interaction determines the scenes of the program and their related script ideas. A production storyboard is produced by the Producer working on his/her own but using the planning documents that were approved by the client. The storyboard is simply a visual presentation of what each scene of the proposed program will look like. We need to digress for a moment and point out that the term visual means simply small sketches of what the scene will look like. Don't worry about your sketching ability. These sketches can be extremely crude and still be very successful.

The third sub-stage in the design process is the preparation of the script that represents the verbal components of the proposed program. These scripts may take two quite different forms depending on the type of people who are delivering the information. An outline script (similar to the content outline) is appropriate for those talent who are (1) content experts able to expand upon the topic in an ad-lib way, or (2) unable to memorize an verbatim script. A verbatim script is much more appropriate for talent who are professional performers and used to the memorization of materials and their delivery.

These three sets of documents the treatment, the storyboard, and the script are used for different people in the production process. The treatment is designed for the client. It gives the client the opportunity to put his/her stamp of approval on what the program will look like before you get into the expensive production stage. The storyboard is used by the production crew. The Cameramen will see the types of shots that they are expected to get. The Audio Technical Director will see what type of music or sound effects that they have to plan for. The Assistant Director (Switcher) can tell ahead of time the type of special effects that will be needed. The script is used by both the Talent and the Audio Technical Director. It gives the Talent an advanced organizer as to what he/she will have to say during the program. It also gives the Audio Technical Director the opportunity to determine how many mikes will be used and where they will be placed.

Now let's take a more specific look at the various substages of the design stage of the production process.

THE TREATMENT.
WHAT WILL THE PROGRAM LOOK LIKE?

EXPOSITORY (A STRAIGHT PRESENTATION OF INFORMATION.)

DRAMATIC (A PRESENTATION WITH A STORYLINE.)

HUMOROUS (A PRESENTATION WITH A TOUCH OF COMEDY.)

DEMONSTRATION (A HOW TO DO IT PRESENTATION.)

OTHER TYPES AND COMBINATIONS.

THE TREATMENT

The treatment is a written description of what the proposed program will look and sound like. One of the first things that the Producer must decide when producing a treatment is the overall style of the message. A few of the more common styles would be (1) expository, (2) dramatic, (3) humorous, and (4) demonstrations. The expository approach is a straight forward presentation of the information. This is used quite extensively in the instructional types of programs. The dramatic style is not limited to the productions of plays and stories. A dramatic program might be effectively used to present a problem and then to propose a solution. It might well be that a segment of a production would cut away to a dramatic episode to make an important point. The dramatic style is one that utilizes a story line and dialogue between two or more performers. The humorous style is attractive to many Producers. This can be excellent for entertainment types of programs but it can also be successfully used to make a point within what might otherwise be an expository presentation. Remember that good humor is one of the most difficult styles to use. Demonstrations are good for instructional programs but can also be used for informational programs. These demonstration type of productions stress the how-to-do-it or the how-it-was done approach.

The treatment is designed by the Producer using the various planning documents as a basis. The completed treatment is then sent to the client for approval, rejection, or suggestions. Once the client has approved the treatment it becomes the basis for the production.

Example

The program will open with a shot of a glass of water and the Talent. The Talent will say something to the effect that "This water is millions of year old." Then drink some and close with "It still tastes delicious."

There will be a quick cut to the opening titles which will be displayed over music.

Cut back to the Talent and the water glass after the titles and the Talent will explain why the water is millions of years old. The Talent will explain that there is no new water in the world and that the water we have is continually purified through natures system called the water cycle. The Talent will then walk to the display board where the water cycle is on display. Using the diagram the Talent will point out the four stages of the water cycle: evaporation, condensation, precipitation, and percolation. As each new word is introduced it will be supered across the bottom of the screen. Once the four stages have been introduced the Talent will then describe the process that occurs in each stage. Visuals used to explain the various processes will be shown. These will include studio cards or 2 $\times$ 2 slides of the liquid to vapor process of a teakettle, various types of condensation, various types of precipitation, and various types of surface water.

When the Talent has completed the explanation of the four stages of the water cycle they will walk to the vocabulary chart and review the new words introduced during the program. This will include evaporation, condensation, precipitation, and percolation. The Talent will summarize the process and emphasize that the water cycle is nature's way of purifying the only water that exists in the world.

A cut to the closing titles over music will conclude the program.

This is an example of a treatment for a proposed program on the water cycle. This is shared with the client and then becomes the basis for all of the other design documents. Time spent on the preparation of the treatment will pay off in a much better production.

THE STORYBOARD

TALENT: INTRO. TO
MILLION YEAR
OLD WATER.

MEDIUM SHOT OF
TALENT AND THE
WATER GLASS.

MUSIC:

THE
WATER
CYCLE

TITLE CARD.
WATER CYCLE

MUSIC:

FEATURING
DR. JOHN
SMITH

TITLE CARD.
TALENTS NAME.

TALENT: EXPLAIN
THE MILLION YEAR
OLD WATER.

MEDIUM SHOT OF
TALENT AND GLASS.

TALENT: EXPLAIN
THE WATER CYCLE
AS A PURIFICATION
SYSTEM.

PAN TO - - -
LONG SHOT OF THE
TALENT AND THE
DISPLAY BOARD.

TALENT: FIRST
STAGE - - -
"EVAPORATION".

EVAPORATION

SUPER
EVAPORATION

TALENT: SECOND
STAGE - - -
"CONDENSATION".

CONDENSATION

SUPER
CONDENSATION

TALENT: THIRD
STAGE - - -
"PRECIPITATION".

PRECIPITATION

SUPER
PRECIPITATION
(CONTINUED)

THE STORYBOARD

There are basically two types of storyboards. The one shown on the opposite page is an example of a production storyboard. This type of storyboard is commonly used as a communication device between the Producer and the people in the production crew. The second type of storyboard is what is normally called the developmental storyboard. This type is usually done on 3 × 5″ cards. Each card represents a single scene in the proposed production. The cards are pinned to a bulletin board type of surface so that they can be manipulated. This manipulation is the key to the utilization of the developmental storyboard. In this case more than one person is involved in the development of the various shots and scenes of the projected program. Often this group may be the production crew or it may be the Producer and the client. The cards can be shifted from position to position, they can be added to or subracted from, and the individual scenes can be changed. During the process of interaction you, as Producer, will have to play a major role. This is important because you are supposedly the one with the expertise in the production area. The results of the developmental storyboard become a production storyboard. The Producer will translate the 3 × 5″ cards into a communication to the production crew. Note that in each case there are three components of each scene: (1) the script idea, (2) the visual, and (3) the description of the visual.

The script idea is just that, an idea. It is more like the content outline than the exact words that the Talent will use. Note on the opposite page that we are just covering the idea. The actual words will either be ad-libbed by the Talent, using an outline script, or presented exactly, using a verbatim script. There is just enough information there to get across the idea of what is going to be said.

The second element of the storyboard—the visual—is the one that seems to bother most people. The usual response is I CAN'T DRAW WELL ENOUGH TO DO A STORYBOARD. Well, in the first place the quality of drawing is not important. It is not necessary to do fine art work; all you have to do is represent the scene that will eventually become part of the finished product. Very rough sketches can be successfully used as storyboard visuals. This is especially true when you consider the third part of the storyboard—the visual description.

The description is just that—a description of the visual component of the story-board. Notice on the opposite page that this includes the technical description (close-up, medium shot, long shot, etc.) as well as the non-technical description (Talent and glass of water, Talent at display board, etc.). This description of the visual goes a long way to covering up for any concerns that you might have about your ability to draw.

The completed production storyboard then becomes a communication between the producer and the production crew. It is literally a blueprint for the production. The Video Technical Director can judge what will be needed in terms of time. The Audio Technical Director now knows how many mikes will be needed and where they will have to be placed, also what music and/or sound effects are necessary. The Switcher can check on special effects that are needed such as the supers of the names of the stages of the water cycle. Everything is there with the exception of the actual script and this is the next concern in the design stage of the production process.

THE SCRIPT

I.   INTRODUCTION TO THE WATER CYCLE
    A.   THE MILLION YEAR OLD GLASS OF WATER.
    B.   IT'S STILL USABLE (DRINKABLE).
II.   TITLES, WITH MUSICAL BACKGROUND.
III.   THE FOUR STAGES OF THE WATER CYCLE.
    A.   EVAPORATION STAGE
    B.   CONDENSATION STAGE
    C.   PRECIPITATION STAGE
    D.   PERCOLATION STAGE
IV.   EVAPORATION STAGE OF THE WATER CYCLE.
    A.   CHANGE OF LIQUID TO VAPOR.
    B.   SUN IS THE HEAT (POWER) SOURCE.
    C.   THE TEAKETTLE EXAMPLE.
V.   CONDENSATION STAGE OF THE WATER CYCLE.
    A.   CHANGE FROM VAPOR TO LIQUID OR SOLID.
    B.   AT THE GROUND LEVEL
        1.   DEW ON THE GRASS
        2.   FOG AT GROUND LEVEL
    C.   ALOFT (IN THE AIR)
        1.   CLOUDS
    D.   FORMED AROUND DUST PARTICLES
VI.   PRECIPITATION STAGE OF THE WATER CYCLE.
    A.   PRECIPITATION IN LIQUID FORM
        1.   RAIN, SHOWERS, DRIZZLE, ETC.
    B.   PRECIPITATION IN SOLID FORM
        1.   SNOW, HAIL, ETC.
VII.   PERCOLATION STAGE OF THE WATER CYCLE.
    A.   ALONG THE SURFACE
        1.   WATER FLOWS IN STREAMS AND RIVERS.
        2.   WATER STANDS IN LAKES AND OCEANS.
VIII. SUMMARY AND REVIEW
    A.   OF THE WORDS (PHASES OF THE CYCLE).
    B.   OF THE WATER CYCLE IN GENERAL.

AN OUTLINE SCRIPT

A VERBATIM SCRIPT

TALENT: This glass of water is over one million years old!
        (drinks the water)
    And it still tastes delicious.
MUSIC: (over title cards)
TALENT: Yes, this glass of water is over a million years old and
yet it still tastes delicious. Actually all of the water
that now exists in the world today is over a million years
old. There is no new water in the world. The reason that
we can use this water over and over again is a process
called the WATER CYCLE. The water cycle is natures way
of continually purifying the water supply of the world.
Without this we would have all died off a long time ago.
    (walk to the display board)
This is a diagram of the water cycle. There are four
major phases in this cycle. The first stage is called
evaporation.
    (pause)
Evaporation is the process where liquid is changed to a
vapor. The next stage is condensation.
    (pause)
Condensation is where the vapor rises and it changes
back into a liquid or even a solid form.
The third stage is precipitation.
    (pause)
This is where the liquid or solid falls back to earth.
The last stage in the water cycle is percolation.
    (pause)
Here the liquid runs-off along the surface or under the
ground. These four stages evaporation, condensation,
precipitation, and percolation form natures water cycle.
Let's look at these stages in a little more detail. The
evaporation stage actually begins with the sun. The
sun is the heat source that changes the liquid into a
vapor. It is very much like what happens when you put
a teakettle on the stove. The stove heats the liquid
and changes it into

THE SCRIPT

Once the treatment has been approved and the production storyboard has been prepared we are ready for the final step in the design stage of the production process. We are ready to prepare the script which will provide the words, music, and sound effects that will be used to complement the visual aspects of the program. Basically there are two types of scripts that you will deal with: (1) the outline script and (2) the verbatim script. The selection of which type of script to use is a function of the type of Talent that you are dealing with.

The outline script (see example on the opposite page) is very similar to the content outline. It is normally used with Talent that have not had training in the memorization and/or delivery of lines in front of a television camera. This is very appropriate for use with classroom teachers and students. In either case the Talent must be sufficiently knowledgable to ad-lib about the topics that are indicated in the outline.

The verbatim script is more normally used with trained Talent who not only can memorize their lines but also can deliver these lines in front of a television camera (see the example of the opposite page.) This verbatim script not only specifies the exact words that the Talent will use but also his/her movements and delivery.

The preparation of the outline script begins with the content outline. Once it has been approved by the client it forms the basis for the script. You may need to add some bridges between the ideas but actually little more than that needs to be done. There are some problems that you, as Director, will find when you are directing a program from an outline script. First, since the Talent will be ad-libbing they may use slightly different words in the rehearsal than they do in the actual production. As Producer/Director you will need to identify key words or phrases that will allow you to cut from one scene to another at the appropriate time. Second, the necessity of covering all of the information may require the use of cue cards to remind the Talent of the points in the outline script.

The preparation of the verbatim script poses different types of problems. Your first task will be to expand the content outline and to begin to develop the dialogue for the script. It is necessary that you take care with the vocabulary level to ensure that it is appropriate for the grade level of the audience. Another concern in preparing a verbatim script is the simple fact that you must write to be heard, not to be read. Most of your writing training has been aimed at developing materials that are to be read by others. Now you must switch and write materials that are designed to be heard. The use of a verbatim script poses other problems for the Producer/Director. You will need to spend some time in assisting the Talent to deliver the lines that you have prepared. You will also need to spend a great deal of time in rehearsals to make sure that the words, movements and shots are coordinated for the best possible effect.

Probably you will begin with the outline script simply because it is the easiest to produce and it is more appropriate for the type of Talent that you will be working with. But even in a program that is primarily developed from an outline script there are times that a verbatim script might be appropriate. Often a program will call for an off-camera Talent—someone to deliver lines while he himself will not be seen. This is a very appropriate use of a verbatim script. In this case the Talent can just read the words that you have written and need not worry about memorizing the lines. The key to successful writing is simply practice, practice, and more practice.

PRODUCING THE MESSAGE AN OVERVIEW.

DOCUMENTS

ELEMENTS

ASSEMBLY

GET IT ALL TOGETHER.

THE PRODUCTION STAGE: AN OVERVIEW

Where are we in the production process? We have completed both the planning and the design stage. This means that the client has approved the content outline, the audience description, and the instructional objectives. You have selected the appropriate medium to deliver the message to the intended audience. The treatment has been approved and used to develop the storyboard and the script for the proposed production. Now we are ready to actually produce the program. Well, not quite. We are in the production stage but there are three sub-stages and only one of them is the production of the message. These three sub-stages are (1) the preparation of the production documents for the crew, (2) the preparation of the elements for the production, and (3) the assembly of these elements into the final production.

The production documents are intended to ensure that all of the equipment, materials, and personnel are on hand and ready when the actual production begins. These documents include the shooting schedule, the prop and equipment list, and the set or studio diagram. These documents are prepared by the Producer and used to keep the crew informed of the who, what, why, when, and where of the production. The prop and equipment list is just that a listing of the materials and equipment list is just that a listing of the materials and equipment that will be needed for the production. Nothing is as frustrating as arriving on location and finding that an essential prop or a vital piece of equipment is either not there or is not working. The set or studio diagram is simply a map of the area where the shooting will take place and shows the location of the Talent, props, and equipment. This diagram will be used by the production crew to set up the various items in the shooting area and to relieve the pressure on the producer.

We need to point out that the second and third sub-stages of the production stage will be different depending on the type of television production that you are using. There are two quite different television production techniques. The first is what we might term "live" production. In this situation the program is taped from beginning to end without any interruption. This is the way television was originally done and is the way that most current "live" productions are done. The second way is through electronic editing. In this case—the "edited" productions—the individual scenes are produced and then edited together electronically. This system is becoming more and more popular as the electronic editing systems begin to approach the capability of the film editing equipment and the laboratories that service them.

In the live productions the second aspect of the production stage is simply the production of the various components of the message. These would include the audio tapes that provide the music for the opening and closing of the productions, studio cards for the titles, and even the various instructional materials that are used during the program. The assembly of these components plus the Talent and the production crew take place during the "live" production. The edited productions are quite different. Here the individual scenes are shot, usually out of order and sequence. Then these scenes are assembled through electronic editing. While the production of the elements and the assembly of the elements occur in both types of production they are quite different situations.

Thus, in the production stage of the production process we are concerned with more than the actual production of the message. There are actually three aspects that we are engaged in: (1) the preparation of the production documents to prepare the production crew, (2) the production of the elements necessary for the final production, and (3) the assembly of these elements into the final product.

THE DOCUMENTS

THE WATER CYCLE

SHOOTING DATE: FRIDAY, JUNE 15, 1979. 5:30 in the evening.

PLACE: We will be shooting in room 148C of the Payne
Building at 5055 North Park Place, Tempe, Arizona.
NOTE: You will have to come in the back door
since the building will be closed.

PRODUCTION CREW:
Director	Les Satterthwaite
Assistant Director	Mary Smith
Audio Tech. Dir.	John Jones
Video Tech. Dir.	Jean Johnson
Floor Director	Charlie Chase
Asst. Floor Dir.	Charles Robinson
Camera one	Ralph Ferguson
Camera two	Paul Parker

ASSIGNMENTS: Mary Smith will be responsible for making sure
that the equipment is in good shape and placed
according to the set diagram. Charlie Chase
will be responsible for the collection and the
arrangement of the set elements and props. The
studio cards will be produced by Charles
Robinson.

SHOOTING SCHEDULE.

PROP AND EQUIPMENT LIST FOR
THE WATER CYCLE:

THE EQUIPMENT: We will use the standard TELEMEDIA
production unit. We will need one
mike. A 2x2 carrousel slide projector with screen.

THE PROPS:
Studio card	THE WATER CYCLE
Studio card	FEATURING DR. SAM SMITH
Studio card	A TELEMEDIA PRODUCTION
Wall chart	Diagram of the WATER CYCLE (see Dr. Smith for details)
Wall chart	Vocabulary---the four stages of the water cycle
Glass of water	
Pedestal for the glass of water, approx. 32" tall	
Super card	EVAPORATION
Super card	CONDENSATION
Super card	PRECIPITATION
Super card	PERCOLATION
2x2 slides	Dew
2x2 slides	Fog
2x2 slides	Rain
2x2 slides	Snow
2x2 slides	Teakettle and steam

PROP/EQUIP. LIST.

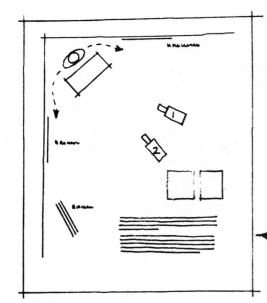

SET/STUDIO DIAGRAM.

THE PRODUCTION DOCUMENTS

These three documents are prepared by the Producer and distributed to the crew to keep them informed about the upcoming production. The main function of these documents is to allow the Producer some freedom to work with the Talent. To do this certain responsibilities must be shared with the rest of the production crew. These documents will do just that. The shooting schedule provides the entire crew with information about the production. The prop and equipment list is given to the Assistant Director (Switcher) and the Floor Director who are responsible for the props and equipment. The studio diagram is given to the same people so that they can arrange the materials in the appropriate places.

Let's look at the shooting schedule a little more closely. There are a number of very important questions that it must answer. First it must tell the production crew WHAT the production is that they will be shooting. It must also tell them WHEN the proposed production will take place. The WHERE is also important, not only the street address but, if necessary, a map on how to get there. The shooting schedule should also let the crew know WHO will be working in what position. A listing of the various crew positions and the people who will fill these roles and responsibilities is essential. Then of course there is always the "special" information that is needed to ensure a smooth production. This shooting schedule should be prepared and distributed well in advance of the scheduled production. Many of the crew members will need to get things done well in advance of the production date. For example, the Floor Director or the assistant must prepare the studio cards and the Audio Technical Director must prepare the music tapes well ahead of time.

The prop and equipment list is just that, a listing of the various props and equipment that are needed for the production. The equipment part of the list should be devoted to special equipment that is needed. Commonly used production equipment might simply be listed as "the system." The prop list is vital. Here you should not only include the items that the Talent will manipulate during the production but also any set items such as furniture, pictures, drapes, etc. that are necessary to provide the desired environment for the production. The prop list should also include the various studio cards and instructional aids that will be used during the program. This serves both as a collection list and as a list to check that everything necessary will be on hand for the production.

The set or studio diagram is simply a map of the area in which the production will take place. It provides the Floor Director with information as to where the props and set elements will go. It provides the Assistant Director with information as to where the various pieces of equipment should be placed. This is a very important document simply because time is vital in television production. If the Producer must be concerned with all of the minor details then he/she cannot be as concerned with the important things in the production. It is essential that the Producer/Director be free to work with the Talent and to get ready for the difficult job of directing the program.

The documents shown on the opposite page are the first sub-stage in the production stage of the production process. They are designed to communicate with the production crew and to assign various roles and responsibilities. They ensure that when the production is due to be taped everyone will know his/her job and that everything will be where it should be. It is a vital set of documents, vital to the smoothness of the proposed production.

THE ELEMENTS

FOR LIVE PRODUCTIONS

STUDIO CARDS

AUDIO

INSTRUCTIONAL AIDS

FOR EDITED PRODUCTIONS

PRODUCTION OF THE ELEMENTS

Remember there are two different types of production: "live" and "edited." The way that we approach the production of the elements is a function of the type of production we are doing.

Production of Elements for a "Live" Program

In this situation we are concerned with the production of the various components of the message that need to be completed before the live production begins. One thing that we need before we begin the production is the music, sound effects, and other audio information that is necessary for the production. While these are available on records, it is difficult to cue up records during a live production and it is advisable to transfer this information onto audio tape for use during the production. This poses one real problem and that is copyright. It is against the law to use most music in this way. However, there are records that are designed for this purpose. Sound effects records are usually designed to be transcribed onto audio tape. While you can use copywritten music for practice programs, it is not wise to use them for programs to be used outside of your school. The safest way is to use the school band or orchestra and original music. It is also best to make sure that you have written permission from the writers and performers before you use their product. Another set of elements that needs to be produced before the production is the studio cards. These are normally used as opening and closing titles. Specifics of their design and production are provided earlier in the book. The various instructional materials needed for the production should also be produced ahead of time. For details on the design and production of simple instructional materials to be used on television consult GRAPHICS: SKILLS, MEDIA, AND MATERIALS by Les Satterthwaite and published by Kendall/Hunt. There may be other items that need to be produced for specific production but the audio, the studio cards, and the instructional materials are common items.

Production of Elements for an "Edited" Program

In this situation the production of the elements means the production of the various scenes intended for the final program. These scenes may be shot in the same order that they will be used in the actual production but more commonly they will be shot out of sequence and rearranged into the proper order during editing. This situation is not common in the public schools today. This is primarily true because of the cost of true assemble editing equipment. This is not true in industrial or even broadcast production situations. More and more the industry is moving to the portable cameras and the expensive editing equipment. In a very real sense this simply electronic film production. It is an individual creative effort rather than the group effort that is commonly associated with "live" television production.

No matter which type of production is the end result this part of the production stage is concerned with the preparation of the elements that will eventually make up the final program. The care that is taken at this stage will affect the final production. Sloppy title cards will create a poor "set" for the entire production. Audio recordings that are less than perfect will create a poor impression of the final product. Once the various elements have been prepared we are then ready to move into the final part of the production stage—the assembly of the elements into the final product, the program.

ASSEMBLY

OF LIVE PRODUCTIONS

OF EDITED PRODUCTIONS

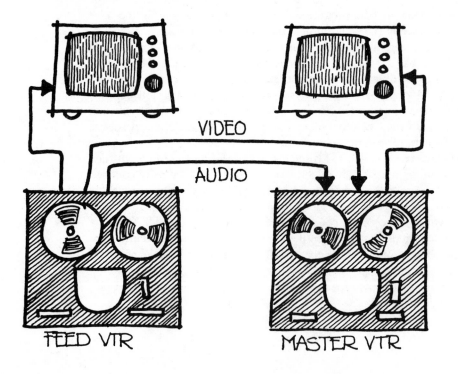

VIDEO

AUDIO

FEED VTR

MASTER VTR

ASSEMBLY OF THE ELEMENTS FOR A PRODUCTION

This third sub-stage of the production stage is what we normally think of when we think of production. At least in the live production situation this is the READY ON CAMERA ONE, READY ON CAMERA TWO, ROLL VIDEO that is normally associated with television production. It has taken a long time to get here if you have followed the entire production process. Yet without the planning documents, without the design the production would not have nearly the potential that it now can have. The results will be well worth the effort that has been put into it.

Assembling the Elements for a "Live" Production

This process is described in the previous two sections of the book, SINGLE CAMERA PRODUCTION and MULTI-CAMERA PRODUCTION. All that needs to be said at this time is that there is a lot to learn. The production process up to this point has prepared you for a predictable production. Now the operation of the equipment and the activities of the crew members will bring all of these documents to life in the actual program.

Assembling the Elements for the "Edited" Production

We will not cover the process of editing in the remainder of the book since it is not commonly found in the public schools. Nor can we cover it in detail in this short amount of space. However, we will take the time to provide a very rough overview of the editing process. First, there are two types of editing: (1) assemble or add-on editing, and (2) insert or full editing. The latter is limited to very expensive editing systems costing thousands of dollars. The former can be done with the same equipment that you use for normal television production. In an editing system you need two video tape recorders and two television monitors. The video tape recorders must have a pause mode. This means that the heads of the VTR must continue to rotate but the video tape does not move through the system. One VTR will be the feed or play system and the other will be the master or record system. Each television monitor will be attached to a separate video tape recorder. The audio and video output from the feed or play VTR must be attached to the input of the master or record VTR.

From this point on the process is relatively simple. The master VTR is placed in passive record mode. (It is in record but the tape is not moving through the machine.) The play or feed VTR is cued up to the opening scene. Back up the feed VTR past the opening scene and then put it into play mode. As the image begins to appear on the monitor of the monitor release the pause control of the master VTR and it will record the opening segment. Once you have done this repeat the process until the various scenes have been reassembled into the order and sequence that is depicted in the production storyboard. Unfortunately this process will not ensure clean edits. This means that quite often you will get a disruption of picture at each edit point. This disruption is called a "glitch" and is one of the disadvantages of this type of editing.

The insert or full editing systems eliminate these picture disruptions but most public schools simply cannot afford the cost of the system. This is one of the major reasons that edited productions are not common in schools.

In either case—a "live" or an "edited" production—you now have a product. The production is completed and is on video tape. Is this the end of the production process? No! There is still one very important stage left in the production process—evaluation. The opportunity to evaluate the production that we have completed. It is our opportunity to learn from our own mistakes.

EVALUATION

TECHNICAL EVALUATION

SHARP/CLEAR

GOOD SOUND

CONTRAST

ARTISTIC EVALUATION

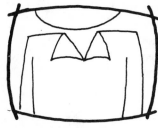

COMPOSITION

STUDIO CARDS

PACING

INSTRUCTIONAL EVALUATION

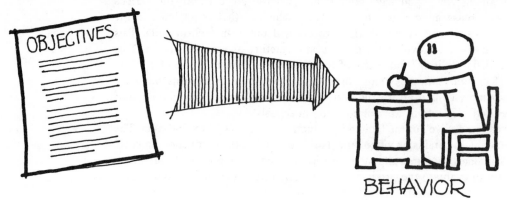

OBJECTIVES

BEHAVIOR

EVALUATING THE COMPLETED MESSAGE

We have finally arrived at the end of the production process. The last stage in this process is evaluation. There are three aspects of this evaluation: (1) the evaluation of the *technical* aspects of the message, (2) the evaluation of the *artistic* aspects of the message, and (3) the evaluation of the *instructional*, informational, or entertainment aspects of the message.

Technical Evaluation

This is the point at which you evaluate the technical aspects of the production. This evaluation is the responsibility of the Producer/Director. However, it is not uncommon to involve the entire production crew and even the client in on this. Even with all of these people the final decision is up to the Producer/Director. Do we keep the production or do we re-do it?

What are some of the technical aspects that we need to evaluate at this point? First, is the picture sharp and clear? A fuzzy picture can be just poor focusing on the camera or it can be an electronic problem. Another concern is the quality of the sound. The audio portion of a television program is often the aspect that is given the least attention and yet it is vital to a good production. Is the sound sharp and clear? Is the sound at an appropriate volume level for playback to a large audience? The contrast of the picture is also another concern. This is often a function of an inappropriate lighting situation or poor adjustment of the f-stops on the cameras. A television program with poor contrast creates a very poor impression of the technical quality.

Artistic Evaluation

This is a little more difficult than the technical evaluation of the picture and sound quality. Here we are concerned with the various intangibles that make a television program "good." Composition is one artistic quality that is relatively easy to evaluate. If the Talent's head is consistently cut off, as shown on the opposite page, this is an example of poor composition. However composition is a concern in moving shots such as pans and tilts as well as the more common static shots. An artistic evaluation is also concerned with the quality of the studio cards and instructional aids that are shown during the program. The quality of these materials may directly affect the percieved quality of the entire program. The pacing of the program is another aspect of the artistic evaluation. Is the program too fast or too slow? Does it seem to drag or does it rush past so fast that some students might not get the information that is being presented? All of these are concerns of the artistic evaluation of the program. Like the technical evaluation the final decision rests with the Producer/Director. However, it is not uncommon to ask the opinions of the production crew and even the client.

Instructional, Entertainment, and/or Informational Evaluation

This aspect of the evaluation process is concerned with whether the program is doing or will do what it was intended to do. In this case we look back to the goals or objectives developed in the planning stage of the production process. Here the client must make the final determination. He/she can do this in anticipation, "I THINK IT WILL ACHIEVE THE GOALS OR OBJECTIVES," or in retrospect "I GAVE THEM A TEST AND THEY DID WHAT WE SAID THEY WOULD BE ABLE TO DO." The former is a judgement on the part of the client and the latter is the result of actually eliciting responses from learners after they have been shown the program.

Evaluation is the final stage and in many ways the most important stage. It allows you as Producer/Director to learn from your mistakes and to improve future productions.

CHAPTER V.

TELEVISION UTILIZATION

IDEAS AND APPLICATIONS

BROADCAST
DISTRIBUTION SYSTEM

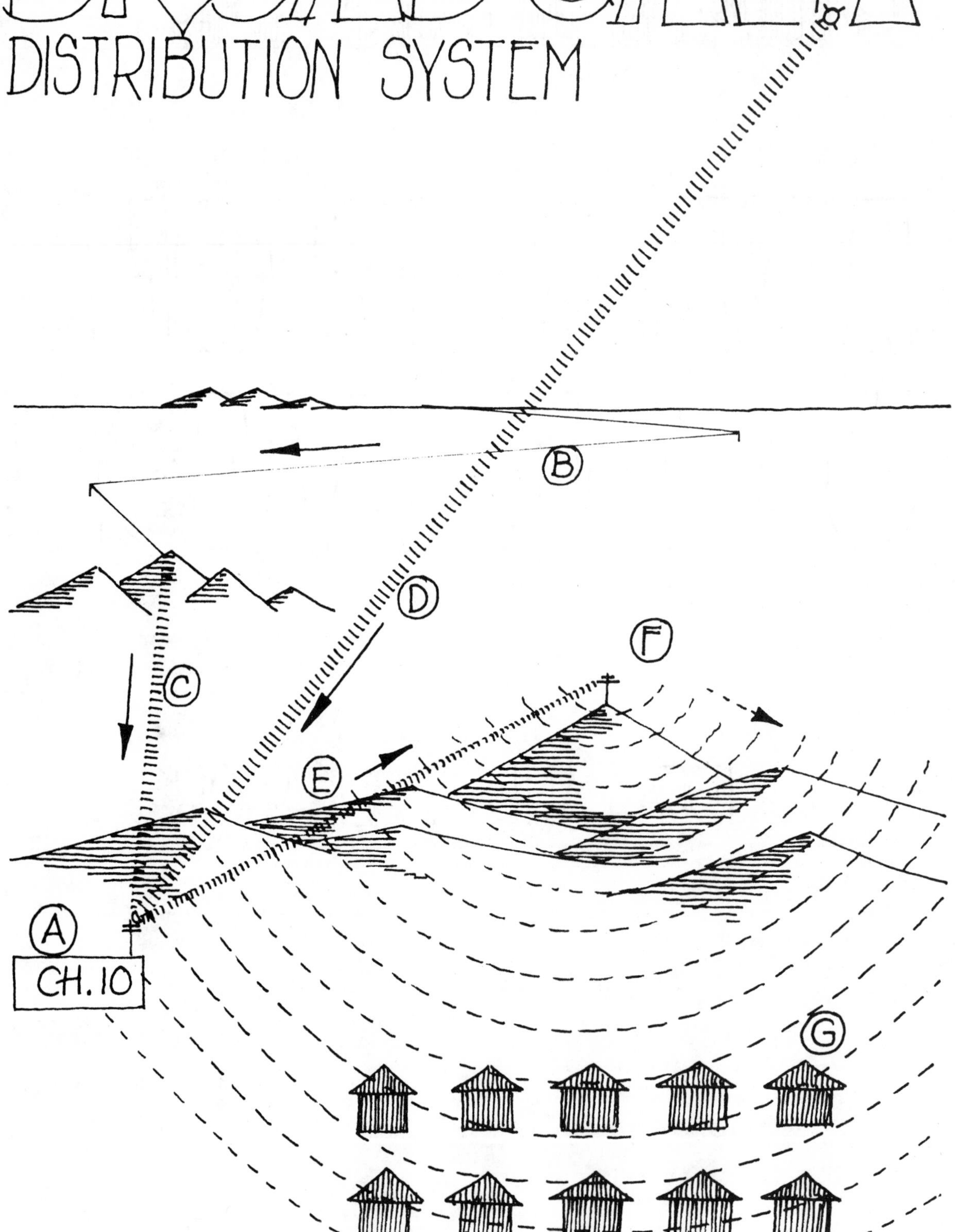

A
CH.10

B

C

D

E

F

G

BROADCAST TELEVISION, A DISTRIBUTION SYSTEM

When you sit in your living room watching the dancing images on the tube, chances are that you are watching "broadcast" television. The term broadcast simply means that an open signal is being set through the air and that any television receiver within range that is tuned to the proper frequency or channel can pick up the signal. These broadcast signals originate from two quite different types of television stations. The commercial stations concentrate on entertainment to attract the largest possible audience and to increase the value of the air time that they sell. The public television stations also send out broadcast signals but they deal with a different type of program content and seek to serve a much smaller and more specific audience. Since they cannot sell air time (commercials) they exist on grants and taxes and can afford to seek out these specialized audience and provide instructional and informational programming which is, hopefully, still entertaining.

How do these signals that are broadcast from the transmitter of the local station get there—where do they come from? Networks such as NBC, ABC, CBS and PBS (the Public Broadcasting System) provide much of the programming that you watch. These signals are sent cross-country through cables (B) or rented telephone lines, or through microwave transmissions (C) which send a narrow beam closed signal. These incoming signals arrive at the local television station (A) where they are either recorded on video tape for delayed playback or immediately sent by microwove (E), to the stations transmitter (F). The transmitter is located as high as possible to increase the area that the signal serves. The broadcast signal is a line-of-sight signal and this means that the higher you can get it above ground the larger the area that will be able to receive the signal. From the stations transmitter the signal is sent through the air over a specific frequency (the channel that is assigned to that station). Any receiver within range of the station that is on and turned to the proper frequency (channel) will now pick up and display the signal.

In some cases the station originates the program. A good example of this would be the evening news. Here the program is produced in the studio of the local station and sent to the transmitter for distribution to the audience. Another source of programming for the stations are syndicated shows. These are programs that either were on the network or never made it to the network. They are on film and are shipped by mail to the local station where they are put on a film chain and translated into electronic signals and sent out over the system. Network programs, locally produced programs, and syndicated shows make up the bulk of the programming for the commercial broadcast stations. These programs are designed to attract the largest possible audience since the amount of money that a station can charge for their air-time (the commercials) depends on how many people are watching.

Consider the fact that by the time a young person has graduated from high school he/she has watched an average of 15,000 hours of television. For the same amount of time he/she has only spent 11,000 hours in the classroom. The only activity that will consume more of their time is sleeping. Is it any wonder that so many people are expressing concern over the impact that television is having on our society. Many people have expressed concern that our society is developing into a world of passive viewers—they are absorbed by the television programs. This book is intended to help you change from a passive viewer to an active critic; to remove the magic of television so that you can not only know how a program is produced but to also produce your own. So that you can react to the programming you watch rather than just absorb it.

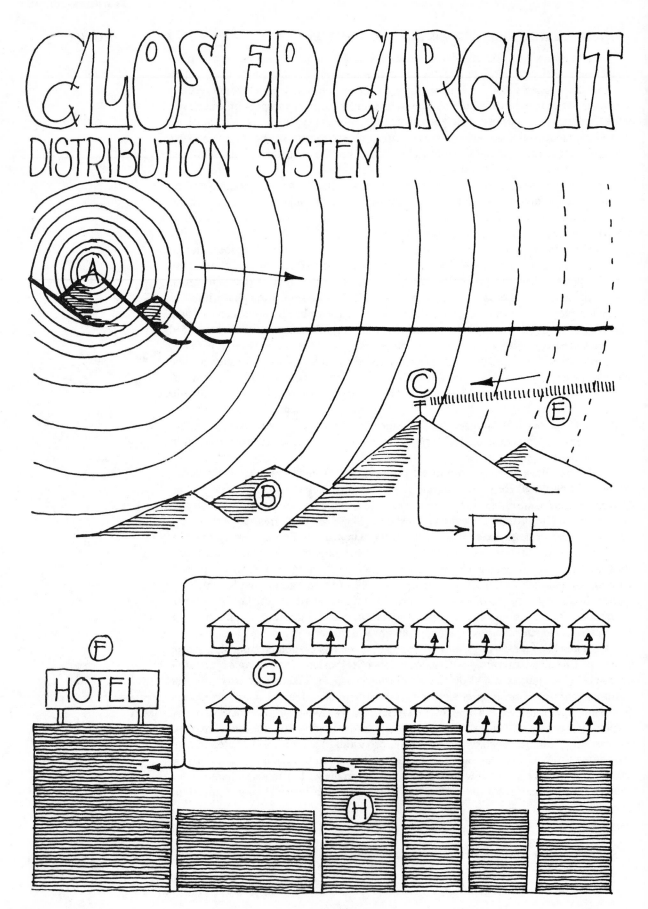

CLOSED CIRCUIT
DISTRIBUTION SYSTEM

CLOSED CIRCUIT TELEVISION AS A DISTRIBUTION SYSTEM

Let's go back to our broadcast distribution system for just a moment. If you remember we indicated that the broadcast television signal is a line-of-sight signal with a limited range. What about those TV receivers who at the edge of the reception area (on the fringe) or who are blocked from the broadcast signal by mountains or other natural objects that interfere with the transmission. In our diagram on the opposite page the stations transmitter (A) is broadcasting its signal but the mountains (B) are blocking that signal and the community shown in the foreground cannot receive it.

Each home owner could build a television antenna tall enough to reach over the mountain and capture the broadcast signal. However, this is impractical. Rather a group of people work together and put an antenna (C) on the top of the mountain then run separate cables to their individual houses. In this case a closed circuit signal is sent by wire to each home who participated in the erection of the community antenna. This is the way cable TV was born. It originated from desire to pick up a fringe signal and amplify it for a better picture or to overcome some sort of natural obstacle to the TV signal. In either case the result was that homes that previously could not pick up a television signal were now being served. Soon people decided that there was money to be made in cable TV and they would erect the TV antenna and charge a monthly fee for those who wanted to be part of the system. To make the offer even more attractive the owners of the cable TV system would link up with other sources through either cable or microwave links (E). Soon even more programming was added. In some cases local programs produced in a studio were added to the systems and in others films were translated into appropriate electronic signals through a film chain.

Eventually communities that were already well served with broadcast signals explored the possibilty of closed circuit cable systems. The concept of cable television became as common as the concept of broadcast television. Special cable systems began to be developed. Hotels and motels found that cable television was a way to distribute current motion pictures to their rooms and to attract more customers. Business and industry found that cable television systems could be used to enhance either their security or their safety. Now from a central location people could monitor all areas of a plant for criminals or fire. Hospitals found this a suitable technique for sharing information from the operating room. Now the staff could have front row seats as new techniques and skills were demonstrated. Soon even the schools were exploring the possibility of utilizing closed circuit TV as a means of distributing informational and instructional programs to their classrooms.

Cable television systems that are privately owned and that are not run for a profit do not have the same type of controls exerted over them that do those that are profit oriented. This means that the Federal Communications Commission (FCC) does not exert the same degree of control that they do over broadcast stations or commercial cable companies. This also means that these distribution systems do not have to have the same signal quality requirements. This results in less expensive equipment and puts the possibility of a cable distribution system and associated production equipment well within the range of public schools. Also as applications for cable television and related production facilities increase it opens an entirely new source of employment for those who are trained in television production and distribution techniques.

DELIVERY SYSTEMS

PHYSICAL DISTRIBUTION

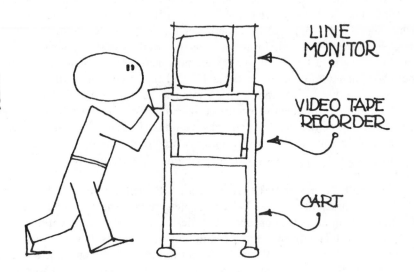

LINE MONITOR

VIDEO TAPE RECORDER

CART

ELECTRONIC DISTRIBUTION

TELEVISION DELIVERY SYSTEMS IN THE SCHOOL

Within a school system (building or district) there are two basic types of delivery systems. First there is the physical delivery system where the video tape and the playback equipment is moved from room to room as it is needed. The second type of delivery system is the electronic delivery system that send the television signals over wires to those learning spaces where there are perament monitors. There are advantages and disadvantages to each of these systems.

The Physical Delivery Systems in the School

The physical delivery system consists of the tape and the playback equipment. The playback equipment includes (1) a video tape player or player/recorder, (2) a line monitor, and (3) a cart to allow the system to be moved from place to place. You can use either a video player or a video player/recorder in the system. The video players are less expensive than the combination player/recorders but they can only be used for playback. On the other hand the player/recorder is more expensive but it can also be part of a production system or it can be used to record materials off the air. The line monitor should be a 24–25″ color set that will serve as both a monitor and a receiver. This means it should be capable of receiving broadcast signals from the local broadcast stations and it should also be capable of receiving signals from a video tape recorder. The monitor/receiver and video tape recorder should be mounted on a cart to allow you to move it from place to place.

The addition of a single camera and a microphone will turn this delivery system into a single camera production unit. As the system is expanded the components can be used as part of the electronic distribution system. Ideally you would begin with a couple of systems and when you reached the point that these could not meet the classroom needs you would expand into an electronic distribution system. The main disadvantage of the physical distribution system is that you cannot send the same signal to a variety of locations.

The Electronic Delivery Systems in the School

This is basically a closed circuit television system that originates, distributes, and displays a signal to the learning spaces in the school. The origination may be video tapes and a video tape player, a filmchain and motion pictures, a television studio and a live signal or any combination of these. The signals go to the head-end equipment which feeds an electronic signal throughout the system. This head-end equipment can send multiple signals over the same wire. Thus one class may be watching a film, another may be watching a locally produced video tape, the third may be watching a commercially produced video tape, and a fourth may be watching a live studio production. Or a single signal may be sent to all stations simultaneously. The classroom teacher simply selects the signal that is desired by tuning in the appropriate channel on the monitor/receiver in their classroom.

The main advantage of this type of system is the ability to send a common signal to all learning centers. This would be excellent for a morning news program or for announcements from the administration. The system could also be used after school as a means of communicating with the instructional staff and even for providing in-service and even university training programs. The disadvantage of this system is simply the cost. While the cost will vary widely depending on the number of channels desired, the nature of the feed system, and the number of viewing stations, it may cost as much as $60,000. However, it is possible to start small and then develop the system as the need for it increases.

PRODUCTION SYSTEMS

SINGLE CAMERA

MULTICAMERA

PRODUCTION SYSTEMS IN THE SCHOOL

A distribution system is just one component of an overall television system. In addition you need to consider some sort of production component. This production component can be an inexpensive single camera system or a more professional multicamera system. Each of these systems has certain advantages and disadvantages.

The Single Camera Production System

There are two types of single camera systems: (1) the portapak and (2) the studio system. The portapak is a portable unit that is designed to be used by a single individual. The single camera studio system increases the production potential by increasing the number of student who can be involved in the production process and increasing the things that can be done during the local production. The portapak systems are an end in themselves. They cannot be interconnected with other components to expand the system and they use a different type of video tape recorder than either the studio systems or the delivery systems. On the other hand the single camera studio system can be expanded into a multicamera system at a later date. This is especially true if some consideration for later expansion is made when the original equipment is purchased. The video tape recorder that is purchased for a studio system will work as part of a multicamera system or as part of the delivery system. The monitor can be used either as part of the production system or as part of the distribution system. The camera (if the right type is purchased) can become part of a multicamera system.

For more details on the single camera systems see Chapter I, The Portapak System and Chapter II, The Single Camera Studio System. The single camera studio system is a good place to begin the development of a local production system for your school.

The Multicamera Production System

The multicamera system is the ultimate in production facilities. While these are available either in color or in black and white most school applications can be best met with the black and white systems. The use of color requires the purchase of additional lights and also limits the production unit to a fixed studio system or portable/ system. The fixed studio system simply means that the production equipment is permanently installed in a studio-control room complex designed specifically for television production. On the other hand the portable system can be moved from place to place and a fixed studio is not absolutely essential. The portable system still requires AC power but it can be moved to any location where AC power is available. In this situation you can do an instructional program on chemistry in the chem lab , you can do a feature on the football team either on the football field or in the locker room, or you could do a program from the principal's office if that type of set were required. With a fixed studio system all of these would be impossible. The personnel, sets, props and all of the other requirements of the production would have to be brought into the studio—and the studio has limited space. It would be very difficult to show the football team in action in even the largest studio.

There is more information about the multicamera system in Chapter III The Multicamera Production System. Since costs will vary from place to place and from week to week we have avoided giving even approximate costs. Your best bet is to contact a local vendor who has experience in the design and installation of television systems and have them make an estimate.

APPENDIX A.

DEVELOPING A TELEVISION PRODUCTION/UTILIZATION FACILITY FOR YOUR SCHOOL.

1. ON YOUR MARK!

2. GET READY!

3. GO!

CONVINCING THE ADMINISTRATION.

DEVELOPING A COST ESTIMATE.

DEVELOPING A CURRICULUM.

ON YOUR MARK!

There are a number of reasons why you might want to develop a TV production training program in your school. First, TV production is a lot of FUN! Unfortunately most school districts will not consider new curriculum additions just on the basis of their being fun. This is especially true when TV production is going to require a considerable initial outlay of money. To get the administration to consider TV production training in your school we need to provide the administration with some valid academic and social reasons to consider this addition to the school offering.

You might begin by pointing out that by the time a student has graduated from high school he/she has spent an average of 15,000 hours in front of the television screen and only 11,000 hours in the classroom. The only activity that consumes more of a student's time is sleeping. This statistic is amplified by the fact that during most of these 15,000 hours the student is a passive viewer of information. This passive reception of information is not in the best interests of either the student or the nation. It is part of our responsibility as teachers to assist students to take a more critical role in reacting to the media.

Parents, teachers, and even legislators are expressing grave concern over the impact that television is having on young people. They have suggested approaches ranging from more parental control to federal action controlling the content of television programming. Most of the suggestions entail a great degree of outside control. Unfortunately there will come a time when this control will have to be lifted and we will then have a group of people that have little experience in controlling their own behavior. Over the past five years in working with students from the third grade to graduate school I have observed that students who are trained in television production techniques change from the role of passive viewer to that of active critic. Apparently once a student has been involved in a television production experience the media has lost some of its "magic" and he/she now is more in the position of being able to critically analyze what he/she is watching.

If this is not enough to convince the administration of the value of a program in television production you might consider the career education approach. The field of cable television is opening all sorts of new positions for people trained in telecommunications. Schools, businesses, industry are all beginning to utilize closed circuit production and distribution facilities. Of even more importance is the general training in work skills. As a member of a production crew the student will be actively involved with the need for individual responsibility, promptness, group cooperation, leadership, and many of the other skills that are common to a wide range of careers. In addition the feedback characteristic of the television system allows student to see the immediate results of their behaviors. The fact that the vast majority of the experiences will be positive provide the opportunity for a definite growth in the student's self-image.

Since a television crew has a variety of levels of leadership this type of training will also allow students to determine that level that is most appropriate for them. They may be comfortable in the role of Producer/Director with all of the responsibility and authority. Or they may prefer the secondary leadership roles of Floor Director or Switcher. Or they may find that they fit better into the roles which have limited degrees of responsibility and authority. Students will also find television production an excellent way to bring together other areas of the curriculum and to provide meaning to other less exciting subjects.

GET READY!

Once you have sold the administration on the idea of a course in television production training you will have to help them sell the idea to the school board. Obviously you will have to provide them with some valid reasons for including such a course in the curriculum but you will also need to provide them with some good estimates of what this program will cost. This is not easy since the cost of a complete production and distribution system may run as high as $100,000.00. Obviously there are few school districts in these times of tight budgets that will even consider such an expense. However, it is possible to develop a five or ten year program that will make the expenses easier to deal with. The prices we are going to use are very general; they will differ widely—not only from place to place but also from day to day. At best these should be considered as guides.

Phase One (A Single Camera Studio System)

1-Black and white viewfinder television camera, with zoom lens remoted to the rear, capable of accepting internal and external sync.

1-Pan head, tripod, and dolly for the above camera.

1-Video tape recorder (¾″ cassette)

1-Microphone and audio extension cable.

1-24″ color line monitor.

1-Set of cables to interconnect the system.

1-Equipment cart to carry all except the camera and accessories.

(estimated price $3500.00)

Phase Two (Increasing the Audio Capability)

1-Professional audio mixer (4–5 channels) with VU meter.

1-Cassette audio tape recorder with digital counter.

1-Cables to interconnect the system.

2-Microphones and audio extension cables.   (estimated price $500.00)

Phase Three (Increasing the Video Capability)

1-Black and white viewfinder television camera compatable with the first one purchased. (plus accessories)

1-Set camera monitors plus preview monitor.

1-Video switcher with sync generator.

1-Portable console base.

1-Intercom system with six headsets.   (estimated price $6,000.00)

Phase Four (Beginning your distribution capability)

1-Head-end equipment for four channels.

1-Wiring to connect 10–12 learning spaces.

12-24″ color monitors.

1-Video tape recorder to feed the system.   (estimated cost $40,000.00)

Phase Five (Completing the distribution system)

1-Addition to head-end equipment to provide eight channels.

1-Set of wiring to complete the distribution system.

12-24″ color monitors.

1-Film chain.   (estimated costs $30,000)

Phase Six (Completing the production system)

1-Black and white viewfinder television camera compatable with the previous two (plus accessories)

1-Character generator.

1-Video tape recorder.   (estimated cost $3,000)

PROGRAM 1.   THE TELEMEDIA EXPERIENCE   (ONE DAY)

This program is designed as a one-day experience to acquaint groups of students (24–30) with the equipment, crew positions, and techniques that are needed in the production of simple multicamera programs. The main emphasis will be on removing the "magic" from television and turning the students from passive receivers of television information to active critics of what they see.

OBJECTIVES: Students involved in the program will—

1. Name, describe the function of, and operate the major pieces of production equipment including (a) cameras, (b) mikes, (c) video switcher, (d) audio mixer, and (e) video tape recorder.
2. Name and describe the function of the various crew members including (a) the Producer/Director, (b) the Video Switcher, (c) the Audio Technical Director, (d) the Video Technical Director, (e) the Floor Director, (f) Cameramen, and (g) Talent.
3. As a group design and produce at least four original, simple, multicamera productions.

SCHEDULE:

8:30– 9:00	Introduction to TV and TV equipment.
9:00–10:30	Demonstration of and practice with the equipment.
10:30–11:00	Introduction to the crew roles and establish the crews.
11:00–11:30	Demonstration of producing/directing a program.
11:30–11:45	Crew A shoots and crew B plans. (The same program)
11:45–12:00	Crew B shoots and crew A plans. (The same program)
12:00–12:30	——LUNCH——
12:30– 1:00	Planning the afternoon programs.
1:00– 1:15	Crew A shoots and crew B plans.
1:15– 1:30	Crew B shoots and crew A plans.
1:30– 1:45	Crew A shoots and crew B plans.
1:45– 2:00	Crew B shoots and crew A plans.
2:00– 2:15	Crew A shoots and crew B plans.
2:15– 2:30	Crew B shoots and crew A plans.
2:30– 2:45	Crew A shoots and crew B plans.
2:45– 3:00	Crew B shoots and crew A plans.
3:00– 3:30	Critique and evaluation of the productions.

LOGISTICS:

This program can be either a single or a multicamera experience. The multicamera experience will involve more students and is more appropriate to the above objectives. If you have a portable multicamera production system you can take it to the students classroom. If your multicamera system is a fixed studio system you will have to bring the students to the studio. While the program can be offered in a single classroom there is an advantage in having the shooting take place in one room and the planning in another. The training director will handle the production and the classroom teacher will supervise the planning.

SCOPE AND SEQUENCE:

8:30– 9:00	Introduction, television and its equipment.
	Broadcast TV (pages 214–215)
	Cable TV (pages 216–217)
	Multicamera equipment (pages 89–91)
9:00–10:30	Demonstration of and practice with the equipment.
	Train two students on the cameras (2).
	Train one student on the audio system.
	Train one student on the video switcher.
	Have these students train other students until all have explored each piece of equipment.
	Supervise and monitor training period.
10:30–11:00	Introduction to the crew roles and set the crews.
	The multicamera crew (pages 92–179)
	Randomly divide group into two crews (A and B).
	Define the role of Producer/Director and have each crew "elect" their Producer/Director.
	Talk briefly with the elected Producer/Directors about leadership and selection of people.
	Producer/Directors appoint their crews.
11:00–11:30	Demonstration of producing/directing a simple show.
	Utilize crew A as the production crew (with crew B observing).
	Select a simple topic such as HOW TO FOLD A PAPER AIRPLANE.
	Do a walk-through with the talent and identify the various shots you will want. Inform the cameramen of their shots and let them practice.
	Check the other crew member to insure that they know what to do and how to do it.
	Run a rehearsal of the program and evaluate the tape.
	Modify if needed and shoot the program.
11:30–11:45	Crew A shoots and crew B observes.
	Crew A shoots the same program as you assist the Producer/Director.
11:45–12:00	Crew B shoots and crew A observes
	Crew A shoots the same program as you assist the Producer/Director.
12:00–12:30	——LUNCH BREAK——
12:30– 1:00	Planning the afternoon programs (by crews).
1:00– 1:15	Crew A shooting and crew B planning.
1:15– 1:30	Crew B shooting and crew A planning.
	(the rotation schedule continues until 3:00)
3:00– 3:30	Critique and evaluation of the programs.
	Show the complete set of programs that were produced during the day. Emphasize ways in which they have improved. Identify the best show of the day.

PROGRAM 2.   THE ADVENTURE CENTER EXPERIENCE   (ONE WEEK)

This program is designed as a one-week career experience that will introduce a group of students (24–30) to the equipment, crew positions, and techniques of television production. Emphasis will be placed on the various careers in telecommunications and the relationship of television production to other curriculum areas (science, language arts, etc.). The students will be divided into crews and will rotate through all of the crew positions experiencing job related skills such as leadership, group interaction, individual responsibility, cooperation, promptness, etc.

OBJECTIVES: Students involved in the program will—

1. Name, describe the function of, and operate the major pieces of production equipment including (a) cameras, (b) mikes, (c) video tape recorder, (d) video switcher, (e) audio mixer, (f) audio tape recorder, and (g) intercom system.
2. Name, describe the functions of, and operate in each of the various crew positions (a) Producer/Director, (b) Video Switcher, (c) Audio Technical Director, (d) Video Technical Director, (e) Floor Director, (f) Cameraman, and (g) Talent.
3. Produce and direct at least one program and serve in the production crew for 10–12 other productions.

SCHEDULE:

The First Day—
9:30–10:00	Introduction to TV and to TV equipment.
10:00–11:30	Demonstration of and practice with the equipment.
11:30–12:00	Introduction to the crew roles and establish the crews.
12:00–12:30	——LUNCH BREAK——
12:30– 1:00	Demonstration of producing and directing a program.
1:00– 1:15	Crew A shoots and crew B observes.
1:15– 1:30	Crew B shoots and crew A observes.
1:30– 2:00	View and critique the productions.
2:00– 2:30	Discuss program ideas for the next day.

The Second Day   *—(through the fourth day)*
9:30–10:00	Crew A shooting and crew B planning.
10:00–10:30	Crew B shooting and crew A planning.
10:30–11:00	Crew A shooting and crew B planning.
11:00–11:30	Crew B shooting and crew A planning.
11:30–12:00	Crew A shooting and crew B planning.
12:00–12:30	——LUNCH BREAK——
12:30– 1:00	Crew B shooting and crew A planning.
1:00– 1:30	Crew A shooting and crew B planning.
1:30– 2:00	Crew B shooting and crew A planning.
2:00– 2:30	Viewing and critique of productions.

(Use 20 minute shooting/planning periods for classes of 30)

The Fifth Day—
9:30–10:15	Crew A, final production.
10:15–11:00	Crew B, final production.
11:00–12:00	Crew A, final production.
12:00–12:30	——LUNCH BREAK——
12:30– 1:15	Crew B, final production.
1:15– 2:00	Viewing and critique of final productions.
2:00– 2:30	Summary and close of program.

SCOPE AND SEQUENCE: *THE FIRST DAY*   NOTES

9:30–10:00	Introduction to TV and to TV equipment.
	    Broadcast TV (pages 214–215)
	    Cable TV (pages 216–217)
	    Multicamera equipment (pages 89–91)

10:00–11:30	Demonstration of and practice with the equipment.
	    Train students on the camera (2).
	    Train student on the audio system.
	    Train student on the video switcher.
	    Have these students train other students until they have all explored each piece of equipment.
	    Supervise and monitor the training period.

11:30–12:00	Introduction to the crew roles and set the crews.
	    The multicamera crew (pages 92–179)
	    Randomly divide the class into two crews (A/B)
	    Define the various crew roles and establish the rotation schedule. (See next page)

11:00–12:30	——LUNCH BREAK——

12:30– 1:00	Demonstration of producing/ directing a TV program.
	    Utilize the first crew on rotation schedule.
	    Select a simple topic such as HOW TO FOLD A PAPER AIRPLANE.
	    Do a walk-through with talent and identify shots.
	    Inform the cameramen of their shots.
	    Check the rest of the crew to make sure they know their jobs.
	    Shoot the program.
	    Rewind, view and critique the production.

1:00– 1:15	Crew A shooting and crew B observing
	    Crew A shoots HOW TO FOLD A PAPER AIR-PLANE.
	    Stay with the Director and assist him/her.

1:15– 1:30	Crew B shooting and crew A observing.
	    Crew B shoots HOW TO FOLD A PAPER AIR-PLANE.
	    Stay with the Director and assist him/her.

1:30– 2:00	Reviewing, view, and critique the productions.
	    Emphasize positive aspects.
	    However, point out places for improvement.

2:00– 2:30	Discuss program ideas for the next days shooting.
	    Talent #1 on the rotation schedule will come up with the idea for that program.
	    He/she will give the idea (written) to the director on the schedule as soon as possible.
	    Help kids generate some ideas (news, interviews, commercials, etc.)

	DIRECTOR	SWITCHER	AUDIO TD	VIDEO TD	FLOOR DIR.	CAMERA 1	CAMERA 2	ASST. FL. DIRECTOR	TALENT 1	TALENT 2	TALENT 3	TALENT 4
PROGRAM 1	A1	A2	A3	A4	A5	A6	A7	A8	A9	A10	A11	A12
PROGRAM 2	B1	B2	B3	B4	B5	B6	B7	B8	B9	B10	B11	B12
PROGRAM 3	A2	A3	A4	A5	A6	A7	A8	A9	A10	A11	A12	A1
PROGRAM 4	B2	B3	B4	B5	B6	B7	B8	B9	B10	B11	B12	B1
PROGRAM 5	A3	A4	A5	A6	A7	A8	A9	A10	A11	A12	A1	A2
PROGRAM 6	B3	B4	B5	B6	B7	B8	B9	B10	B11	B12	B1	B2
PROGRAM 7	A4	A5	A6	A7	A8	A9	A10	A11	A12	A1	A2	A3
PROGRAM 8	B4	B5	B6	B7	B8	B9	B10	B11	B12	B1	B2	B3
PROGRAM 9	A5	A6	A7	A8	A9	A10	A11	A12	A1	A2	A3	A4
PROGRAM 10	B5	B6	B7	B8	B9	B10	B11	B12	B1	B2	B3	B4
PROGRAM 11	A6	A7	A8	A9	A10	A11	A12	A1	A2	A3	A4	A5
PROGRAM 12	B6	B7	B8	B9	B10	B11	B12	B1	B2	B3	B4	B5
PROGRAM 13	A7	A8	A9	A10	A11	A12	A1	A2	A3	A4	A5	A6
PROGRAM 14	B7	B8	B9	B10	B11	B12	B1	B2	B3	B4	B5	B6
PROGRAM 15	A8	A9	A10	A11	A12	A1	A2	A3	A4	A5	A6	A7
PROGRAM 16	B8	B9	B10	B11	B12	B1	B2	B3	B4	B5	B6	B7
PROGRAM 17	A9	A10	A11	A12	A1	A2	A3	A4	A5	A6	A7	A8
PROGRAM 18	B9	B10	B11	B12	B1	B2	B3	B4	B5	B6	B7	B8
PROGRAM 19	A10	A11	A12	A1	A2	A3	A4	A5	A6	A7	A8	A9
PROGRAM 20	B10	B11	B12	B1	B2	B3	B4	B5	B6	B7	B8	B9
PROGRAM 21	A11	A12	A1	A2	A3	A4	A5	A6	A7	A8	A9	A10
PROGRAM 22	B11	B12	B1	B2	B3	B4	B5	B6	B7	B8	B9	B10
PROGRAM 23	A12	A1	A2	A3	A4	A5	A6	A7	A8	A9	A10	A11
PROGRAM 24	B12	B1	B2	B3	B4	B5	B6	B7	B8	B9	B10	B11

*Assign each student a code number A1–A2–A3 (Crew A) or B1–B2–B3 (Crew B). The schedule above will show them their crew position for each program.

**To expand this schedule for classes larger than 24 add additional talent on the horizontal axis and additional programs on the vertical axis.

SCOPE AND SEQUENCE: THE SECOND DAY

During the second day of the Adventure Center Program the bulk of the activity will be devoted to student productions. Each student Producer/Director will be given a period of time (30 minutes for groups of 24 to 20 minutes for groups of 30) to walk-through the production with the talent and then produce and direct the program. You will shoot programs 1–8 during this period. As instructor you will need to work closely with the Directors. See the rotation schedule on the opposite page for crew positions.

THE THIRD DAY

Same as the above except—
You will shoot programs 9–16 during this period.

THE FOURTH DAY

Same as the above except—
You will shoot programs 17–24 during this period.

THE FIFTH DAY

9:30–10:30	Preparation for Final Productions.
	The crew will select the Producer/Director for this.
	May be a new idea or a reshoot of a previous show.
	The Producer/Director picks their own crew.
10:30–11:15	Crew A final production
	(same as the above)
11:15–12:00	Crew B final production
	(same as the above)
12:00–12:30	——LUNCH BREAK——
12:30– 1:15	Crew A final production number two
	(same as the above)
1:15– 2:00	Crew B final production
	(same as the above)
2:00– 2:30	Viewing and critique of the final productions

This program is designed as a one-semester experience for 24 students that will assist in the development of skills in the design and production of television programs. The emphasis will be on working with clients (teachers or administration) in the design and production of program materials that can be used for instruction, information, or just entertainment through the school's delivery system. Ideally the graduates of this course will form production crews that will develop programs for the students, teachers, and administration of the school even after the course is over.

OBJECTIVES: Students involved in this course will—

1. Name, describe the function of, and operate the major pieces of equipment including (a) cameras, (b) mikes, (c) video tape recorder, (d) video switcher, (e) audio mixer, (f) audio tape recorder, and (g) intercom system.
2. Name, describe the responsibilities of, and serve as a crew member in each of the following positions: (a) Producer/ Director (b) Video Switcher, (c) Audio Technical Director, (d) Video Technical Director, (e) Floor Director, (f) Assistant Floor Director, (g) Cameraman, and (h) Talent.
3. Produce and direct at least four programs and serve as a crew member in at least 40 other productions.
4. Descibe the form and function of the various stages and documents in the production process.
5. Plan, design, and produce a short production for a client (student, staff, faculty, or administration).

GENERAL DESCRIPTION:

The class will be a standard 50 minute class period. It will meet five days a week for 15–16 weeks. The exact length should obviously be adjusted to the length of the semester in your school. The class size should be limited to 24 students and you may even want to begin with a class size of 12. The class should be oriented to learning by doing. There will be some aspects that will require the presentation of information but the bulk of the class should provide the students with the opportunity to produce television programs and learn from the critiques of their productions. If you emphasize that we all make mistakes but that we can learn from our mistakes these critiques will provide a good learning experience.

The course is divided into six segments: (1) an introduction, (2) producing opening and closing for TV programs, (3) the production process, (4) producing a scripted program, (5) producing a program for a client, and (6) producing a final project. The introduction and the production process segments are presentations using segments of the text as a guide. The remaining four segments are production activities. During these four segments you will make an assignment. The students will rotate through a production schedule with each student having 15–20 minutes to produce his/her program. These programs will be critiqued by the entire class and should provide an excellent learning situation.

SCHEDULE (SPECIFIC)

WEEK ONE
Introduction to the course
Introduction to television
Introduction to equipment
Introduction to the TV crew
ASSIGNMENTS

WEEK TWO
Opening/closing (2)
Opening/closing (2)
Opening/closing (2)
Opening/closing (2)
Opening/closing (2)

WEEK THREE
Opening/closing (2)
Opening/closing (2)
Opening/closing (2)
Opening/closing (2)
Opening/closing (2)

WEEK FOUR
Opening/closing (2)
Opening/closing (2)
Program critiques
Program critiques
Assignments

WEEK FIVE
Production process
Production process
Production process
Scripted shows (2)
Scripted shows (2)

WEEK SIX
Scripted shows (2)
Scripted shows (2)
Scripted shows (2)
Scripted shows (2)
Scripted shows (2)

WEEK SEVEN
Scripted shows (2)
Scripted shows (2)
Scripted shows (2)
Scripted shows (2)
Scripted shows (2)

WEEK EIGHT
Program critique
Program critique
Assignments
Client programs (2)
Client programs (2)

WEEK NINE
Client programs (2)
Client programs (2)
Client programs (2)
Client programs (2)
Client programs (2)

WEEK TEN
Client programs (2)
Client programs (2)
Client programs (2)
Client programs (2)
Client programs (2)

WEEK ELEVEN
Program critique
Program critique
FINAL PROJECT (1)
FINAL PROJECT (1)
FINAL PROJECT (1)

WEEK TWELVE
FINAL PROJECT (1)
FINAL PROJECT (1)
FINAL PROJECT (1)
FINAL PROJECT (1)
FINAL PROJECT (1)

WEEK THIRTEEN
FINAL PROJECT (1)
FINAL PROJECT (1)
FINAL PROJECT (1)
FINAL PROJECT (1)
FINAL PROJECT (1)

WEEK FOURTEEN
FINAL PROJECT (1)
FINAL PROJECT (1)
FINAL PROJECT (1)
FINAL PROJECT (1)
FINAL PROJECT (1)

WEEK FIFTEEN
FINAL PROJECT (1)
FINAL PROJECT (1)
FINAL PROJECT (1)
FINAL PROJECT (1)
FINAL PROJECT (1)

WEEK SIXTEEN
FINAL PROJECT (1)
Program critique
Program critique
Program critique
Program critique

NOTES

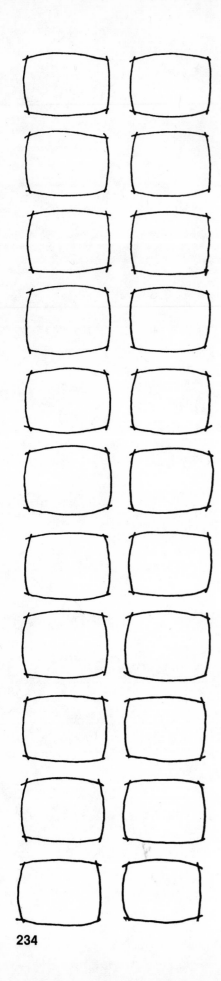

234